ALBANIA'S CAPTIVES

Pyrrhus J. Ruches

ARGONAUT, INC., PUBLISHERS
CHICAGO MCMLXV

737 NORTH MICHIGAN AVENUE
CHICAGO, ILLINOIS 60611

FIRST PRINTING

LIBRARY OF CONGRESS CATALOG CARD NUMBER: 65-15465

MANUFACTURED IN THE UNITED STATES OF AMERICA

DATE DUE

4-7-05	
11-30-4	

PREFACE

There was a time not too long ago when Eastern Europe to the average American was no more than the setting for romantic novels. Otherwise—like David Lloyd George—most people were innocent of the difference between Silesia and Cilicia. Two world wars and numerous conflicts later, we cannot afford that innocence any longer.

Balkan border disputes, in that never-never time of innocence, were the special province of the disputants themselves and of a meager handful of foreign specialists whose reports were lost in libraries and dustbins. Yet it was one such dispute a half century ago that triggered World War I. Because the wrong country annexed Bosnia and Herzogovina, four empires and an entire social order perished forever. In their wake arose the totalitarian monoliths of our times who by war and subversion threaten the very foundations of American democracy and Western Civilization. And the end is far from sight.

Such an open sore, left by the Great Powers after the retreat of the Turkish Empire from Europe, was the partition of the Greek province of Epirus between Greece and Albania. The northern portion of the province became "southern Albania." Its people became—and still are—Albania's captives.

Because boundary disputes are more than a question of which color shall stand on a map—because there, in such places, fester the sores that ultimately poison the world—the problem of the Northern Epirote Greeks, those captives of Albania, cannot be ignored.

Because I am an American with a stake in our struggle with a tyrannical world order, because I have served my country during one phase of that conflict—the Korean War—as a member of the U.S. Marine Corps, and because I am a member of America's free press as a newsman, I believe the facts in the case deserve to be known. And I believe that they should be acted upon.

New York City
October 1964

Pyrrhus J. Ruches

TABLE OF CONTENTS

INTRODUCTION

Wars and revolutions, declared and undeclared, rock the world with explosions from southeast Asia to America's Caribbean doorstep. Brezhnev and Mao Tse-Tung haggle bitterly over the most effective way of burying us while our statesmen and generals ponder the fate of freedom in Viet Nam, Zanzibar, Cuba and many other actual and potential points of danger.

As this war of titans continues, Red Chinese emissaries in Peking's tiny European satellite—Albania—are ensconced undisturbed within visible distance of Italy and the Mediterranean. Ships bearing thousands of peaceful tourists, Americans and Europeans, to Greece and Dalmatia brush past China's silent outpost every summer, blissfully unaware of the nearness of peril.

Many events have brought to an illusory halt the overt turbulence of this part of the world—Europe's traditional tinderbox. These include the Tito-Stalin break, Greece's defeat of the Red forces once arrayed against her and the breakdown of the once monolithic Soviet empire with Stalin's death and the Hungarian revolt. But, as any close student of the area can witness and as the free world's diplomats and generals are aware, to their sorrow, the undercurrents which may yet swell into open conflict have not been done away with.

Although no one can deny categorically that a limited conflict may not spread into the beginning of World War III, it appears that America's foes—at least in Moscow—are well aware now of the consequences of such a turn. They prefer geographically limited but—to us—costly flareups. Given the technological advances of modern warfare, no isolated area of the world has primary strategic importance in a general war. In a limited conflict, however, no area—least of all the southern Balkans—can be written off in our enemies' plans for such operations.

In view of this, Albania's strategic importance is unquestionable despite the shaky pacts between America's Balkan allies and the presence of a U.S. fleet in the Mediterranean. As either a base of attack or a privileged sanctuary, Albanian territory has the advantage of standing athwart the mouth of the Adriatic and along the Greco-Yugoslav frontier. As long as Albania holds this territory, this cannot be otherwise.

Included within the Albanian state created in 1913 by interests other than those of its inhabitants, this territory—Northern Epirus—holds an important key for our fortunes in the Adriatic and southern Balkans.

The dangerous potentialities of continued occupancy of Northern Epirus by Red China's Albanian allies were amply demonstrated not only in the so-called civil war in Greece, but in one striking instance in 1947. On May 15 of that year, Albanian coastal installations fired upon the British cruisers *Orion* and *Superb* from the shores of Northern Epirus. On Oct. 22, continuing to defy international law, the Albanians mined the Corfu Channel. As a result, 45 British seamen died and considerable damage was incurred aboard the *HMS Saumarez* and *HMS Volage.*

Such were some of the recent results of an historic freak created by boundary makers on the eve of World War I, when present boundaries were so arbitrarily and hastily drawn that villages on one side of the border found that their fields had become part of another country.

Because no historical, ethnographic, military or economic reasoning exists for this act, we can understand what happened only in the context of the history of the whole of Epirus. The separate history of Northern Epirus actually commences with the creation of the Albanian state in 1913.

The name Epirus (Epeiros) means the "mainland," a name given to distinguish the area from the belt of the Seven Dorian islands. In earliest times, Epirus was inhabited by the same Dorian tribes dwelling in Macedonia and Thessaly. These, with the Ionians and Aeolians, formed the primary subdivisions of the Greek nation.

Strabo observes that "some go so far as to call the whole country Macedonia, as far as Corcyra, at the same time stating as their reason that in tonsure, speech, short cloak (chlamys), and other things of the kind, the usages of the inhabitants are similar." These Doric tribes, descending in the dawn of Greek history from their original settlements in the Epiro-Macedonian lands, formed the bulk of the population of the states of Boeotia, Acarnania, Thessaly and the Peloponnese.

Ancient Epirus and Macedonia, twin states by reason of

customs, language and the familial affiliations of their rulers, were the great reservoir of Doric Hellenism. Characterized by conservatism, simplicity, rigid tradition and bravery in battle, these Dorians and their descendants proved to be a unifying and revitalizing factor in every period of Greek history. Their finest accomplishment was the spread of Hellenistic culture from the Mediterranean to the banks of the Indus.

The history of Epirus as a Greek highland, however, did not cease with the passing of the ancient world. Continuously since Homeric times, it has stood guard as an Hellenic outpost against northern invaders and has periodically infused vitality into Greece as a whole by its human resources.

Yet unredeemed Northern Epirus, regarded by many as "more Greek than Greece," is still awaiting the removal of an alien yoke. Before we delve into the story of how this has come to be, let us have a look at Northern Epirus, its Greek inhabitants who demand union with Greece and their opponents who have thwarted this burning desire.

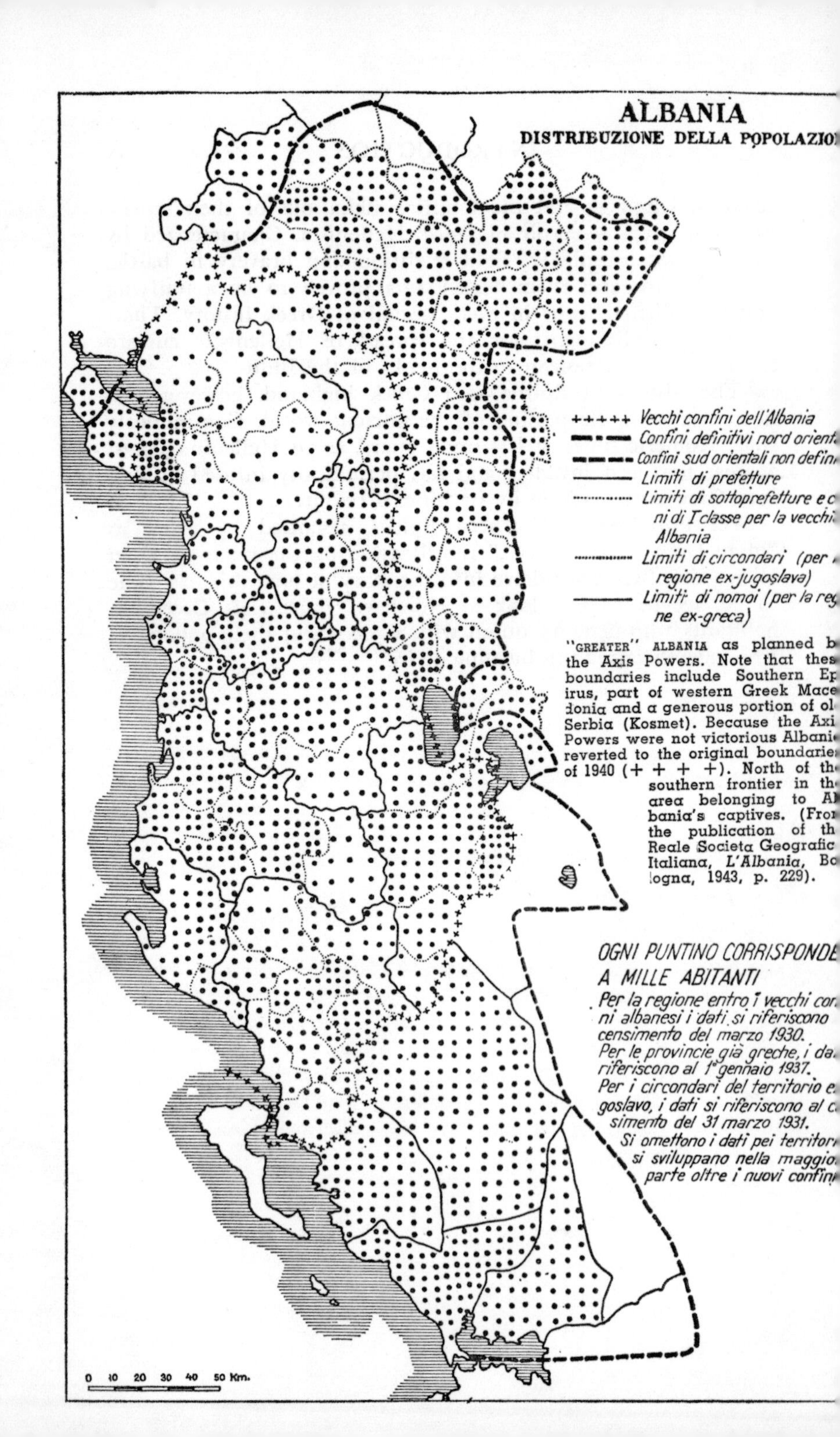

"GREATER" ALBANIA as planned b the Axis Powers. Note that thes boundaries include Southern Ep irus, part of western Greek Mace donia and a generous portion of ol Serbia (Kosmet). Because the Axi Powers were not victorious Albani reverted to the original boundarie of 1940 (+ + + +). North of th southern frontier in th area belonging to Al bania's captives. (Fro the publication of th Reale Societa Geografic Italiana, *L'Albania*, Bo logna, 1943, p. 229).

Chapter I

THE TRUE NORTHERN EPIRUS

"It is an ancestral custom of the Epirotes to fight not only for their own country, but to endanger themselves for the sake of their friends and allies." —DIODORUS SICULUS

The Geography and the People

The historic boundary of Epirus in the north is the course of the Genousas or "Shkumbi" River as it flows from Lake Ochrida to the Adriatic. Complex changes, however, have shifted this boundary more than once in over twenty trouble-filled centuries. The Roman period pushed Hellenism north to the Via Egnatia while barbarian invasions and the Turkish conquest forced the Greek element further south to the Apsus or "Semeni" River. This, in the earlier part of this century, was the northernmost point of the actual Northern Epirote population.

The Italian scholar Giovanni Amadori-Virgilj, as a result of his exhaustive investigations, stated that, "In the Semeni valley begins the true Albanian population."[1] The formal Greek claim is more modest, consisting of only 3,000 square miles, the borders of which run between the Adriatic mouth of the Aous or "Viossa" River and Lake Ochrida.

The Turk who, to give him his due, hardly can be called pro-Greek, gave us the last statistics of the Northern Epirote population that cannot be accused of either Albanian or Greek bias. His 1908 census revealed, in the Sandjaks of Argyrocastro and Korytsa (Greece's minimum claim), a population of 128,050 Greek Christians and 95,661 Moslem Albanians.

The Albanians refute this accurate count by acknowledging a fictitious Greek "minority" of "about 30,000." This is done arbitrarily by making language the sole criterion of nationality. Unsuspecting outsiders may not know that only about 47,000 of

[1] Amadori-Virgilj, G., *La Questione Rumeliota e la Politica Italiana*, 1905, p. 295.

the total Greek population of Northern Epirus speak Greek exclusively. The rest, who spoke an Albanian patois in the home only, were bilingual until a generation ago when their Greek schools were forceably closed by the Albanian government. Even today, however, older bilingual Northern Epirotes are literate almost exclusively in Greek.

Those Greek schools, about which more later, were supported in the face of inhuman obstacles by the voluntary contributions of the Northern Epirotes themselves. Greece did not exist as a state when they began. Afterwards, not only did Greece not spend a single obol for education in Ottoman Epirus, but the reverse is true. The industry and genius of these largely Albanophone Greeks endowed Greece with some of the finest educational facilities in Athens and Constantinople (Istanbul).

Should the Albanian criterion of nationality stand, Switzerland, Austria and Belgium would have no right to independence, Alsace-Lorraine should be German and the United States should rejoin the British Empire—with the exception of those Spanish-speaking areas which we should hand over to Madrid.

By far the majority of Northern Epirotes known to me are equally at home in both Greek and Albanian and sometimes find it easier to express themselves in the latter. Yet there are few more fervently Greek than they. The same ties with Greece exist among them as existed among the former inhabitants of Cappadocia and the Pontus who have since been resettled in Greece and who once spoke Turkish almost exclusively.

On the reverse side of this question there are the Bulgarophone Pomaks, the Grecophone Macedonian "valaas," the Grecophone one-time "Turko-Cretans" and "Turko-Chiotes," etc., all of them speaking little or no Turkish and every one of them an Ottoman Turk to his dying breath.

But, say the Albanian apologists, Greece is in effect claiming Northern Epirus because Athens considers its Christian inhabitants to be Greeks by virtue of a common church. While the overwhelming majority of Northern Epirotes are proud to be considered both Greek and Orthodox, Greece is far from claiming them on the grounds of religious ties. Greece does not claim Belgrade, Sofia, Bucharest or Moscow because the Slavs and Rumanians are Orthodox. Greece claims Northern Epirus because the Northern Epirotes are Greek.

No refutation is risked in stating that not a single Northern Epirote in a position to choose would become an Albanian should Greece renounce her claim tomorrow. The proof of this is written clearly in the history of the past forty years, to say nothing of the last twenty centuries.

The Greek Culture of Northern Epirus

Today the Greek schools of Northern Epirus are empty, the churches desecrated, the people terrorized. What they were like and what their expressed desires were before the successive waves of terror swept over this luckless people is a matter of record. No less a scholar than the world eminent Arnold Toynbee testified, without reservation:

> "Greek nationalism is not an artificial conception of theorists, but a real force which impels all fragments of Greek-speaking populations to make sustained efforts toward political union within the national state; the most striking example of this attractive power is afforded by the problem of Epirus (Himara, Argyrocastro, Korytza) ...
>
> " 'We are Greeks like everyone else, but we happen to speak Albanian, some of us,' said the Northern Epirotes to me.
>
> "The influence of Greek culture and its latent powers found expression in Epirus in a universal enthusiasm for education which has opened to individual Greeks commercial and professional careers of the greatest brilliance and has often led them to spend the fortunes so acquired in endowing the nation with further educational facilities.
>
> "Public spirit is a Greek virtue; there are few villages which do not possess monuments of their successful sons, and a school is an even commoner gift than a church, while the State in Epirus has done nothing to help the Greeks.
>
> "The school house, in fact, is the most prominent and substantial building in an Epirotic village, and the gains which their alliance with the Greek nation has brought to the Greek Epirotes are symbolised generously throughout their country. For the Epirote the school is the door to fortune and to his future. The language he learns there makes him a member of a nation, and opens to him a world wide enough to employ all the talent and energy he may possess if he seeks his future at Patras or Peiraeus, or in the great Greek communities of Alexandria and Constantinople. While if he stays at home it still affords him a link with the life of civilized Europe through the medium of the ubiquitous Greek newspaper. The Epirote then has become Greek in soul; he has reached the conception of a national life more liberal than the isolated existence of his native village through the avenue of Greek culture, so that 'Hellenism' and nationality have become for him identical ideas, and when at last the hour of deliverance struck, he welcomed the Greek Armies that marched into his country from the South and from the East after the fall of Jannina in the spring of 1913, with the same enthusiasm with which all other enslaved fragments of the Greek nation greeted the consummation of a century's hopes."[2]

[2] Toynbee, Arnold, *Greek Policy Since 1882,* p. 26 et seq.

Toynbee is by no means unique in his evaluation of the Hellenic sentiments and culture of the Epirotes. Among others, the special war correspondent of the London *Daily Telegraph,* Capt. A. H. Trapmann, had a chance to gather first-hand observations during the Balkan Wars of 1912-13. He called Epirus:

> ". . . the province perhaps in which Greek blood runs more wildly patriotic than in any other province of Greece. History tells us of the Chimarriots, that Greek seaboard colony that has never yet owed allegiance to any alien conqueror; Byron tells us of the Suliots, who preferred wholesale death to subjugation; and one has no need to look further than the ranks of the Greek Army of today to find out how truly Greek is the spirit of the people of Epirus. In modern times, indeed, many of those who have done most for Greece have sprung from Epirot stock.[3]
>
> "The Westerner, especially the Englishman, is very proud of his own personal honour; but the honour of the Epirot is the honour of Hellas—neither more nor less. However clean the personal honour of an Epirot might be, he would count it soiled if at the same time he was not doing his utmost to keep untarnished the honour and traditions of the Hellenic race.
>
> ". . . It is for this reason that I foresee troublous times ahead for those misguided folk who desire to force the Epirot to accept an alien rule.
>
> ". . . The Epirot is more Greek than the Greeks of the Hellenic Kingdom. He is slower to anger, and the hard conditions of life make it impossible for him to be idle . . . The blood that ran in the veins of the ancient Spartans runs strong in his veins to-day. I for one am convinced that he will fight bitterly and to the end against annexation to Albania."[4]

Northern Epirotes Abroad, the Men and the Movement

Since the days of the Sublime Porte, Epirotes have migrated to the four corners of the earth. Memories and hopes have made them preserve a small part of their homeland in their hearts. Wherever they may be, they band together in their common sorrow and their passionate determination to see their brethren united again beneath the banner of free Greece.

The descent of the Bamboo Curtain has stilled temporarily the voice of Northern Epirus, but her exiled and emigrated children are in a position to echo its sound in a chorus thousands strong.

From the roster of Greek statesmen, diplomats, scientists, teachers and writers—indeed, from the elite of present-day Athens and the whole of Greece—the names of distinguished

[3] Trapmann, A. H., *The Greeks Triumphant,* 1915, p. 120.

[4] *ibid,* pp. 128-130.

Northern Epirotes whose fondest memories are those of the villages beyond the border in which they were born can be compiled.

The influence of Northern Epirotes in Greece in keeping alive their issue before the Greek public cannot be minimized. No less than 30,000 arrived as refugees following World War II. Another 5,000 had crossed the artificial border and settled before 1939. Their political organization, which enjoys the respect of the press and all non-Communist parties in and out of government, is the "Northern Epirote Central Committee" (K.E.B.A.). Its founders include the exiled Metropolitan Bishop of Argyrocastro, Panteleimon and the late Metropolitan Bishop of Korytsa, Evlogios, both born in the district of Korytsa. How widespread this organization is may be judged by its components:

A. CENTRAL COMMITTEE, Athens.
B. Provincial Committees:
  1. Thessalonica
  2. Ioannina
  3. Corfu
  4. Patras
C. Affiliated Organizations:
  1. Northern Epirote Society, Athens.
  2. Northern Epirote Society, Larissa.
  3. Union of Northern Epirote Volunteers and Reservists.
  4. Northern Epirote Student Youth.
  5. Union of Northern Epirote Refugees.
D. Affiliated Regional Societies:
  1. Selasphorus Society of Korytsa, Premeti and Kolonia.
  2. National Chimarriote Federation.
  3. Union of Liountziotes.
  4. Union of the District of Delvino.
  5. Polytsaniote Brotherhood.
  6. Soteriote Brotherhood.
  7. Drovianiote Brotherhood.
  8. Union of Dropolitans.
  9. Pogonion Federation.

In former times, large colonies of Northern Epirotes could be found in the large cities of the Russian Empire, Rumania, Turkey and Egypt. In Constantinople, they were numbered among the business and intellectual elite of the Greek community.

Today there are Northern Epirote societies in Egypt (*Pan-Epirotic Brotherhood of Alexandria*, the *Northern Epirote Society of Cairo*, etc.), Turkey, France, South Africa, the Congo,

Great Britain, Australia, Argentina, the United States and elsewhere.

Well over 15,000 Northern Epirotes and their families are integrated in the thriving Greek-American community and its religious and fraternal organizations. As loyal Americans, they have served the Stars and Stripes in every conflict since World War I, several with exceptional distinction. Hopeful that the quality of freedom they enjoy will be ultimately extended to the land of their birth held captive by Albania, they are extremely sensitive to any current that affects the future of Northern Epirus.

The expression of Epirote-American solidarity is the Panepirotic Federation of America, composed of the following societies:

1. *Epirotic Society Anagenesis,* New York, N.Y.
2. *Chimarriote Society Akrokeravnia,* New York, N.Y. and Washington, D.C.
3. *The Amazons of Pindos Ladies Epirotic Society,* Detroit, Mich.
4. *Ladies Society "Choros Tou Zaloggou,"* Worcester, Mass.
5. *Daughters of Epirus Society,* Chicago, Ill.
6. *Daughters of Epirus,* New York, N.Y.
7. *Epirotic Society D. Doulis,* Peabody, Mass.
8. *Epirotic Society Dodona,* Chicago, Ill.
9. *Epirotic Society Dodona,* Cleveland, Ohio
10. *Enosis Benevolent Society,* Worcester, Mass.
11. *The Epirotic Defense,* Akron, Ohio.
12. *Epirotic Society of Concord Dryinoupoleos Vasilios,* Concord, N.H.
13. *The Heroines of Pindus,* Philadelphia, Pa.
14. *Epirotic Society L. Tzavellas,* Fitchburg, Mass.
15. *Epirotic Society The Liberation,* Chicago, Ill.
16. *Epirotic Society of Michigan,* Detroit, Mich.
17. *Polytsaniote Society Omonia,* Brockton, Mass.
18. *Society of Epirotes Omonia,* Upper Darby, Pa.
19. *Epirotic Society Pavlos Melas,* Southbridge, Mass.
20. *Epirotic Society Profitis Elias,* Southbridge, Mass.
21. *Pyrrhus Benevolent Society,* New York, N.Y.
22. *Benevolent Epirotic Society St. Nicholas,* Chicago, Ill.
23. *Ladies Epirotic Society Souliotissai,* New York, N.Y.
24. *Epirotic Society Spyro-Melios,* New London, Conn.
25. *Epirotic Society of Wisconsin.*
26. *Zagoron Epirotic Society,* Worcester, Mass.
27. *Digenis Epirotic Society,* St. Louis, Mo.
28. *Epirotic Society Pindos,* Boston, Mass.
29. *Ladies Epirotic Society,* Concord, N.H.
30. *Epirotic Benevolent Society of St. Louis,* Mo.
31. *Epirotic Youth Society,* Chicago, Ill.
32. *Epirotic Youth Society,* Detroit, Mich.
33. *Young Epirotans Society,* New York, N.Y.

Chapter II

AN ALBANIAN GALLERY

For Brutus is an honorable man;
So are they all, all honorable men . . ."
—SHAKESPEARE, *Julius Caesar,*
Act II, Scene 2

Who are the Albanians?

It is little less than remarkable that the Northern Epirotes, whose industry and learning rejuvenated modern Greece, should have become the unwilling captives of Albania, regarded by many knowledgeable foreign observers as the most backward nation in Europe.

It is not my intention to heap scorn upon the Albanians because they have had the misfortune to enter the Twentieth Century little more advanced than they left the First, but it is a fact that must be recognized. It explains much about them and the quality of leaders they have produced—as well as the misery to which their rule has reduced Northern Epirus.

Most historians look upon the Albanians as the modern descendants of the Illyrians, an ancient people once settled between the Julian March (Istria) and the northern frontier of ancient Epirus. Napoleon reminded the world of the location of the primary homeland of the ancient Illyrians when he renamed Croatia Illyria during its brief French occupation.

Only negative evidence can be cited in favor of the Illyrian descent of the modern Albanians. Although Greek influence in ancient times extended through the area of Albania proper *(Gegnija)* it is conspicuously absent today with the sole exception of Elbasan. Elbasan's local dialect shows a heavier Greek influence than that of Shkodra, for instance, because the town was in the direct path of the Via Egnatia, the Roman road which marked the farthest direct Greek penetration in late Roman times.

In the south, the "Albanians" are a linguistic and religious phenomenon rather than an ethnic one, a fact to which I shall refer again later.

Among the Ghegs, the true Albanians, the cultural influence of classic times is conspicuous by its absence. The Albanians entered the Twentieth Century without even a common alphabet. All of the books printed in the language—curiosities even among the Albanians of 1900—would hardly fill a short library shelf.

The ancient name "Illyria" is unknown in popular speech, the interesting term "Shqypnija" being used instead. Yet the term is recent. The descendants of the Shkodrans who fled to the Dalmatian island of Zara, for instance, speak the Gheg dialect of the 15th Century. Their name for Albania is "Arbnija" and that of their language "Arbnesh."

Some scholars have attempted to derive the current name of Albania from "rock" or "eagle," while others indicate the similarity of the Italo-Albanian word "shkupeta" (musket) and and its derivative, "shkupetar" (from the Italian "schiopetto") to the national name. If so, it is an admirable description of the Albanian tribes to the present day.

A dissenter from the Illyrian theory—for the support of which not a single indisputably Illyrian text has ever been unearthed—is Giuliano Bonfante, professor of Romance Languages at Princeton University and an authority on the Albanian language. It is his opinion that:

> "... The Albanians and Rumanians seem to have been one and the same people—the ancient Dacians or Thracians ... If the Albanians and Rumanians were one people, the Albanians are not autochthonous in Albania, but came from the East before the eleventh century of the Christian era, presumably from Rumania, ancient Dacia, or Bulgaria (ancient Moesia), which were inhabited by Thracians. This origin is indicated, also by many other linguistic considerations."[5]

Regardless of what they were originally or where they came from, the Albanians, according to a modern Russian diplomat who had occasion to know them during his tenure as a member of the International Control Commission of 1913-14, were known in the middle ages when:

[5] Cf. *Collier's Encyclopedia,* article *Albanian Language.*

". . . Byzantine historians represented the Albanians as a wild folk, nomadic, going from place to place with their flocks, pillaging towns. In the fullest sense of the word, 'viri malignantis naturae,' as they were described by Venetian historians."[6]

Almost on the eve of their dubious nationhood, the Albanians were described by Sir Charles Elliot, British ambassador to the Sublime Porte for many years and an expert on then European Turkey:

"Albania presents nothing but oppositions. North against South, tribe against tribe, bey against bey. Even family ties seem to be somewhat weak, for since European influence has diminished the African slave-trade, Albanians have taken to selling their female children to supply the want of negroes."[7]

Almost a hundred years before, John Cam Hobhouse (Baron Broughton) had visited the court of the notorious Ali Pasha and had written of Albanian domestic life:

"I feel no great inclination to speak of the morals of the Albanians. Their women, who are almost all of them without education, and speak no other than their native tongue, are considered as their cattle, and are used as such, being, except the very superior sort, obliged to labour, and are often punished with blows. They have in truth rather a contempt, even an aversion for their females; and there is nothing in any of their occasional inclinations which may be said to partake of what we call the tender passion. Yet all of them get married who can, as it is a sign of wealth, and as they wish to have a domestic slave."[8]

Karl Marx, or in this case his ghostwriter Engels, was able to observe that the Albanians of his time, *"according to all we know of them, (are) as yet unprepared for civilization."* He added:

"Their predatory habits will force any neighboring Government to hold them in close military subjugation, until industrial progress in the surrounding districts shall find them employment as hewers of wood and drawers of water . . ."[9]

The war correspondent of the London *Daily Telegraph* in Epirus during the Balkan Wars (1912-13) also described the Albanians:

[6] Petriaew, A., "Albania and the Albanians," *Russkaya Mysl;* Vol. V, 1915, Petrograd.

[7] Elliot, Sir Charles, *Turkey in Europe,* London, 1908, p. 403.

[8] Hobhouse, John Cam, *Journey Through Albania,* Vol. I, p. 129

[9] *N.Y Tribune,* Apr. 7, 1859

"As a race the Albanian is essentially martial, but he lacks the idea of cohesive nationality, the ambition of self-government. Albania is not a country, but rather a series of small countries where every kingdom is a nation itself, and where the nearest mountain range forms the horizon of national ambition. For three thousand years the Albanian has never been possessed by a nobler ambition than that of robbing his neighbor . . . In all the history of the races in the world there is no parallel to Albania. It is merely a series of valleys inhabited by semi-civilized bandits, without education, without cohesion or the least ambition for national existence or legislation . . . There is nothing in the Albania of today to give the least vestige of hope that she possesses one single qualification or desire to become an autonomous self-governing state. It happens to suit Europe to endeavour to create the impossible, but it is seldom in the history of the world that a state which has not had sufficient homogeneity to create itself has proved itself worthy of nationalisation."[10]

The same writer predicted with perfect accuracy that the Albanian leaders:

"during the next few years . . . will have the delight of intriguing against their king and of playing off the divided interests of Italy, Austria and Greece, not to mention those of Serbia and Montenegro."[10a]

It may be argued that the Albanians were just emerging from Ottoman rule. Almost a half century has passed since. Behold then the testimony of their friend who lived in their midst in World War II, Julian Amery, then member of a British mission to the Gheg chieftain Abas Kupi and later Conservative M.P. in England:

"Indeed, save for the short-lived rule of Skanderbeg, there had never been an independent Albania until modern times. It is therefore small matter for surprise that the Albanians have hardly acquired a national or state consciousness; nor indeed, outside of the towns and the coastal plain, has nature encouraged, or their way of life given rise to, social organization in any form."[11]

There is said to be a code of the hills, the mediaeval *Qanun i Leks Dukagjinit,* supposedly regulating the interminable Albanian blood-feuds. Amery observed by personal experience:

". . . It was honoured as much in the breach as in the observance . . . what most impressed us in the way of life of the Albanians was not the stray survivals of their ancient customs but the extent to which they lived without law at all."[12]

10 Trapmann, Capt. A. H., *The Greeks Triumphant,* pp. 5-6

10a *ibid,* p. 132.

11 Amery, Julian, *Sons of the Eagle,* p. 7

12 *ibid,* pp. 9-10.

The main passion of the Albanian is *baksheesh,* and his musket has always been for sale to the highest bidder.

> "Such indeed had been the influx of gold and arms into the mountains in the past hundred years that it was perhaps not too much to say that the whole economy and strength of many of the clans had become dependent on subsidies received for 'political services' from the Central Government or foreign powers."[13]

This, in brief, is the Albanian, his culture and his country. His political allegiance is bought, sold and exchanged for a price.

Albania's Leaders Today

In Soviet Russia Stalin's death caused Minister of the Interior Beria to be executed as a traitor. In Russia's smallest satellite it raised Minister of the Interior Mehmet Shehu to a commanding position.

Shehu is a native of Malakastra, Berati who was decorated for his part in the International Brigade during the Spanish civil war. He became a communist while at a French military school. His father was a minor prewar politico. After Spain he was sent to Moscow where he was graduated from international communism's military college. Today he reigns as Premier while the Peking ambassador and his staff rule the country.

Enver Hoxha is still Secretary of the Albanian Communist Party, and therefore technically the primary government figure.

Self-appointed Colonel-General, General, and then Generalissimo Hoxha, "Our Enver" as the Red press of the Albanian People's Republic has called him, was born into a Moslem family of some prominence in his native Argyrocastro. His uncle Hussein, the local Mufti, was unusually tolerant and even served the Northern Epirotes as one of their deputies to the Greek Parliament prior to the election of December, 1915. His nephew proved to be a totally different sort of creature.

Sent first to study at the University of Naples, Hoxha was expelled for academic deficiencies and subsequently was sent to France's Montpelier University. There he frittered away his time and the family pocketbook in excursions to the nightspots and fleshpots of Paris' Latin Quarter. There he found himself compelled to undertake a piece of Albanian highway robbery at the expense of some unwary Greek student friends.

[13] Amery, *ibid.,* pp. 9-10.

When Hoxha's Greek school chums appeared ripe for fleeceing he forged bank statements to prove he had money coming. Claiming temporary insolvency, Hoxha pleaded for a quick loan to be as quickly repaid. Having amassed in this wise over a thousand francs, he skipped out on his victims who never saw him or their money again.

It is said that Hoxha met Tito in Paris when Yugoslavia's present dictator was doing Comintern work as a gunrunner for the Spanish Republic. At the time they may have met it was doubtful that they could have envisioned the use one would be to the other later. Hoxha was heard of next as a secretary in Albania's Brussels legation but didn't last there for very long. When Hoxha returned home he opened a coffee-house and tobacco shop in Argyrocastro. Hoping to redeem the prodigal his relatives secured for him a position as French instructor at the Lycée of Korytsa. He was later forced to terminate his teaching career abruptly after a transfer to the Valona Commercial School. The academic authorities removed him for inefficiency.

After the Nazi-Soviet pact Hoxha joined the chorus of supporters of Il Duce's "greater Albania" and actively collaborated in Durazzo and Tirana as protegé of then Propaganda Minister Ramadan Bicaku.

When Tito founded the Yugoslav National Liberation Front following Hitler's attack on Russia he made use of Hoxha as his Albanian stooge. In 1943 Hoxha took to the hills as "Colonel-General" of an assortment of officers who, with an eye to the emerging Allied victory, suddenly decided to blossom forth as "popular democrats." The rest is current history.

The Albanian Emigrés and the West

What of the Albanians abroad? What of those men to whom the West has given credence and who might be restored to rule? It would be easy to delude ourselves that we have here knights in shining armor to fight an anti-bolshevik crusade.

On August 26, 1949, Greece cleared the last armed Communist nests from her side of the Albanian frontier. That same day in Paris a gentleman named Midhat Bey Frashëri proclaimed the organization of a "National Committee for a Free Albania." What had happened was that the "Legality Party" of ex-King Zog and "Balli Kombëtar" or the "Nationalist Front" of the late Midhat Bey had joined hands. An unholy wedding was consummated between Zog and the quislings who had helped topple him from power ten years before. Judged by non-Albanian standards it was a strange alliance. Stranger things were still to come.

Midhat Bey Frashëri was the son of Abdyl Bey Frashëri, one of the participants in the Ottoman-sponsored Congress of Prizren in 1878. His career began in the Young Turk Party which, coming to power in 1909 with fair promises for the Empire's Christian minorities, concluded with the "elimination of the Armenian question by eliminating the Armenians." During the twenties he was Albania's Minister to France and Greece. With Ali Klisura (Këlçyra), one of the trio who offered Albania's crown to Victor Emmanuel in 1939, he co-founded Balli Kombëtar, becoming its first president.

Frashëri's brother, Mehdi, was the co-regent of Albania with Lef Nosi and Andon Harapi in 1943-44 during the Nazi occupation. Mehdi's son Vehbi was Undersecretary for Foreign Affairs and passed through occupied Athens twice, carrying suitcases filled with German gold for the use of Hitler's fifth column in neutral Istanbul.

Under his presidency, Balli Kombëtar received supplies and 17,000 guns, as well as 600,000 napoleons (12,000,000 gold francs) from the Nazis. These were used to arm the Ballist "chetas" which functioned as semi-official anti-guerrilla bands. With the help of the Fascist militia and S.S. these bands acted to execute hundreds of Northern Epirote Greeks, regardless of age, sex or political affiliations. A detailed account of these operations is given in the latter part of this book.

Ballist headquarters were in German-occupied Tirana. Brigadier "Trotsky" Davis, head of a British miltary mission, met Frashëri at Mt. Dajti near Tirana trying unsuccessfully to persuade him to make a break with his Axis masters. Midhat, however, preferred to remain faithful to the Ballist pledge given by Ali Klisura in writing to General Dalmazzo on March 15, 1943, cementing Balli to the Axis. After this the BBC denounced Balli Kombëtar as a collaborationist and the British dropped leaflets openly naming Frashëri and his friends as war criminals.

When the Germans retreated the Ballists went with them to Shkodra. From there some proceeded with the Germans as far as Vienna, while the bulk, including Frashëri, paid the Nazi general in command 10 napoleons (200 gold francs) each to be conveyed to Brindisi.

Throwing themselves upon British mercy, Midhat and 120 other Ballists in this group were disarmed and sent, in the company of German prisoners, to the Grumo detention camp. At Grumo Midhat Bey was lodged in a stable and drew rations in line with his defeated Nazi comrades. Two British sergeants interrogated the Ballists to prepare legal briefs for their forthcoming war crimes trial. All the money of the detained Ballists was confiscated and a special commission came from Communist Albania to have them repatriated for trial. Then, quite suddenly, the repatriation proceedings were dropped and charges against the Ballists were later mysteriously withdrawn.

After six months at Grumo these Ballists were sent to the DP camp at Santa Maria di Leuca where they celebrated their release with a feast and a round of speeches.

Then began the big buildup of Balli Kombëtar as a wartime resistance group. Playing upon the credulity of British and American correspondents to whom Albania was a patch on the map and her history during World War II even more obscure, a "Mihailovitch" legend was built around Midhat and Balli. This fairy tale can be dispelled by any non-political person who has lived through the Nazi-Fascist occupation of Albania.

So well did Balli and its new sponsors succeed that, four years later, Midhat was president of a British and American supported National Committee for a Free Albania. At London he stayed at the Barclay Hotel as a British Government guest. He died, aged 69, at New York's Winthrop Hotel on October 4, 1949.

His successor to the presidency of the National Committee for a Free Albania, and, at first, to the presidency of Balli, was Hasan Aga Dosti. During the war Dosti served the puppet government in various capacities. From December, 1941 to May, 1942, he was Minister of Justice and Education in the quisling cabinet of Mustafa Mërlika-Kruja, leaving this post to become President of the Criminal Division of the Tirana High Court, a post he held up to August 18, 1943.

For a time an important faction of Balli Kombëtar, headed by Ali Klisura, had split in exile with Midhat's faction and remained outside the National Committee for a Free Albania and in close collaboration with the *Blok Independente,* a group of even more distinguished antecedents. Despite half-hearted attempts toward early reconciliation, Midhat Bey (and later Hasan Aga) and this ultra-rightist clique remained at odds.

Apart from personal clashes, the difficulties between the

Bloc and the Frashërists lay in Midhat's post-war pose as an "agrarian democrat". Even on paper this phrase has a disturbing sound to the private and very feudal interests of the Bloc leaders, the very *crème de la crème* of the wartime puppet governments of Albania.

In December, 1953, without authorization by the Balli Kombëtar faction he headed, Dosti concluded negotiations with the Bloc and exchanged sides.

Up to the time they kissed and made up Dosti and the Bloc were freely exchanging verbal brickbats. The latter's organ called Dosti a "philo-communist"[14] with Dosti returning the compliment by screaming "fascists", "collaborationists" and "Judases", citing names, dates and places to prove his point.[15]

Now Dosti abandoned the so-called "Balli of the Agrarians" and cast his lot with the "Balli of the Beys". The new NCFA "Statutes", signed by him and his enemies of the day before, called upon the UN to recognize the reorganized Committee as a provisional UN-sponsored commission to rule Albania provisionally should the Communists be ousted and to supervise free elections. The audacity of these former pals of the Axis is stupifying.

The upshot was that Dosti, at a special convention of the Frashërists in Italy, was judged *in absentia* and removed from the "Balli of the Agrarians". At the same time, the convention withdrew recognition of the NCFA and set up a dummy Frashërist "Democratic NCFA" headed by Abas Ermenji, former chief of the Ballist "chetas", and other Frashërist members of the old NCFA.

The new NCFA included the son of Mussolini's first puppet premier of Albania, Mussolini's appointee as Minister to Berlin and later "Minister of (Axis) Liberated Territories", the Minister of the Interior in the last German-sponsored government, a member of the delegation which presented the Albanian crown to Victor Emmanuel in 1939, etc. A year later, in Paris where the first NCFA had been announced, the reorganized NCFA quietly expired, leaving the field clear for the "Balli of the Agrarians". Apparently, the Western supporters of these Albanian committees were becoming a little tired of the use to which their support was being put—to provide the means for the continued

[14] *L'Albanie Libre,* Rome, It., Mar. 1, 1951, p. 2.

[15] *Flamuri,* Rome, It., Mar.-Apr. 1952, p. 8.

internal squabbles of a cynical group of ex-fascists.

Charges and countercharges have also issued forth from Belgrade and Rome in the chess game between Tito and Italy over Adriatic ascendency. To both, Albania's future disposition has been a burning question. Two days after Midhat Frashëri announced the formation of his NCFA, Tito, not to be outdone, made public the existence of a "Liberation Committee" of Albanians in Yugoslavia. As originally announced, this organization consisted of a headquarters at Skoplje, a military base at Peç (Ipek) and a political committee at Prizren, only nine miles from the Albanian frontier.

The political organizer of this committee was Dushan Mugosha, a name not entirely unknown in the history of Albanian Communism. He was, with Miladin Popovic, one of the two official emissaries sent to unite Albania's microscopic Communist groups in 1941. To them is credited the founding of the Albanian Workers' Party on Nov. 8, 1941. Until the end of World War II, Mugosha and his co-emissary were the actual rulers of Albanian Communism.

At the outset, the Tito group contained a motley quiltwork of personalities. These included several leftovers from the persons formerly subsidized by Yugoslavia before World War II in opposition to Zog, several turncoats who had successively served the quisling regime, Hoxha and then Tito and one of Mussolini's co-regents of the Kingdom of Albania.

The close proximity of Kossovo-Metohija ("Kosmet") to the Albanian border has sometimes given Tito thoughts of invading Albania and placing his own stooges in power. Rumors indicate that he might even accomplish this without invasion, provided he makes a compromise with the Soviet Union in which Albania would be Russia's payoff for Tito's cooperation.

Being wiser in the ways of double-dealing than the Anglo-Americans, Tito placed little faith in the Albanian tribal chieftains from the start. Even the surveillance exercised by the trusty Dushan Mugosha and Tito's OZNA could not assure him the loyalty of men like Kryeziu, Bajraktari, Kaloshi, Elezi, Ulqinaku, etc. Thus, a conference of Titoist Albanian refugees at Prizren in June, 1951, set down a more positive Titoist line. In March 1953, Tito made his first big bid for Albania.

Just prior to this, two secret conferences, it was reported, had been held at Prishtina. Tito's handpicked Albanian figurehead then was a genuine Titoist ex-mathematics instructor named

Apostol Taanefi. Units of the Yugoslav army were reportedly moving into Albania in the disguise of Albanian guerrilla units. The Russians became alarmed and were said to be ready to flee Albania at a moment's notice.

The Albanians in the West and their supporters were no less disturbed, and accordingly tried to show that they too were carrying on activities within Albania. The *Paris Presse* of March 12, 1953 reported that planes, purported to have come from Italy and bearing the markings of the NCFA, dropped more than leaflets into Albania.

Italy too, has fished in Adriatic waters. The issue of Trieste was only half the story. The future control of the Adriatic mouth—Albanian-held Northern Epirus, is the reverse of the same coin. Behind each Albanian emigré group stands either Italy or Yugoslavia, with the West generally standing by the former. All the antagonists insist that only Greece's refusal to join in a guarantee of the Albanian frontiers of 1939, i.e. renounce Northern Epirus, bars their way. This Greece cannot do without disowning a part of herself.

Disentangling the Truth

In international diplomacy truth, unfortunately, is often hidden in a vessel within a vessel and held up to the light only in part. In all fairness to the Albanians as much as to the Greeks, it is the author's purpose at this point to consider the whole problem of Albania's borders with as much justice to Albania as to Greece.

The union of Northern Epirus with Greece would be a solution to more than one Balkan difficulty. As a last measure of objection to the restoration of Northern Epirus to Greece the Albanians are advancing certain arguments apart from their insistence that the territory belongs to Albania.

The latest variation of these arguments is that, as long as the Albanians fear the annexation of Northern Epirus by Greece, they are hindered from an anti-Communist uprising. This version has been repeated by the late king Zog, by Hasan Dosti's NCFA, by the Balli Kombëtar and has found echo in the capitals of Italy, Yugoslavia, Britain and the United States.

The argument, strangely enough, is rarely heard from recent refugees who have fled Albania. If these refugees advance any reason for the lack of a successful anti-Communist insurrection to date it is the nature of the Communist régime itself. When sources of supply are controlled at the primary level, making possession of a few grams of bread above the Government dole a cause for arrest, where the secret police is ever present, where the family itself is disrupted and brother dares not trust brother, spontaneous revolt is an impossibility. The Albanians abroad, by claiming otherwise and placing the onus of failure on Greece's pursuit of justice, are trying to blackmail the West by sheer bluff.

The second argument, seemingly the most impressive, is that Albania is too small to survive as an independent state without Northern Epirus. If Albania, a nominally independent state since 1913, has been unable to preserve the least semblance of actual independence during its entire history, of what importance to that independence could Northern Epirus really be?

It is difficult to convince the Albanians that the loss of Northern Epirus would be, for them, a blessing in disguise. Yet there are aspects of this many-faceted question that easily make it so. To wit: Northern Epirus is the reason that Albania is valuable to every would-be master of the Adriatic and the Balkans. The liberation of Northern Epirus from Albanian rule not only would benefit the Northern Epirotes, but would allow Albania to attain a degree of security heretofore unknown.

Whatever the merits of this argument for the Albanian people, it cannot fail to meet the antediluvian opposition of the "beys", "agas", "bajraktars" etc. whose comfortable incomes have been derived from the sale of their duped followers' lives to foreign aggressors.

The final Albanian objection to Greek annexation of Northern Epirus is that Greece would thereby acquire a Moslem minority. However, were the provocations of foreign propaganda removed and artificially sustained enmities laid aside, there would be little in the life of this religious—be it noted, not racial —minority to raise conflicts with the rest of the local population. After all, thousands of Moslems live in Greek Thrace in absolute equality with their Christian fellow citizens, elect their deputies to the Greek Parliament and observe whatever religious obligations they have in freedom. The measure of their contentment may be judged by the petition by their fellow-Moslems in the part of Bulgaria immediately adjacent who asked to be taken into the Greek fold at the end of World War II.

In the last analysis, the Moslems of Northern Epirus—members of the Bektashi sect which is regarded with abhorrence by other Balkan Moslems—have known for over a century that Greece would some day receive her just due. General Makrigiannes, the doughty semiliterate author of a memoir masterpiece that is an important primary source on the Greek Revolution, recalled the events of his stay in August, 1821 with Ismail Bey Konitza.

Ismail Bey, an ancestor of one of the founders of the Albanian nationalist movement in the United States, addressed himself thus to an audience of Albanian pashas and beys who had gathered in his home:

> "Pashas and beys, we will lose. We will lose! This war is neither with the Muscovite nor with the English nor the French. We were unjust to the *raya* and robbed him of both wealth and honor. Thus our eyes were darkened and they have taken up arms against us. And the Sultan, that ass, doesn't know what is happening to him. Those about him deceive him, and this is the beginning of our kingdom's downfall."

Answering the objection that the pashas of other Ottoman provinces were gathering to help put down the Greeks, Ismail Bey wisely warned that these strangers, "will go back to their country, but we will remain here."

When Makrigiannes was ready to leave him, Ismail Bey told him to let the Greek insurgents know he wished them success. "Let them be just," were his parting words, "and there will be an end so that we Turks as well can rest, for God has made a ruin of our kindom because we have departed from His justice."[16]

Today, the only ones who stand to lose anything from a readjustment of the Greco-Albanian boundaries are a handful of now-exiled feudarchs who long for a return to the Ottoman or Zogist days. The Greek quarrel has not been with the Albanian tribesmen eking out a savage existence in the mountains of Mati and the Malesija. The future of these Albanians is—or should be—their own and Greece wishes them well and God-speed. But the Northern Epirotes—and their brothers in the Greek state—reject any solution which would force them to remain unwilling subjects of any Albanian state whatsoever.

16 General Makrigiannes, **Memoirs.** Ed. Vlabogiannis. Athens 1947. Vol. I.

The Albanian-American Scene: The Local Boys

The handful of Albanians in this country are no more than that. In order to give weight to their public statements their spokesmen have not been above claiming that there are 30,000, 40,000 or even 50,000 Albanians living in this country.

There are no real statistics on this subject. The United States census does not even list an Albanian nationality. It lumps together a number of miscellaneous European nationalities ("Other Europe") as 86,375. The number for all other and not reported (Asiatic, European and other foreign-born whites) is 146,833. The closest estimate would be, on the basis of deduction from scanty evidence, a probable total of not more than 2,500 or 3,000 Albanians in the United States.*

Those of the Albanian immigrants who interest themselves in "old country" politics have long been the political football of several small cliques of Albanian politicos.

The first sign of political stirring among these immigrants was the one-man newspaper *Kombi* of Soterios Petsis. Petsis, who began publication of his newspaper in 1906, was a turncoat Greek from Korytsa and a graduate of the University of Athens.

Constantine Chekrezi, another of the local "professional patriots", gave us a fair idea of its reception in his book, *Albania, Past and Present* published about forty years ago:

> "The people to whom he (Petsis) sent the newspaper, gratis at the beginning, wondered what it was for; they not only had never seen any Albanian newspaper, but were also entirely illiterate. Consequently, Mr. Petsis, who was at the same time editor, publisher, manager and printer, was obliged to go and explain in person what that shabby sheet of paper was meant to be."

Chekrezi added that, at that time, there were not more than 20 Albanians in the United States who knew how to read and write!

For many decades the Albanian nationalist movement in America, if not the world, could be summed up in one name— "Vatra." This was the largest of several tiny organizations revolving around two or three personalities. It was fortunate, however, in possessing the undoubted talents of two of the slickest manipulators of Balkan intrigue, Fan Noli and Faik Bey Konitza.

*Census figures are for non-listed nationalities, U.S. Census of 1950.

The late Faik Bey was one-time Ottoman Consul-General in the United States. He and his brother Mehmet were Moslems from Konitsa, Greece. The Moslems of this area were "albanised" quite late and there are living witnesses to the fact that the mother of Mehmet and Faik rarely was heard to speak any other language but Greek.

A founding father of "Vatra", Faik Bey was later Albanian Minister to Washington. Mussolini's occupation of Albania disturbed him not at all, and he remained at his post for a while in the pay of the Italian Embassy. In 1940, as the whole civilized world was applauding the Greek David's inspired defense against the Axis Goliath, he issued the following Rome-inspired statement to the press:

> "And now Italy is about to step in with the announced intention to right the accumulated wrongs done to the Albanian nation and to restore the natural and historic limits of Albania . . . The question is whether the former Turkish province of Janina was and always has been an integral part of Albania. If it is truly so, does this truth automatically cease to be a truth because the Italians affirm it? The plain fact is that Italy has here a good and strong case, because her interest happens to be identical with a long over-due act of justice toward Albania. *For once, the avenging gods are on the side of Caesar's legion.*"[17]

In this manner did the Albanian Bey stand by the side of the Italian Duce and his unspeakable accomplice in Berlin.

Faik Bey departed this life in December, 1942, but he was survived by Fan Noli, the most unusual "Albanian" on earth. The power behind "Vatra" and its editorial organ *Dielli,* Noli was likewise founder and, until recently unchallenged, Bishop of the Albanian Church in America.

A close-up of Fan Noli is in order. To begin with, he is not an Albanian. He was born in the Greek village of Imbrik-Tepe near Adrianople. It is possible, as he claims, that he is descended from Albanophones. There were several Albanian-speaking villages in the Silivri district of Adrianople that were famous for their quality of yogourt which their natives peddled in the streets of Turkish cities. Be that as it may, His Reverence's name is not Fan Noli, but the very Greek Theophanus Stylianos Mavromatis. We have an account of his early life:

> "... when he left the village of Ibrik-Tepe, in the year 1900 his name was Theophanus Mavromatis, which is Greek. A petition came to the gov-

[17] Konitza, Faik, "Background of the Italo-Greek Conflict," Wash. D.C., 1940 (my italics, P.J.R.).

erning body of the high school at Adrianople with reference to this young man. The kindly person, one Vergadis, who presented it, explained that Theophanus, an assistant in an ironmonger's shop, had had some trouble at his school, but being a youth of promise who had no material resources Vergadis said that he would be most grateful if the good professors would accept him."[18]

When he was graduated from the Greek high school at Adrianople, he worked in several Athenian theatres before joining the staff of the newspaper *Acropolis.* He left Athens abruptly for Rumania when a warrant for his arrest on fraud charges was issued.

He was probably bitten by "albanomania" in Bucharest. At that time, the Rumanian government was subsidizing certain Albanians in hopes of setting up an Albano-Kutzovlach condominium in the southern Balkans under a descendant of Hospodar Ghica. Propaganda in Kutzovlach, a corrupt half-Romance sister tongue to Rumanian, was primarily published at the press of the Albano-Rumanian society "Deturia".

Fan Noli then went to Alexandria, Egypt, where he was a teacher of Greek.

"He then emigrated to America, became a shop assistant and worked very hard. His next move was into the church; the Russian bishop, who at that time was the spiritual father of all Greek Orthodox Christians in the States, consented to ordain him, and the new priest thereupon adopted his Albanian name, though one of his former Adrianople professors is of the opinion that Fan Noli is less of an Albanian than himself."[19]

To Fan Noli's intellectual credit, which is considerable, may be mentioned the fact that he was graduated from Harvard and is the translator of Shakespeare, Ibsen and other classic playwrights into Albanian.

In 1909, three years after coming to America, Fan Noli established *Dielli,* which became the organ of "Vatra", founded a few years later, in 1912 by Noli and Konitza. Their tiny following was and is principally, though not exclusively, Moslem.

The policies of "Vatra", needless to say, completely dominated by Konitza and Noli, were then pro-Austrian. Albania's emergence as Austria's puppet in 1913 was hailed by them with loud applause. This enthusiasm for Austria continued until the very day the Central Powers fell to pieces.

[18] Baerlein, Henry, *Under the Acroceraunian Mountains,* p. 75.

[19] *Ibid,* p. 76.

To sell their point of view to the American press, Noli and Konitza, excellent propagandists themselves, needed a native American front. It is at this point that, for a brief time, Greenwich Village's "Professor Seagull", self-styled bohemian and "ex-Albanian expert," entered the scene. Joe Gould, famous as author of the *Oral History of the World* and for his barroom antics, became Fan Noli's one-man publicity department.

"In 1913, in an Albanian restaurant in Boston named the Scanderbeg, whose coffee he liked, he became acquainted with Theofan S. Noli, an archimandrite of the Albanian Orthodox Church, who interested him in Balkan politics. In February 1914 Gould startled his family by announcing that he planned to devote the rest of his life to collecting funds to free Albania. He founded an organization in Boston called the Friends of Albanian Independence, enrolled a score or so of dues-paying members, and began telegraphing and calling on bewildered newspaper editors in Boston and Manhattan, trying to persuade them to print long treatises on Albanian affairs written by Noli. After about eight months of this Gould was sitting in the Scanderbeg one night, drinking coffee and listening to a group of Albanian factory workers argue in their native tongue about Balkan politics, when he suddenly came to the conclusion that he was about to have a nervous breakdown. 'I began to twitch uncontrollably and see double', he says. From that night on his interest in Albania slackened."[20]

We also are told:

"During the First World War Bishop Fan Noli was known to the American Intelligence Office as a staunch pro-German, and President Wilson issued a decree in 1918, discharging all Albanians from the United States Army."[21]

For some time after the war "Vatra" continued to agitate for the return of Austrian-sponsored Prince Wied to the Albanian throne. Fan Noli then decided to make himself a bishop.

"At Whitsuntide 1918 he appeared in New York before an assembly of Christian and Moslem Albanians. He told them that there was a general desire to have a true Albanian bishop, but that Greek intrigues had vetoed this. (The Russian Church authorities had said, quite rightly, that he was under the jurisdiction of the Greek Patriarch.) 'Well!' he cried and—his friends were prudently scattered among the audience—'what shall we do?' 'The people,' they answered, 'can elect kings, they can elect bishops!' 'What shall we do?' cried Fan Noli. 'You shall be our bishop!' Thereupon he retired, it is said, and coming back in episcopal robes he was hailed by the people with cries of *Axios, Axios!* ('He is worthy!'). And as he gave the benediction they crossed themselves, except the Moslems, who, *bien entendu,* saluted in their own fashion."[22]

20 Mitchell, Joseph, *McSorley's Wonderful Saloon,* p. 82, N. Y., n. d.

21 Cassavetes, N.J. (ed.), *Greek Northern Epirus,* p. 20

22 Baerlein, *op.cit.,* p. 76.

From the start, "Vatra's" leaders inflamed the simple minds of their peasant followers with chauvinistic speeches claiming not only Northern Epirus, but Jannina and Preveza as well for Albania. It will be well to remember that, even now in its pro-Communist phase, "Vatra" has never ceased to preach this type of propaganda.

The end of the First World War and the subsequent discussions of national claims at the Peace Conference sent Noli scurrying to France as self-appointed spokesman of all the Albanians in America.

In order to give his statements gravity he was not above telling the Peace Conference, and later the League of Nations, that he spoke in the name of an Albanian-American community with no less than thirty churches and schools. Nothing daunted, he retained his composure when confronted by depositions attained from responsible city authorities in the United States, proving that most of these churches and schools had, like Athena from Zeus, sprung full-blown from His Reverence's brain. The debunk was the work of the present Panepirotic Federation's predecessor, the Pan-Epirotic Union of Boston.

Fan Noli had, in the meantime, found a new protector in Italy and "Vatra" went through the first of many changes in "party line". In 1921, Noli left for Albania where he succeeded in obtaining ordination from Metropolitans imported from Yugoslavia for the purpose, and thus became a legitimate bishop. He named himself to the See of Durazzo, but, since the Albanian church was not then autocephalous, the Oecumenical Patriarchate regarded the matter as an irregular usurpation of an area of its jurisdiction. Fan Noli was never recognized by the Patriarchate as exercising episcopal jurisdiction either in Albania or the United States, however valid his episcopal orders since the consecration in Durazzo.

Noli, a "professional patriot" with ambitions, continued to look to Italy. Ahmet Bey Mati, afterwards King Zog, was then premier of Albania by the grace of Yugoslavia. In June 1924, with the blessings of Mussolini, Fan Noli, Mustafa Mërlika-Kruja and their pro-Italian followers heaved Zog out of the country. Then, the Greek pot-mender of Imbrik-Tepe of other days became premier of Albania. His six-month premiership with Italian backing was productive of several agreements with Italy that paved the way for Mussolini's later death-grip on Albania's economy.

Fan Noli was driven out when Zog returned triumphantly at

the head of an army of 2,000 Yugoslavs, 800 White Russians and the tribesmen of Mati who flocked to their leader as soon as he crossed the border. Noli eventually found himself an exile in Vienna.

While there, the history of this Balkan Tallyrand took yet another turn. Without concrete support for the moment, Fan Noli began flirting with the Bulgaro-Macedonian branch of the Comintern ("IMRO United"), then headed by Dimitar Vlahov, later vice-premier of Yugoslavia and president of the "Macedonian People's Federative Republic." When the Comintern decided it had no need of him, he and the Bolsheviks parted company and he subsequently returned to the United States to pick up once more the reins of his politico-religious offices.

From 1933 Noli became pro-Zogist. Certain opposing Albanians claimed that Italy, then backing Zog, had resumed her subsidies to Fan Noli. From 1939 his course was less sure, but he did not openly renounce Zog. "Vatra's" membership became sharply divided between King Zog and the Italian-run Fascist government of Shevket Vërlaci. An openly pro-fascist faction temporarily set up a rival "Vatra" in Detroit.

America's entrance into the war encouraged Fan Noli to maintain his pro-Zog position. There were now no Italian subsidies and Allied policy temporarily seemed to favor Zog.

In 1942 another force, the "Free Albania Central Committee" with headquarters in Boston, entered the field. Its founder, Constantine Chekrezi, had been a member of "Vatra" and had returned to Albania where he was a minor politician. In 1935, 80 peasants rose in the abortive "Fieri revolt". Chekrezi was among the leaders. This revolt, an Italian-inspired disturbance, had for its ulterior purpose the forcing of Zog's hand into conceding the Myzeqe valley, Albania's best agricultural district, to 10,000 Italian colonists Mussolini wished to settle there in return for an Italian loan.

Chekrezi went to Italy, then to France and afterwards to the United States. The "Free Albania Central Committee" and *Liria,* its weekly organ, declared themselves anti-Zogist and a feud with Noli, ever the grand vizer of Albanian-American politics, ensued.

Only in one particular did Noli and Chekrezi, as well as Albanian politicians in all other camps, see eye to eye. This was the necessity of blocking any Greek attempt at a hearing in respect to Northern Epirus. Noli and the FACC were both willing to back any post-war Albanian government that could succeed in this objective. It was this outlook that eventually was to reconcile the two under the aegis of Stalinism.

In 1943 Enver Hoxha appeared on the Albanian scene. While "Vatra" preferred to be cagey, the FACC went wild over Moscow's stepchild and openly proclaimed him the "people's hero" of the hour. "Vatra" was numerically and financially stronger, but the FACC enjoyed more prestige in Washington thanks to the leftist sentiments of some officials in America's wartime administration. The same people who sabotaged our Eastern European policy, helped the Communists enslave the eastern European nations and caused the present muddle through appeasement of Stalin were then busy promoting the NOF, the EAM and Hoxha. Chekrezi and Noli were asked to join hands and receive joint recognition as Albania's spokesmen in America. Chekrezi accepted, but Fan Noli procrastinated until such a program became futile.

When it became evident that the Greek case for Northern Epirus would receive due consideration at the peace settlement, Fan Noli prepared to make another about face. The drive for recognition of Communist gangster Hoxha became a drive to keep Greece from re-entering Northern Epirus. "Vatra" and the FACC began to vie with each other in singing Hoxha's doxologies. John T. Nasse, President of the FACC, demanded that America, Britain and the Soviet Union support the Albanian Reds "to save Albania from dismemberment by its enemies and give official recognition to the democratic government of Gen. Enver Hoxha."[23]

Fan Noli conducted a "Fund Drive for the Preservation of Albania's Boundaries." He went to the Paris Peace Conference in the same role as Albanian-American spokesman he had so successfully essayed in 1919, but with indifferent results. His enemies have asserted that no account of how a part of the $14,000 he raised has ever been given and that $11,000 of that sum was neither spent nor accounted for.

Fan Noli, until his death in Ft. Lauderdale in 1965, stood recognized as Albanian Communism's leading spokesman in America. The original NCFA (Zog-Balli), tried to overlook his sellout to Communism as a temporary aberration. While attacking *Dielli* and "Vatra" they tried to court Noli himself into their

23 Vide *Liria,* Boston, Mass., July 27, 1945.

camp. The attempt failed miserably. They then tried to take the Church from under him.

In 1950 several priests bolted from Noli's rule. Their leader, a certain Paul V. Rado, denounced Noli as a pro-Communist and this group requested a new bishop. Hastily ordained in Istanbul, Bishop Marko Lipa was sent to America to assume an as yet non-existing see.

The ordination of Lipa forced Noli to make even clearer his own stand. A statement by Noli as Bishop of the Albanian Church in America was published by the official organ of the Albanian Communist Party:

> "On October 31st (1950), the Tirana daily *Bashkimi*, published a statement of the Albanian Orthodox Episcopate in America protesting against the new Bishop, Marko Lipa, sent by the Patriarchate of Constantinople to organize an Albanian Episcopate in the U.S.A. Lipa was 'an agent of the Monarcho-Fascists and of the U.S. Intelligence Service.' Albanians in the U.S.A. should keep their allegiance to the Albanian Church directed from Albania."[24]

Fan Noli, despite some losses to Lipa, had really not too much to worry about. The Fan Nolists' Church has only a microscopic Christian flock. Not the least of its support comes from Moslem Albanians who look upon it as a propaganda weapon against the Northern Epirotes. Lipa, who is trying to play a similar game, must be content with a few scattered malcontents he has been able to attract from Noli.

There is one very good reason why both Lipa and Noli attracted so few Christian followers—the Orthodox in America who originated within the boundaries of the present Albanian state—about 15,000 of them—would no sooner attend an Albanian Church than enter the Kaaba of Mecca. They are completely integrated into the Hellenic-American community of which they are an indistinguishable part. Those who fancy that Lipa's presence in America, with or without the spiritual benediction of the Patriarchate, would in any way change the situation are supporting a chimaera against a mirage.

[24] *East Europe* (pub., London, England), Nov. 16, 1950.

Chapter III

NORTHERN EPIRUS AND THE GREEK REBIRTH

The Seed is Sown

Ancient Epirus and its 70 cities had a place of prominence in the affairs of the Greeks from the days of Neoptolemus, its Homeric hero-king, to Pyrrhus' invasion of Italy, which left the term "pyrrhic victory" to posterity. In time, Epirus fell to Rome which in turn, transformed by history, became the so-called Byzantine Empire—Roman in name and Greek and Christian in fact.

Afterward, barbaric invasions of Greece followed wave upon wave. When the Fourth Crusade fell upon Constantinople and momentarily eclipsed the Byzantine Empire, Epirus became the rallying point of continental Greece and came within an inch of becoming the empire's restorer. In the restoration that followed, the Despotate of Epirus disappeared and all of Epirus passed into Greek hands with the exception of a coastal strip held by the Sicilian Normans.

By 1349, Epirus, along with much of Macedonia and Thessaly, endured the Serbian occupation of Tsar Dushan, in whose wake little feudal states ruled by foreign adventurers and maintained by mercenary troops sprung up.

It was during this dark period that hellenized Albanians settled in parts of Epirus where their mingling with the decimated but culturally superior native population produced the Albanian patois—a half-Greek speech in its unliterary state—which survives in Northern Epirus to this day.

Albanian-speaking Epirotes, induced by the Paleologus Dynasty—Byzantium's last—to settle in southern Greece, have kept their Albanian jargon to this day. They are a proud Greek people whose heroes in the Greek War of Independence—Miaoules, Koundouriotes, Bouboulis, etc.—are the heroes of all of Greece.

Ottoman power, weakly opposed by fragmented Greece, reached Epirus before the fall of Constantinople itself. In October, 1431, Ioannina, which became the provincial capital under the Turks, surrendered to the forces of Murad II led by Sinan Pasha. The major portion of Epirus became a fief of the Ottomans, but scattered, semi-autonomous clusters of villages resisted.

By 1452, a year before the fall of Constantinople, the Turks held all the major centers, but Chimarra resisted and managed, until 1518, to keep out both the Turks and the Venetians who held adjoining territory. Even after capitulating to superior Ottoman forces, the Chimarriotes managed to preserve their internal administration into the 20th Century. Such is the prelude for the dark days of Ottoman rule that followed.

The Ottoman Yoke

Had not the greater tyranny of the modern totalitarian states appeared in our own days we could scarcely believe the condition of Greece under the Ottomans. The 18th century Englishman William Eton, in his *Survey of the Turkish Empire,* 1798 (Vol. II, p. 76), remarked:

> "Conquered Greece polished Rome, but the conquerors were Romans. Conquered Greece did not polish Turkey, for the conquerors were Turks. The insensibility of these barbarians is astonishing; living amid the effulgence of genius, they have not caught one spark; they gaze with unfeeling stupidity on the wonder and boast of art, on their glorious monuments, and conclude they were built by genii, and then destroy them, to burn the marble for lime to make stucco for their own tasteless houses; where ignorance, tyranny, superstition and gross sensuality do dwell, in sad and stupid pomp, or issuing out with savage fury, lay waste the country round, and imbrue their hands in the blood of the helpless, murdering those they have conquered without remorse. Thus, the finest countries in the world have become deserts; part inhabited by savage beasts, and part by more savage men; the poor aborigines sulking in hiding places like the timid hare (which epithet the Turks give them in derision) while those beasts of prey roam abroad."

Of the condition of the Greek people under this regime of nomad herders of men the same British observer wrote:

> "This degradation and servility of their situation has operated for centuries, and has consequently produced an accumulated effect on the mind; but were this weight taken off, the elasticity and vigour of the soul would have wide room for expansion, and though it cannot be expected that they would at once rise to the proud distinction of their former heroes, they would doubtless display energies of mind, which the iron hand of despotism

has long kept dormant and inert. It is rather astonishing that they have retained so much energy of character, and are not more debased; for like noble coursers, they champ the bit and spurn indignantly the yoke; when once freed from this, they will enter the course of glory. *The truth of these observations will appear, whether we consider the Greeks in their common character as one people, or whether we consider them according to their local and peculiar distinctions.* [italics mine]"[25]

Islamization and apostasy

The intolerable yoke of the Ottoman rested heavily upon Epirus. While conversions by the sword to the conqueror's faith could not fail to take place, it is a wonder and a tribute to the majority of Epirotes that they remained constant in their deep-rooted Christian faith and in their Hellenic ancestry.

The very first conversions were a result of the battle of Baghdad between Turkey and Persia in 1639. Until 1640, four fifths of the Epirotes had remained Christian, but during that year 50,000 were made to forsake Christianity.

The incident is curious enough to bear repeating. In the course of the Turko-Persian war (1623-1639), a religious war, inasmuch as Sunnite Turks and Shiite Persians contended for the mastery of the lands of Islam, Sultan Murad IV called for bodies of Christian troops to fight for him under their own commanders. A liberal share in the booty was promised, but all such Christian formations had to fly the Prophet's banner. Any other colors flown in this Moslem religious war would be regarded as an unforgivable affront to Islam.

A body of Greek Spahis, numbering 12,000, was composed of Northern Epirotes from Delvinon, Rhiza, Argyrocastron, Konitsa and Premeti. As the tide of battle went against the Sultan's forces at Baghdad, the Epirotes saw a weak point in the enemy ranks and led a wild charge. In the confusion of battle someone gave the order for the standard-bearer to unfurl the flag of St. George. Into the Persian ranks, with their Christian flag ever in front, the Epirotes hurled themselves. The Persians broke and retreated.

However grateful Murad might have shown himself to the Christians for his victory, he was constantly reminded of his word by the *Sheikh-ul-Islam* and the ulemas who had stood about his throne. Moslem honor was wounded and would be avenged. The order was given that the heaviest penalties would be

[25] Cited in Comstock, John L., *History of the Greek Revolution,* pp. 75-76.

exacted on those Epirote participants who failed to embrace Islam. Their whole families were likewise to abandon Christianity. As a result the first major apostasy occurred in Epirus.

Other conversions were made at sword's edge later. Yet Islam was, and for all the outward fanaticism of its followers still is, only skin-deep in many parts of Epirus. For example, in the Kourvelesi district, where Christian customs survive as local superstitions, the folklorist and ethnologist will discover many curious things. The very name of the Moslems dwelling there, *Liab*, is derived from the expression *la besën* which can be translated as "apostasy" and is equivalent to the Latin *lapsus*. When their flocks are ailing these Liabs are as wont to call upon Christian priest as a Moslem hodja. They do likewise to have their crops blessed and their popular Moslem saint, "Baba Ali of Tepeleni", is a thinly disguised St. Elias. Other strange survivals of Orthodox Christianity can be cited in this respect.

Genuine Turkish administrators in Epirus were few and far between. Since the Ghegs of nearby Albania had become, mostly through their own free will, Moslems, there existed a large body of co-religionists of the new converts in the neighboring northern provinces. As the Ottomans pressed Islamization, so much firmer became the faith of those who stood steadfast in Christianity and, as is natural, greater grew the chasm between the Christian and his apostate brother.

As a reward for apostasy the former Christians were granted the confiscated lands of the stubborn Orthodox. With these grants went Ottoman titles such as "bey" and "aga".

These new Moslems adopted the loosest kind of Mohammedanism, the Bektashi creed, regarded by more conservative Moslems as a heresy. The dervish order around which the Bektashlis cling is a mystic society of gnostic antecedents philosophically. Its lay followers, with few exceptions, are not only unfeelingly ignorant of its true content, but originally affiilated themselves with it in order to reduce Mohammedanism to the barest externals of Moslem worship. The spread of Bektashism in Albania was due to its convenience ritually in comparison with Sunnite Islam and to its popularity with the Janissaries, most of whom were recruited from the western Balkans.

The last major forceable conversions to Islam before the persecutions of Ali Pasha took place between 1733 and 1740. Afterwards, the Sultan abolished the recruiting of Janissaries in

Epirus, instituting a per capita tax, the notorious "haratch" instead. Koutsi, at the outskirts of Kourvelesi and Chimarra, was probably the last entire village to turn Moslem. Its conversion took place in 1818.

The First Revolts

Uprisings in Epirus took place in 1495, 1585, 1612 and 1684. The latter marked the first serious attempt to enlist the aid of Orthodox Russia, the sole powerful state in the world with a Byzantine heritage—the "Third Rome".

Having risen, the Greeks of Palea Arta (near Valona) and Chimarra sent a mission headed by Panos Matsiles and Elias Christophorus to Prince Orlov to obtain financial aid (which was given) and military supplies that were promised but not forthcoming. Thus, this uprising also met the fate of its predecessors, but left a lasting impression.

A tradition fixes its date as identical with that of the Greek War of Independence, i.e. March 25 which is Evangelism (Annunciation) Day. The Epirotes preserved its memory by going from house to house and to the fields each Annunciation Day, ringing chimes and exhorting the snakes and vipers to depart. The symbolism is apparent. The custom, which survives in our own times, was even observed in those villages which later became Moslem and forgot the significance of this observance. Both Greek and Albanian versions, almost identical, exist of the verses sung. We give the Albanian:

Ikni gjërpënje, ikni shtërpënje,	Depart snakes, depart vipers,
Sot vjen Vangjelizmoj ba kamë dhe lopatë.	Annunciation comes today with knife and spade.
Do t'u presi, do t'u hedhi	To cut you down, to cast you out
Përmbi udhe, ndënë udhe.	Upon the roads and paths.

The association of Annunciation Day with insurrection against the Turks spread through Greece via Palea-Artan refugees who joined their Albanophone brethren in Attica. Inasmuch as the proclamation of Greek independence in 1821 really predates March 25, it is actually a much older tradition that the Greeks are commemorating. In point of fact, though perhaps unwittingly, they are paying their respects to the Northern Epirote Greek fighters of the memorable revolt of 1684.

The Rise of Argyrocastron

Though founded as an ancient Chaonian town and called "Argyrine" in Byzantine times, it was in the early days of the Ottoman occupation that Argyrocastron began to rise in prominence in the western part of Northern Epirus. At a time of almost universal ignorance in Greece, in 1633, it opened the doors of its first Greek school. Sponsored by Argyrocastran merchants in Venice, it was under the supervision of Metropolitan Callistus of Dryinoupolis. At the time it was founded there were no more than five or six such institutions in the whole of Greece. The school was further enlarged in 1778 by a grant of 4,000 florins bequeathed by Christos Constantinides, a wealthy Epirote merchant in Vienna. Later, a Greek Gymnasium (High School) was founded in 1818 in Argyrocastron by Metropolitan Dositheos and enriched in 1839 by the large endowment of Demetrius Hatzipolyzou, an Argyrocastran who had amassed a fortune in Wallachia.

From Argyrocastron went forth the first pioneer of a Hellenic Epirote revival. He was Sophianus, Metropolitan of Dryinoupolis. (Dryinoupolis is the ecclesiastical eparchy of Argyrocastron and includes Argyrocastron, Delvinon, Chimarra and Tepelini.) During his tenure Islamization became a danger that might have smothered Christianity. Since many villages had just become Moslem, family ties between *muminin* and Christians still existed and mixed marriages had occurred. In such arrangements, the law of the Koran and the Sultan directed that the children be raised in the faith of the Prophet. Had this practice prevailed, Islam's complete triumph was assured.

It was in recognition of this peril that Sophianus resigned his bishopric and became a wandering preacher. Single-handedly he defeated by reason and eloquence a force that had the swords of an empire for argument. The practice of mixed marriages between Moslems and Christians was stopped in the province of Argyrocastron.

Sophianus' last days were spent at the Monastery of St. Athanasius in the village of Polytsani where he taught religion and letters to the village children. Although uncanonized, he is always spoken of by the pious Polytsaniotes as St. Sophianus. From the inscription on the glass-covered casket containing his skull, still preserved in the monastery and venerated as a holy relic, we know he died in 1711.

Here we have the very first stirrings of the Epirote renaissance. Later came the full bloom of Epirote cultural leadership in Moschopolis and Korytsa, and the completion of Sophianus' work by Cosmas the Aetolian. The leadership Epirus was now to show in Greece's most grievous hour was to be panhellenic, for all of Greece was to reap the rich harvest her Northern Epirote sons had sown.

Moschopolis, Korytsa and the Epirote Renaissance

In the century before the Greek Revolution a remarkable upsurge of cultural and material progress, without parallel in the rest of the Greek world, took place in Epirus despite increased Ottoman persecution. Not a small part of this was due to the migration abroad of Epirotes. These men, who went out to Venice, Trieste, Corfu, Austria, France, the Danubian Principalities, Russia and afterwards to Constantinople and Egypt, devoted much of their wealth to the direct aid of their unfortunate compatriots.

The industrious merchants of Moschopolis (Voscopolis) near Korytsa were among the pioneers. An English writer asks:

> "Were not the enterprising natives of Moscopolis familiar in Constantinople and Belgrade, Vienna, Budapest and Leipzig? They had even established in those towns their own Chambers of Commerce and it was generally recognized that both in wealth and culture the Moscopolites had everywhere a prominent position."[26]

The first printing press in Epirus and the second in the whole Ottoman Empire was set up in Moschopolis in 1720 by the monk George Constantinides. The primacy of the remarkably literate and well-travelled Metropolitan Joasaph (1709-1742) saw the establishment of a famous Greek academy and an extensive library in Moschopolis. There were in that town 12,000 stone houses and no less than 23 churches, the best of which were built during Joasaph's tenure. Among these were the Church of the Assumption, built in 1715, St. Athanasius in 1721 and the Church of the Taxiarchs in 1724. All this magnificent work suffered violent sack and destruction by the Moslem Albanians in 1788. Rebuilt as a village and destroyed again in 1916 and during World War II by the descendants of its first despoilers, Moschopolis' sun eventually set. Nevertheless, the

[26] Baerlein, Henry, *Under the Acroceraunian Mountains,* p. 18.

impetus given by Moschopolis to awakening Greece, which was of the spirit, could not perish with the stone and mortar. It is recalled to this day by Greeks in grateful remembrance.

Nearby Korytsa began to flower in the shadow of Moschopolis after the latter's destruction. Korytsa first receives mention in 1487 as a fief granted by Sultan Beyazid II to a local apostate named Iliaz Bey. It remained a village until 1700 when its Church of the Living Source (Zoödochou Pege) was founded. In 1724 the Cathedral of St. George was begun which became the Metropolitan seat after the destruction of Moschopolis. The same year saw the first Greek school there. A new school was erected in 1817, largely paid for by the donation of Paul Antzia, a Korytsaian who had earned a fortune in Poland. More schools were added later in 1836 and 1843, with the grants of still other successful native sons. Much later, in 1856, the celebrated Gymnasium was established with its large library and splendid department of natural sciences. This bore an inscription truthfully proclaiming that, "A great number of students have departed from this school, have dedicated themselves to science and the practical arts and have done honor to Greek intelligence and industry."

Cosmas the Aetolian and the Epirotes

The figure of a humble servant of God, trudging the narrow mountain paths with only a sack containing all his earthly possessions, has passed into undying oral tradition. The time in which he lived is hazy in folk memory, for whenever an Epirote peasant wishes to denote age he says "from the time of Kurd Pasha", yet his memory is still as fresh as it was the August day he met his martyrdom. He is Father Cosmas the Aetolian, the St. Cosmas of a thousand prophecies.

Cosmas was born the son of a weaver at Mega Dendron, an Aetolian village in the Apokouros district near Naupactus (Lepanto). A deacon named Ananias taught him his first letters and from there he went to the Athoniad Theological School at Mt. Athos where he was ordained a monk in 1758.

At the age of 45, he became inspired with a unique mission. Leaving the Holy Mount he went to Constantinople where a brother, Chrystanthus, was teacher of the children of the Phanariot Soutsos. He obtained permission and blessings from Patriarch Seraphim II to become a preacher and, for twenty years, he travelled the length and breadth of Greece preaching the Gospel openly and Hellenism covertly. About 210 schools were founded by him in the villages of northern Greece.

His work in Northern Epirus strengthened a people's sorely tried faith and the fame of his sanctity was heard even among Moslems. Wherever he went a new determination appeared among the Epirotes to preserve their faith and heritage for the coming day of liberation. Village schools multiplied until the poorest hamlet managed to possess a room where the Greek alphabet could be taught, in extreme cases by a teacher who was himself half-literate.

There is a graphic illustration of Cosmas' power in the story told of his second visit to Chimarra in 1777. He had urged the Chimarriotes during his first visit to open a school. They had been unable to find the means to build one so Cosmas, axe in hand, led the Chimarriotes to one of the village chapels that had long fallen into ruin, and with his axe began to demolish it. As he did so, he instructed the Chimarriotes to use the long useless stones to build themselves a school. In this manner the first Greek school in Chimarra was built.

One of the Moslems who had heard Cosmas had the gift of prophecy was a bandit son of the dead Veli Bey of Tepeleni. To him Cosmas foretold a future glittering with promise of power and gold. "Some day you will be lord of all this land," Cosmas told the astounded and delighted robber. "Someday you will even enter Constantinople with a red beard," Cosmas prophesied to the enraptured bey, who achieved in time all that Cosmas predicted. After becoming master of nearly the whole of Greece, he did enter Constantinople, his beard dyed red from the blood of his decapitated head. The name of the grateful blackguard was Ali. In his day of glory he allowed a Greek church to be erected to Cosmas' memory.

Cosmas, whom all honored by prefixing the title of sainthood to his name, received the martyr's crown when seized by order of Kurd Pasha at Berati and hanged on Aug. 24, 1779 in the village of Kaliekoutsi.

The Premature Rebellion

In 1787 Catharine the Great sent an agent named Soteris to travel through all Epirus with Russian funds and manifestos signed by her calling upon the Greeks to revolt.

The call was successful and the Epirotes routed the army of the Pasha of Jannina, slaying the Pasha's son in battle. His armor was later presented to Catharine herself by a Greek delegation from Epirus to St. Petersburg in April, 1790. The heads of the delegation, which requested Russian arms and a Romanov to restore freedom to the Greeks, were Panos Kyris, Christos Lantsiotes and Nicholas Pangalos.

Catharine, thwarted once in her pet "Greek project", was willing to try again. The Epirote delegation was furnished with 1,000 ducats in gold and sent to confer with Prince Potemkin in Moldavia. They arrived in Greece via Vienna that same autumn accompanied by an experienced military advisor in the person of Major-General Tamaras, a Greek in the Russian service.

The general revolt, timed to coincide with a Russian invasion, never occurred because the Prussian King posted 150,000 troops on the Bohemian border, and England, then as now anxious to keep the Russians from the Mediterranean, ordered the British fleet to the Baltic in the spring of 1791. Catharine reluctantly kissed her "Greek project" goodbye and concluded peace with the Sultan who gave his Epirote subjects another taste of Ottoman atrocity.

Ali Pasha, Satrap of Jannina

Meanwhile, in 1788, Ali Bey of Tepelini, an Albanian ex-bandit, became master of the Vilayet (Province) of Jannina, by fraud and bribery obtaining *ex post facto* recognition from the Shadow of Allah by greasing liberally the palms of the Empress Mother, the Divan of Viziers and the heads of the Janissary Odjaks (Battalions).

After the Janissaries became a hereditary institution they began to occupy much the same position under their rulers as the Praetorian Guard had to the "Barrack Emperors" of ancient Rome. They cowed a line of weakling sultans whom they elevated and deposed at will. Ali grasped this fact and used it once he became master of Jannina. As long as the Janissaries ruled in Constantinople he would be master of Epirus. His rule, from 1788 to 1822, the first 32 years by the Sultan's weakness and the last two by his scimitar's edge, was an unbroken tragedy for the Epirotes. Had the Hellenism of the Epirotes not become the example for all of Greece it would have perished under Ali, but it withstood his test of fire and sword and remained unscathed. Soon its spark was to kindle the fire of Greek Revolution.

All during this time the Epirote hills were an armed camp. The Greek Klephts continually harassed the masters of the plains from their mountain hideouts. The Turk had been encamped in Europe for three hundred years. During this time his administration had been more in the nature of an occupation of enemy territory than a subjugation of a conquered province. The Greeks, especially the Epirotes, had handed down a spirit of resistance through sporadic revolts and ceaseless guerrilla activity.

If the hills belonged to the Klephts, the plains belonged to Ali Pasha. He paid lip-service to the Porte and proceeded firmly to make and unmake his own rule—a rule marked by excesses of cruelty that still make Greek blood run cold. Autonomous in fact, the "Lion of Jannina" received semi-official French and British delegates at his court. One of these, the learned member of the French Academy and Napoleon's envoy, Pouqueville, described Epirus under the Albanian ex-bandit's rule:

> "Since 1740, the Epirotes had preserved a sort of semi-independence. But, when in 1788 Ali became the Satrap of Jannina, the Epirotes were subjected to a most cruel persecution. Ali devestated Epirus. He robbed the churches and the ancient temples to make grotesque palaces and mosques.
>
> "The province which gave Greek letters to all the Greeks under the Turks, the province which had a Greek College, built by funds donated by Caplanis and Zosimas, the province which had produced Meletius, the famous geographer, Soedonis, the Greek grammarian and author of the first Greek dictionary, and Psalidas, the famous mathematician, fell into darkness and her schools were closed.
>
> "The court of Ali Pasha is open to murders, criminals and perjurers. His guards are assassins, his pages are the illegal sons of his depravity, his commissaries are mean Vlachs, ready to commit any crime; his public officials prisoners who take glory in their crimes. Ministers who commit sacrilege against the living God are admitted into the innermost dark council rooms in order to disclose to Ali Pasha the innocence of the poor and the secrets of the confession of the repentant Christian Greek population. Spies, disguised in all forms, seek the property of the orphan, the widow and the weak. Timid virgins, hiding in the dark recesses of bolted chambers, cannot escape his scrutiny. The daughter is snatched from the bosom of her mother; the son, the only support and hope of the family, is taken away by the Albanians; honor, beauty and chastity (male and female) are sacrificed to the most barbarous and shameless passions. Kindness and favors never fall to the lot of good men. And yet, despite all the orgies of impiety, the Greek population holds on tenaciously to virtue and to religious life . . . The clergy, the bishops, monks and the priests, by whom the worship of

Christ was made to survive the fall of the Greek Empire, comforted the Greeks by teaching them that, being born Christians, they should always think of their freedom."[27]

The apostates of Epirus, having adopted Islam, had been cut off from the Hellenic renaissance of Epirus by their act of renunciation. Religiously they had been grafted on to the world of Islam. Linguistically and culturally they had degenerated almost to the barbarism of the truly Albanian Gheg tribes. These neo-Albanians with a vested religious and economic interest in the Star and Crescent in the service of Ali Pasha burned villages and massacred their former Epirote Christian brethren without mercy. If we henceforth refer to the native Albanians of Northern Epirus it is to the descendants of these men whose fathers were once both Greek and Christian that we shall have reference. Such was Ali Pasha himself. Such are the Hoxhas and the Shehus today. The American philhellene Dr. Comstock wrote:

"With regard to his character, there cannot be two opinions: it was one of pure unsophisticated evil, with scarcely a redeeming quality; one of those rank productions of the hot-bed of Turkish despotism which are remarkable only for their enormous growth, not differing otherwise, in a moral point of view, from the vulgarest specimens."[28]

In addition to this prose description of Ali, written some six years after Ali's death, Lord Byron has left us one in verse:

"In marble-paved pavilion, where a spring
Of living water from the centre rose,
Whose bubbling did a genial freshness fling,
And soft voluptuous couches breathed repose,
Ali reclined, a man of wars and woes:
Yet in his lineaments ye cannot trace,
While Gentleness her milder radiance throws
Along that aged venerable face,
The deeds that lurk beneath, and stain him with disgrace.

"It is not that yon hoary, lengthening beard
Ill suits the passions which belong to youth:
Love conquers age—so Hafiz hath averr'd,
So sings the Teian, and he sings in sooth—
But crimes that scorn the tender voice of ruth
Beseeming all men ill, but most the man
In years, have marked him with a tiger's tooth

27 Pouqueville, Charles Françoise, *Histoire de la Régénération de la Grèce.*
28 Comstock, *op. cit.*, p. 138.

> Blood follows blood, and through their mortal span,
> In bloodier acts conclude those who with blood began."[29]

With the unscrupulous acumen the world eventually learned to expect from Albanian politicians Ali played off Napoleon against the British and vice versa. With French help he subdued Preveza, Vonitsa and Buthrotum (Butrinto) in 1797, after which he went over to the British side. He was to exchange sides several more times. Ali took from his erstwhile allies what arms and gold they provided and gave them empty promises in return. He benefited from all of them though, in the end, none benefited from him.

Two attacks Ali launched against the tiny Epirote district of Souli, a republic of mountain villagers. In 1803 he took the rebellious Souli from its gallant defenders who took the road of exile and martyrdom. Among them was the immortal Marcos Botsaris, hero of modern Greece who fell many years later at Messolonghi in the Greek War of Independence.

It is noteworthy that Souli was then an Albanophone pocket in southern Epirus because it calls to mind yet another proof of the allegiance of all Epirote Greeks, Grecophone, Albanophone, Vlachophone and even, in two or three villages near Kortysa, Bulgarophone, to their Hellenic nation. Marcos Botsaris, an exile in Corfu, may have been the compiler of an Albanian dictionary for the use of the British administration, but he fought and died for the only country to which he and his compatriots ever owed fealty, his Greek motherland.

In 1807 Ali made another turnabout and allied himself to Napoleon. This alliance lasted only to 1809 when he finally turned to the British once more. In a series of attacks, first upon the nearby Pasha of Delvino and then upon his fellow-satrap of Berati, he got possession of all of Northern Epirus. With Thessaly and Aetolo-Acarnania in his hands and his relatives installed in other Greek provinces he could almost be called the *de facto* king of Greece.

The most shameful chapter in the west's relations with Ali is that of Parga. The seacoast town, which had placed itself under the protection of the Union Jack, was betrayed in a cash transaction to Ali by Sir Thomas Maitland, the hellenophobe Governor of the Ionian Islands. "Christ was sold for silver and

[29] Gordon, George, Lord Byron, *Childe Harold's Pilgrimage,* Canto II, vs. LXII, LXIII.

Parga sold for gold," according to an old Greek ballad.

On May 10, 1819, the natives of Parga left their hearths, taking with them, according to tradition, even the bones of their ancestors from the graves. They found refuge in the Ionian Islands ruled by the man who had betrayed them.

The worst of Ali's ire, however, was reserved for Northern Epirus where the sword of Islam was felt once more on Christian necks. Already in 1797 he had taken the Dryinus valley of Argyrocastron and the villages of Delvino which had been burned by him and their populations massacred. These villages were now repopulated as Moslem fiefs inhabited by southern Epirote, Thessalian and Macedonian Greeks. Their descendants continued to work the fields for their Moslem overlords as sharecroppers until 1945 when the lands were confiscated by the Bolshevik government of Enver Hoxha. These Greek peasants, a small part of the Greek majority of Northern Epirus, are the so-called "Greek minority" invoked by Albanian propagandists who avail themselves of the fact that these are the only exclusively Greek-speaking Hellenes of that province.

The extent of the carnage and arson which followed Ali's troops into Northern Epirus had to be witnessed to be believed. Pouqueville gives us such an eye-witness account:

> "We came, near Ondessovo, which in 1798 was a beautiful village, and now had only one villa of Ali Pasha. All the inhibitants had been murdered because they were Christian Greeks.
>
> "Then we came upon the town of Hagios Vassilios, the inhabitants of which had also been butchered by the Albanians in 1798 and the town was now nothing but ruins.
>
> "We passed by Nivitsa Bouba, which had been destroyed in April, 1798. As we were approaching Delvino, we heard shots. An Albanian officer returning announced that Ali's forces were taking Delvino. He advised me that 'it was not safe' for me to appear as a Christian. He gave me Albanian dresses. We entered Delvino. Flames were rising from the town. The Albanians had pillaged and set it on fire. The officer informed me that he was showing too much kindness to a Christian. He said that every Mohammedan who shows friendship for the Christian is a dubious character and unworthy of the true Faith of the Prophet.
>
> "We entered Dridgsi. An Albanian crier went out and demanded of the Greek people that each family should bring two lambs, chickens, milk, cheese, butter, eggs, wine, bread, and fodder for the horses.
>
> "It is impossible to describe how difficult it has proved for me to study the Greek people of this province owing to the suspicions of the ruling Albanians. But, my observations have persuaded me that their large numbers, their courage, their industry and their activity will some day change the face of Greece."

It will startle the reader who is unfamiliar with the Balkans to discover that Ali Pasha, the genocidal maniac, is next to the mercenary Skanderbeg as the *beau ideal* of the modern Albanians. The mouthpieces of Albanian propaganda have not been above assuring credulous foreigners that the wretched Greeks would do well to be more respectful to the shade of the great humanitarian and philhellene Ali Pasha.

What is fantastic is that some Europeans, unacquainted with the evidence to the contrary, have taken this hogwash seriously. We do not mean to offend anyone personally by singling out a specimen, but the following deserves some kind of prize:

> "This hero (Ali) made alliances with the Greeks to free his country from the Turkish yoke, but his fierce struggles were in vain. With conspicuous generosity, however, he created a large army and navy for the provinces over which he ruled, and endowed several towns with schools, libraries and other public works."[30]

If the writer of the above drew his sources verbally from Albanians his informants must have been laughing long and loud behind his back.

Parga was the last town taken by Ali's treachery. From that time his days were numbered. Mahmud the Reformer, who now sat on the Ottoman throne, had disposed of the Janissaries by mass decapitation and proceeded to put his ramshackle house in order. Mahmud II was the last great Ottoman Sultan before the "Sick Man of Europe" began his final death agonies.

Ali's gold lost its purchasing power in Constantinople when Mahmud decided his Albanian satrap had become too powerful to escape the inevitable bowstring. Ali was declared an outlaw in 1820. His Albanian mercenaries and most of his family deserted the old tyrant without remorse and joined the Ottoman forces besieging Jannina.

Prostrate but not dead for hundreds of years, a specter rose behind both Ali and the Ottomans to become a plague to both their houses. The defiance of Leonidas and the eloquence of Demosthenes were once more abroad in the land. Striking out for liberty or death in 1821, Hellas proclaimed to the world her resurrection.

30 Mann, S. E., *A Short Albanian Grammar*, p. 10.

Chapter IV

A CENTURY OF HOPE

Epirus and the Greek Revolution

The Epirotes, among the first nationally conscious Hellenes, were ready to lead in Greece's fight. They had been the first to revolt against the Turks and the first to take their place in Greece's spiritual regeneration. Above all, they had been among the founders of the *Philike Hetaeria* (Friendly Society), the secret patriotic organization created by three Greek merchants, two of them Epirotes, in 1814.

The greatest Greeks of the period, as well as the humblest, were enrolled in the Society's ranks. Among them were the Hospodar of Moldavia and Wallachia, the martyred Oecumenical Patriarch Gregory V and the most influential Greeks of Trieste, Budapest, Vienna, Bucharest, Jassy, Odessa, Moscow and St. Petersburg. Many among them were sons of Epirus who gave willingly their money, their time and even their lives for the idea of a resurrected Greece. It would have been beyond their power of prognosis to imagine that Epirus would not receive her due of freedom within an indebted motherland.

The Epirotes had been in a state of readiness since 1818. On Dec. 12, 1820, Marcos Botsaris made his way from Corfu to his ancestral Souli where he raised the flag of revolt. This was a signal for Prince Alexander Hypsilanti, Hospodar of Moldavia and Wallachia, to proclaim his revolt in the name of Greece on Feb. 23, 1821.

This Danubian phase of the Greek Revolution, a fight for Greece fought in far-off Rumania, was as ill-fated as it was singular. In the end, one of the Rumanian chieftains, Todor Vladimirescu, betrayed Hypsilanti to the Turks. Hypsilanti's troops, not a few of them Epirotes, made futile stands against the Turks. We are told of one of these Greek captains, Athanasius Pines of Vouno, Chimarra, who was surrounded by the

Ottomans in a church outside Bucharest. With only 13 men of his band of Epirotes he held the Turks for 32 hours. Two thousand Ottomans, armed with muskets, cannon and bombs, fought the little band at the loss of 800 lives before its members were captured and executed.

These events were a war within a war. Epirus was filled with Ottoman troops fighting the remnants of Ali Pasha's armies while the tyrant himself was shut up in his besieged fortress in Jannina.

In March, 1821, the standard of Greek freedom was raised by Metropolitan Germanus at Patras in the Peloponnesus. Prince Hypsilanti had already sent his brother Demetrius via Trieste to assume leadership of the insurgents. He arrived in Epirus with no knowledge that this brother in Wallachia had failed. In Epirus, Demetrius Hypsilanti was met by Perrhaebius, the agent of the *Philike Hetaeria,* who sent him on to the Peloponnese.

At Premeti, Chormovo, Argyrocastron, Chimarra and elsewhere the Epirotes gathered to fight for freedom. They were ready to enter the field when Mustafa Pasha of Shkodra descended on Epirus with 2,500 Ghegs and was joined by 8,000 in local Albanian Moslem bands. These cut the Epirote units from each other and made organized resistance impossible.

Under such circumstances the only out for the Epirotes was to make their way to Roumeli and the Peloponnesus where the Greek War of Independence was meeting with better fortune. Seven hundred Northern Epirotes rallied to the forces of Caraiscakis. Another 400 made their way to Euboea with their captains, the Argyrocastran Liakos, Stavros and Costas Vassilliou who fell heroically in the battle of Andrilae. Still others took part in further campaigns against the Ottomans.

The provisional Greek government at Corinth, on May 13, 1822, placed the seacoasts of continental Greece still under Ottoman domination in a state of siege, declaring:

> "It proclaims . . . in accordance with the right of nations and of Europe, all the coastal areas which are still held by the enemy in Epirus as well as the Peloponnesus, Euboea, and Thessaly, from Epidamnus (Dyrrachium) to Corona (at the edge of the Chalcidice) in Macedonia in a state of siege."

Ali Pasha, by the same treachery he had dealt others, was finally beheaded by the Ottomans in February, 1822. Anarchy reigned in Epirus. The villages about Pogoniane, Jannina and Konitsa were the field of battle between the Ottoman troops and an ertswhile supporter of Ali Pasha, the Albanian bandit Selihtar Poda.

Poda, after massacring Christian villagers and Ottomans indiscriminately, was put down after Reshid Pasha was appointed Governor of Jannina in 1825. In 1829 Reshid left Jannina to become Grand Vizier in Constantinople. His successor, Selim Pasha, was confronted with the same unruly Albanian elements who plundered Epirus with impunity. Poda, not completely crushed, found an ally in Mustafa Pasha and his Ghegs who were dissatisfied with their share of the war booty. Reshid was forced to return to Epirus to crush the bandits. Reshid's son Emin replaced the inefficient Selim Pasha after the Ottomans had dealt with the Ghegs and bandits in the autumn of 1830.

John Capodistrias and the Liberation of Greece

In 1827, to head off the abnormal international tension the Greek Revolution had caused in post-Napoleonic Europe, the Great Powers joined in and destroyed the Turko-Egyptian fleet at Navarino. Turkey, far from showing strength, proved so feeble that it needed only a common European will to uproot the Ottoman Empire once and for all. Neither France nor Britain, the two allies at Navarino, was anxious to do so for several reasons. To some of their diplomatic confrères the Sultan was a "legitimate monarch" in the age of Holy Alliance. The chief reason, however, was that, should the Ottoman Empire be dismembered, all the Great Powers would close in for a piece of the corpse. This was a situation which all regarded as too explosive to touch, and would continue to so regard it into the 20th century. Henceforth Europe would keep the Ottoman Empire from collapsing suddenly because it was much easier to stand by and see it disintegrate piece by piece.

For these reasons the Great Powers decided upon a course that could not fail to leave the Greeks a bitter heritage. It was as if, in World War II, we had helped the French to liberate the territory of Vichy, France and then had forbidden the French Republic to advance further; then made peace with Hitler and sanctioned Nazi control of half of France to exist side by side with the free Republic.

To a people who had shown themselves willing to die for freedom the Allied note of Oct. 27, 1827 was a blow not easily forgiven or forgotten. The note told the embattled Greek nation:

"We will not suffer any expedition, any cruise, any blockade, to be made by the Greeks beyond the limits of from Volos to Lepanto, including Salamis, Aegina, Hydra and Spetsa . . . We will consider as void, papers given to cruisers found beyond the prescribed limits; and ships of war of the allied powers will have orders to arrest them wherever they may be found."

With this infamy the Great Powers hoped to write *finis* to the episode of Greek Revolution. What they did was force the Greeks to counter with the "Great Idea", the "Megale Idea" of a united Greece which everywhere became the dream of successive Greek generations. Today, after irretrievable losses and a few major gains, only Northern Epirus and Cyprus remain of the unredeemed Hellenic legacy. The Greeks will never rest until these too are brought within the boundaries of their motherland.

The first head of a recognized modern Greek state was a Northern Epirote by ancestry, the Corfiote-born Argyrocastran Count John Capodistrias. Previous to the Greek Revolution he had been no less than Foreign Minister of Russia. Giving up his august position as servant of the greatest empire in Europe, he became head of the struggling Greek nation with all its factions. From 1828 to 1831 he headed the government of the Hellenic state.

The ancestry of Greece's first head of state has not generally been referred to. His family originally went to Istria as merchants, hence the family name. They settled in Corfu where he was born. The Capodistrias ancestral home was standing in Argyrocastron until quite recently. In March, 1913, following the town's first brief liberation, it was decided that the site was to be used for the town's administrative offices, and the then Crown Prince George was present to lay the foundation. On that occasion, the future George II was honored by the Mufti who presented him with a pair of pistols originally belonging to Ali Pasha. The new edifice was never built because of the storm that soon broke upon the luckless province.

Count John was the first to tilt his lance against Europe's diplomatic windmills. Though realizing that the Great Powers were indisposed to hear Greek pleas for a frontier corresponding to the Hellenic ethnic limits, he made a modest demand for at least a minimum settlement. In a memorandum to the Emperor of Russia and the Courts of Europe on Jan. 21, 1830, he pleaded for substantially what Greece still claims officially after 125 years of futile sacrifice. "If one takes into consideration," he wrote, "the history, the still existing monuments, the view of travellers and geographers, Greece must have as a northern boundary a line beginning from the mouth of the Aos (Viossa) and extending to the sources of that river."

Minimal though it was, the Greek demand fell on deaf ears in Europe's foreign ministries, where the wishes of peoples were the least of concerns in dealing with the "Eastern Question". Capodistrias' own ancestral Argyrocastron, and with it all of Northern Epirus, are enslaved to this day.

While leaving church in Nauplion in 1831, Capodistrias was struck down by the bullet of a political assassin. Greece subsequently became a monarchy under Otto of Bavaria and the rump Greek Kingdom began a painful ascent from the ashes.

The Janniote Pashalik and its Rulers

While the Hellenic Kingdom, the hope of the enslaved Greek "rayas" behind the arbitrary frontier, began to put its house in order, Epirus continued to groan beneath a succession of Ottoman Pashas. Under the successor of Emin, Mahmud Pasha, the native Moslem element proved itself anew an incubus on the terrified Christian villagers. The Pashas continued their policy of delegating their rubber-stamp rule to the local "agas" and "beys" of Epirus, who wanted nothing more than to extort and plunder the Christian majority.

A pasha who did not understand this method of administration was soon relieved, for the Albanian Moslems had enough of their own in the Ottoman Court, the Divan, the Army and even the imperial harem itself, to be able to override their local pashas. Dismissal under pressure was the fate of more than one of Epirus' one-year pashas. Thus it happened to a Pasha in 1837. His successor, Mustafa Nuri Pasha, was more tractable and the local feudarchs were unhampered in their activities. This Pasha ruled for only a few months in 1840. He was called to Constantinople to assume a military post and his place was taken by a tyrant named Nuri Osman who ruled until 1844. He was succeeded by Hosref Pasha, another one-year governor. Ziya Pasha likewise lasted a year and was succeeded by Hafuz "the Cross-eyed", afterwards removed in May, 1847, for an alleged affront to the French flag.

The Banditry of Gjon Leka

During the tenure of the new Pasha, Havuz the Circassian, Albanian gangsterism broke out in violent form, reaching a new height and taking on a novel and unique aspect. Havuz unfortunately did not know enough to leave the actual rule in the hands of the local beys as his predecessors had done. He attempted an unheard of thing—forceable drafting of the heretofore irregular Albanian bands and enforcement of taxation among Moslems as well as infidels. Therefore, in 1847, the beys and agas of Epirus, masterminded by the three sons of Tahir Abas, Ali Pasha's onetime field commander, the grandson of Kaplan Pasha of Delvino, Tahir Bey, and Veiz Bushari, all of whom were afterwards exiled to Asia Minor for their role in the affair, decided to teach their governor a lesson.

One of their number, Zejnel Gjon Leka of Delvino, descended upon Delvino with a band of 300 Moslems and demanded in the Sultan's name that taxes be paid over to him and his "soldiers" in recompense for 12 months of alleged service in Syria. Refusing, the Ottoman officials fled Delvino and Gjon Leka swaggered in, extorting food and money from the Christian inhabitants.

This piece of bravado was the signal for the other local beys to take the law into their own hands. So great had these selfsame beys been in the confidence of the Porte that few regular troops had been regarded as necessary to maintain order in Epirus. Having no independent national sentiment, as had the Greek Epirotes, the beys were regarded as the Sultan's right arm.

The pasha, however, also proved he had friends at the Sublime Porte, and much to their surprise Gjon Leka and his friends were officially declared outlaws by the Sultan. A Turkish force was gathered from the neighboring provinces to suppress the rebels. Thus it was that they, rather than their Pasha, had the unpleasant surprise. Their next move in this curious affair, which gives a graphic illustration of the non-existence then of any Albanian national sentiment, was to try to negotiate with the Sultan's antipod, the power whose local representatives were the very "rayas" the beys so despised and exploited. It is curious to contemplate what would have been the result if the Kingdom of Greece, unexpectedly finding the Beys begging to become its local subjects, had been willing to take up their offer and risk another war with Turkey. This petition of the Albanian beys, translated from their curiously phrased and punctuated Greek, is herein published for the first time in English:

"Illustrious primates and notables of Athens in the Greek lands! We embrace fraternally His Majesty Otto, King of Greece, and notify you:

"The speakers of the salutation bring our complaint to you on the spot because we, the below Kazas, have all remained poor people, ruled in a dry and rocky place, with no profession save that of bearers of arms. Since Constantinople ruled, during the preceding Sultans until now, we have shown ourselves submissive to the decrees of the local ruling Vizirs, Pashas, Kaymakams, during the reign of 33 Sultans. For almost 400 years we have shed our blood in every conquest which they have made. He, however, who loves not a king loves not Godliness either. Our old customs have been done away with and new have been imposed in our territory, which is insufferable. They have taxed the twelfth part in each of our Kazas and have judged with favoritism and injustice, not for the sake of God and His Prophet, but by force and internal tyranny, unlike the rule of European kingdoms. Because of this, we have become rebels against our king whom we held as ruler and father of all us Moslems, and we have complained time and again, with pleading and tears, and they would allow us no hearing, not even a petition, since the kingdom takes no pity on us poor beggars.

"Because of this, we are sending you our special envoy to speak with you *viva voce,* with regards to your illustriousness. If your Kingdom's Majesty receives us, that is to say accepts us, the five Kazas will become its subjects, and let him grant us capitulative laws and let us give him likewise our peace. For God's sake, do not be offended by us who also are creations of God, since we were born naked and we will die thus.

"If there is no salvation for us on the side of the Almighty, then let us die from the sword of man if God has willed it to be thus. The below Kazas of Avlona, Delvino, Manahiye, Kurveleshi, Malakastra, Upper and Lower Berati, Tepeleni and Dyshnica, all five Kazas, beg your Kingdom to pity us and not wish us to cease living upon the earth. And if your Kingdom likes us, let it then inform us to form a new administration according to our desires with that guarantee and trust the Kingdom may wish.

"The bearers speak to you *viva voce* and will relate these things to us and may God's will be done.

(Here are appended 47 seals of Beys and Agas.)

"1847, 15 August, in the Kaza of Kurvelesh, Sandjak of Delvino.

"Zejnel Gjoleka, Xhalil Aga (Çelo Picari), Shejko Bullushi, Muharem Bejlule, Abdyl Bej Koka, Lula Çapari, Muhamet Selmani, Muha Pronjo, Zeqir Pronjo, Osman Kuçi, Mehmet Abazi, Aliko Hoda.

"Xhata Selfo, Latif Elmazi, Mane Beqiri, Demze Piçar, Hoda Nivica, Sulo Çobo, Lame Duka, Sadik Bileno, Dervish Kalarati, Lame Peshtani, Sako Malo, Mustafa Braimi, Kapo Lefteri, Lame Hushq, Mustafa Bedo, Myftar Pina, Sheh Duro, Elman Cimbo, Xhafer Demo, Abaz Dino.

"Avlona Sandjak:

"Beqir Velo Kanina, Ladif Sulo Kanina, Mustafa Beba Kanina, Sadik Armeno, Mehmet Muço, Ismail Bekati, Zenko Xhafar Kakbunari, Pasho Selman, Kuçulasi Mavrota, Selim Aga Vlora, Fejzobej, Lato Mamena, Malko

Nelo Lapesi, Mato Çaushi Lapesi, Xhaxha Martollozi, Abedin Sheho, Shadedi Vashori, Ahmet Aga Vashori, Mehmet Qollasi, Osman Rapo Fratali, Beqir Braçano, Lulo Abazi, Zejnel Hodo, Ibraim Çimaro, Lil Qendro, Meta Çobo, Talo Abili, Sinan Dalevishi, Hito Daul Mavrova, Cimba Keçi, Mehmet Trahuvica, Ymer Ali Kudesi, Mustafa Bega, Bega Ismail, Dervish Ali Dukati, Metan Ali Dukati, Kamber Telo Tragjashti, Mahmut Hoda, Dulo Zoto, Braim Muço, Selim Hasani, Haxhi Smokthina.

"Malakastra, two parts:

"Rapus Aga Kabibashi, Shaban Peshtani, Shqekto Hiso Qesarati, Sylejman Çelo Toçi, Osman Bilo, Dula Mato Kalivazi, Xhelil Tura Malivazi, Sadik Luftino, Ramije Komari, Ahmet Matellozi, Mahmut Lamo Lavani, Gjota Lavani.

"Houses:

"1388, Upper Malakastra; 2911, Lower Malakastra; 1011, Rethimi, Myzeqe; 711, Kasaba, Berati; 1730, Nahija, Topaldi; 1339, Skrapari; 500, Tomoriza; 4500, Tepeleni; 4500, Kaza Avlona; 1840, Kaza Delvina."

Even if Greece had wished to accept this desperate petition, it was not possible because of the still alien territory which lay between the Greek frontier and Albania.

When the Turkish force entered Epirus, Gjon Leka's forces scattered and Gjon Leka himself became a fugitive in the hills, soon to be captured and hung on a convenient tree beside a well on the road outside Argyrocastron, still pointed out as Gjon Leka's gallows. Those of his comrades not hanged or sent to Asia Minor were amnestied. The episode then passed into nothing more than tradition and the old order resumed its course.

Northern Epirote Contributions to Free Greece

The eyes of the hopeful Epirotes continued to be turned toward the free Greek state as they patiently awaited the end of the double yoke of the Sultan and his local minions. Though harassed, culture and education among the Christians in the province that had led Greece's regeneration did not die out. Epirotes continued to seek their fortunes abroad and to bestow their hard-earned legacies upon Epirote institutions. Some returned to their villages. Others who did not return made distinguished names for themselves in lands of their adoption. For instance, General Bartolomeo Mitre, who at the age of 41 became president of Argentina in 1962, was the son of a Chimarriote immigrant.

Noble Epirote names were also inscribed with gratitude in the names of the common motherland generation after generation.

"Athens is full of splendid public buildings, gifts of the Northern Epirotes. The magnificient Academy of Fine Arts and the Astronomical Observatory were given by Sinas of Moschopolis (near Korytsa). Bangas of Korytsa left a building worth £20,000 as a bequest to the Greek Navy Fund. The Zappas brothers, who endowed Athens with her exposition grounds and Constantinople with her biggest Greek High School for Girls, were natives of Lambovo, north of Argyrocastro. Zographos (the father of the President of the Chamber of Deputies), founder of a large Greek school at Constantinople, and founder of the Prize Fund for the encouragement of Greek studies at Paris, was a native of Kestorati, near Argyrocastron. Averoff, the donor of the Greek battleship bearing his name and of the splendid Panathenaic Stadium, and Tositsa and Stournara, who endowed Athens with its fine Polytechnic School, were natives of Metsovo. I pass over a long list of generous gifts and endowments by Epirotes to Greece for patriotic Greek aims."[31]

The Schools of Epirus

Thus, even after a sovereign Greek state was established, Epirus continued to be in our own day what Athens prided herself on being in ancient times, nothing less than "the education of Hellas." When contributing to their Greek motherland the Northern Epirote benefactors never forgot their own unfortunate birthplaces. Zographos, for instance, established a college for Greek teachers in his native village of Kestorati. Athens was enriched by Epirote gold, but it was the hard-won gold of Epirotes themselves that enriched Epirus. Northern Epirus' schools were the pride of the province in an age when the majority of the villagers of free Greece continued to be illiterate.

The statistics published by the Oecumenical Patriarchate in 1904 speak for themselves. We give the table below:

SANDJAK	DISTRICT	NO. OF GREEK SCHOOLS	PUPILS
Monastir	Korytsa	41	3,452
	Kolonia	11	390
	Leskoviki	34	1,189
Argyrocastron	Argyrocastron	50	1,916
	Delvino	24	1,063
	Premeti	35	1,189
	Tepeleni	18	589
	Chimarra	3	507
	Pogonion	42	2,061
Berati	Berati	15	623
	Skrapari	1	18
	Liousnia	28	597
	Valona	10	435
Durazzo	Durazzo	3	205
	Total No. Schools	315	Total No. Pupils 14,234

[31] Butler, C. S., *Manchester Guardian*, Sept. 30, 1914.

As late as the time the above statistics were published there did not exist a single Albanian school in the whole of Epirus. The Albanians extricate themselves from this embarrassment by claiming fictitious suppression of their language by Turkey "with the understanding of the Patriarchate." It is exceedingly strange that a people who were actually governors of the Ottoman Empire, who led its armies and whose fair representatives could be found even within the Sultan's "Portals of Domestic Felicity" were so without voice that only the despised "Infidel", the hated and untrustworthy Greek, should have schools.

The lie is clearly not worth repeating, but the Albanians are driven to assert it to hide the truth that to a Moslem Albanian outside of the Ottoman civil service and sometimes within it, literacy was as rare as dying in bed. Reading and writing were for the Greek "raya". The Albanian was too busy plundering and fighting with his fellow Albanian over spoils to bother about such effeminate pursuits as literature.

Indeed, a local legend has it that when God was giving alphabets to the nations, a ragged Gheg, leading a goat by the string, arrived last. God, who had run out of paper, wrote out the first Albanian letters on a fig leaf and gave it to the Albanian. Later, on his way home, the Gheg put down the precious fig leaf to adjust his pigskin buskins and, when he looked up, saw his goat complacently munching the last of the Albanian alphabet.

In marked contrast to the Albanian, the Northern Epirote was devoted to learning and the cultivation of those virtues collectively termed civilization. A French historian of the 19th century bore this witness:

"I have traveled throughout the country of the Epirotes. In the most remote and mountainous districts the newspapers of Jannina or Athens arrive daily. The Epirotes, like the rest of the Greeks, are excellent in the practice of their communal liberties. They have all the qualities requisite for the art of municipal government. Political life is active and eloquence is much prized.

"In Epirus, as throughout Turkey, a Greek village without a teacher, says a proverb, is as rare as a valley without the corresponding hills. In villages where I could not count more than one hundred houses, the teachers showed me their libraries. I could see there the classical collections of Tauchnitz.

"Instruction is not compulsory, but none would consent to deprive his child of an education. The expense of instruction is borne by the parents in each village. Each village has its own treasury, and the money in them comes from a) bequests, b) contributions by the Orthodo- churches, c) gifts of wealthy Epirotes abroad. The budget is arranged according to the calculated expenses for the year. In proportion to the resources of the community, churches are decorated, or new ones are erected; a hospital is endowed; or a first-class teacher is imported from Athens; a young man is sent to the University of Athens, or for studies abroad; a road long neglected by the Ottoman Government is repaired.

"It is a most rare case when two Greek parties appear before a Turkish tribunal to adjust differences. Nothing does so much honor to the Greeks as the good sense with which, without a written law, without constitution, they know how to regulate their municipal affairs. The broadest democracy is the law of these communities. Educational equality is almost perfect. Large fortunes do not create great differences among them. The poor are rare among them. Even the laborer who lives on his wages is never subjected to those hardships so frequent in our Western life. The vivacity of their spirit never changes. At the agora, at the church, at the theater, the merchant, the worker and the rich landowner are almost equals.

"No people erect so many churches and chapels as the Epirotes. It was so with their ancient ancestors before Christianity. Hence this great number of edifices in honor of their heroes, or of the saints. Pausanias, in his description of Greece proper, cites at every step monuments and altars. And I am sure there were many more that he left out. The Epirotes' taste for chapels is inherited from the Ancient Greeks.

"Everywhere the warmest reception is given to strangers. Activity is very great, and fortunes are not rare. A Westerner will find a comfortable home; the rooms vast, well-ventilated, opening almost always to the east, are elegant and simple.

"The people emigrate to foreign lands but never forget to return to their homes. Never is a Greek afraid of a voyage. Motion delights him; and novelty enchants him. And he needs so little to make himself happy anyway. And making a living for a Greek is not a matter which worries him much. He is so ingenious. An Epirote who has seen only his own town or village is very rare.

"If you are a stranger, in the evening they will give you the best entertainment they can, and speak to you of Hellas, of the tyranny of the Turks and the Albanians, of the 'Megale Idea' or Great National Ideal, the union of all the Hellenes with Greece."[32]

Such were the hopeful people who, in the midst of persecution and extortion by the Albanian Moslem servants of the Porte, kept their great dream alive by tireless energy as much as by eloquence. This was the Epirus of which another French writer could testify, "It is the Greeks of Epirus who showed all Greeks how to die for freedom."[33]

[32] Dumont, Albert, *La Turquie d'Europe.*

[33] Houssaye, Henri, cf. *Revue des deux Mondes,* Feb. 15, 1872.

The Revolt of 1878

The Epirotes, to all intents and purposes, could well rephrase the famous Irish revolutionary slogan to read "Turkey's difficulty is Greece's opportunity." Epirus was restless in 1854 during the Crimean War. The better conditions promised at the war's end to the Christian subjects of the Porte by Sultan Abdul Medjid II in the *Hatti Humayun* of Feb. 18, 1856 were to be forgotten like those of the *Hatti Sherif* of Gülhane 17 years before. The Ottoman Sultans, like the Bourbons, learned nothing and forgot nothing.

During the Russo-Turkish War of 1878, armed Epirote bands reappeared in the province. At Plaka, the Ottoman post manned by Albanian volunteers was overcome by an Epirote guerrilla force led by the Abbot Kottikas and an Epirote Greek ex-army officer named Christos Mesios, but the Epirote band abandoned the captured post upon the arrival of 2,000 Ottoman troops from Jannina.

Another band of 150 Epirote volunteers staged the most spectacular of a series of raids in Northern Epirus. They landed under their captains, Lappas and Stephanou, at Hagioi Saranta (Santi Quaranta) and took the town along with the monastery of St. George, the village of Giasta and the historic village of Lykoursi.

Confident of victory, the Epirote liberators remained unmolested until the Ottoman troopship *Mahmudie* landed a Turkish force. The handful of Epirote defenders were forced to evacuate to Corfu. Several members of this Northern Epirote expedition fell into Turkish hands. They were brought to Jannina for execution and were saved only by the timely intervention of foreign ambassadors at Constantinople.

The wealthy international lawyer Kyriakos Kyritsis and his colleague Eleutheriou, who together had the valuable fishery concession at Buthrotum (Butrinto), had secretly outfitted the expedition in Corfu. Kyritsis was born in Stegopolis (the Naoupolis or Stenoupolis of Byzantine times) and Eleutheriou was from the neighboring village of Mingouli. Their villages were part of the Liountzi area between Argyrocastron and Libochovo that numbered among its sons many prominent Epirote merchants and benefactors in Constantinople, including Christaki Zographos. As a result of the ill-fated adventure at Santi Quaranta, the Turkish Government confiscated the Kyritsis-Eleutheriou holdings at Buthrotum when their part in the venture was discovered.

The Epirotes had a long wait ahead before the dream of liberation was to become a brief reality, but every sign on the horizon was noted as an omen of hope.

The Congress of Berlin and the League of Prizren

A Russo-Turkish truce was reached at the village of San Stefano within sight of Constantinople itself. The Ottomans again had come near to losing their empire in Europe, this time to Tsarist Russia which was eager to fulfill a two-fold dream, warm water and the legacy of Byzantium.

Again the Great Powers "mediated" to save the disintegrating Ottoman Empire. Bismarck, from June 13 to July 13, 1878, presided over the Congress of Berlin which was to determine the changes on the Balkan map.

Among other readjustments, the Great Powers decided the cession of Albanian-inhabited Ulqinj (Dulcigno) and the districts of Gusinje and Plava to Russia's stepchild, Montenegro, then ruled by Prince Nikita, the "father-in-law of Europe."

The Turks, anxious to prevent the loss of their faithful "Arnaut Vilayeti", organized among their Albanian subjects a mock "revolt." Hussein Pasha, the Vali of Shkodra, persuaded the Ghegs to form the "League of Prizren", the aim of which was the maintenance of the Sultan's sovereignty over the unified vilayets of Shkodra (Scutari), Kossovo, Monastir and Jannina under a single Turkish Governor-General with Albanian advisers and a local militia under Turkish officers. The Gheg tribal chieftains gathered at Prizren cheered this Hamid-inspired proposal lustily and set about resisting Montenegrin encroachment of their Sultan's territory.

In 1880, the Great Powers put an end to this Turkish plot by a naval demonstration which frightened Sultan Hamid into delivering Dulcigno to Montenegro and dissolving the "League of Prizren." Most of the Gheg chiefs dutifully went home, but the Catholic Mirdites, who were almost alone in taking the ephemeral "League" at face value, were offended, and Prenk Bib Doda, their hereditary chief, was exiled by the Sultan.

At the same time that the Sultan's agents were encouraging what later Albanians were to cite as the birth of Albanian nationalism, it became apparent that the status of the Vilayet of Jannina would be examined at Berlin. Greek desires might even be given a partial satisfaction. For this reason the "League of Prizren" was partially kept alive to frustrate any hopes of the Epirotes for another uprising. A force of 30,000 Moslem Albanians under Abdyl Bey Frashëri helped keep the Northern Epirotes terrified.

The brother of Ottoman Grand Vizier Ferid Pasha, Ismail Kemal of Valona, was sent to Berlin to plead Turkey's fabricated case for the Albanians. Despite Bismarck's disdain for the Sultan's Albanian maneuvers, the Great Powers, for reasons to be made clear presently, decided in favor of Ottoman retention of Epirus. Greece was given only the Epirote town of Arta as a sort of consolation prize.

The effect in Epirus of the decision of the Congress of Berlin survives in a dirge sung by the Epirote mountaineers:

" 'S holon ton kosmon 'xasteria, 's holon ton kosmon helios,
Kai 's ta kaymena Giannena mauro, pachy skotadi:
'Ti 'phetos ekaman boulen okto basileia anthropoi,
Kai ebalan ta synora 's tes Artas to potami."

"In all the world the stars are out, in all the world the sun shines,
And there in wretched Jannina, there is a black, thick darkness:
For in this year they did decide, the men from eight kingdoms,
And set down the boundary line by the river Arta."

Austrian and Italian Imperialism

The great obstacle Greece failed to overcome at the Congress of Berlin was the emergence of Austrian and Italian ambitions in the southern Balkans. For the Italians it was a reawakening of the old Venetian imperialism in the Adriatic symbolized by the mediaeval Doges' annual "Sposalizio del mare". Austrian ambitions were centered about preventing a Slav foothold in the Adriatic, extension of Austrian seapower south of Dalmatia and the curtailment of a strong Italy with ambitions of annexing Austrian Trieste, Fiume and Dalmatia—the inevitable outcome of Italian influence on the Balkan side of the Adriatic.

Bismarck himself hinted at Italian conquest of Albania to Francesco Crispi during the latter's visit to Bismarck at Gastein in 1877. In answer to Crispi's request for Bismarck's position respecting possible Italian conflict with France or Austria, Bismarck pledged support in the case of France, but concluded,

"I am your friend, but I will not break with Austria. If she takes Bosnia you could take Albania."[34]

While talks were going on in Berlin, Italy sent the military topographer Colonel Sironi to Epirus to reach a secret Turko-Italian understanding preventing the Epirote coast outside of Arta from passing to Greece. The Ottomans were only too glad to obtain support from Italy for their continued retention of the Epirote coastline down to the Acheron River.

When Turkey submitted a note in August, 1878, refusing to carry out the Great Powers' decisions, she found support from the Triple Alliance of which Italy had become a member. A conference held between Mustafa Gazi Pasha and the Greek emissary General Scarlatos Soutsos at Preveza was foiled by Italy's consul there. When Vrailis, the Greek Minister to St. Petersburg, sought an understanding at Constantinople, Italian Ambassador Count Corti moved mountains to thwart it.

The Congress of Berlin reconvened from June 16 to July 1, 1880 and actually consented to Greek accession of almost all of southern Epirus. Again Italy was paramount in obstructing more than the token settlement Greece finally received. Licoudis, the Greek military attaché in Berlin, wrote to his father on Jan. 17, 1881, "While during the conference . . . Turkey was not represented, the technical representative of Italy was present, who was worth ten Turkish delegates."[35]

For neither the first nor the last time in history, the rulers of Italy had connived at the expense of Epirote freedom.

Italy, however was but a junior partner of the Triple Alliance, as she was to be chagrined in discovering. In 1895, when Lord Salisbury suggested to the Kaiser that Italy should be supported in Albania and Tripoli in exchange for repudiation of Italian Red Sea claims, the Kaiser replied that France was sure to oppose Italy in Africa and compensation in Albania was out of the question because of preemptory Austrian interests there. Wilhelm had tied himself down to the zigzags of Hapsburg interests and Italy suffered frustration in her hopes to plant her flag on the other side of the Adriatic. This was to be the Allied ace-in-the-hole in swinging Italy from the Central Powers to the Entente in World War I. Meanwhile the Italian empire-makers had to mark time.

[34] Crispi, Francesco, *Memoirs*, Vol. II, Ch. 11.

[35] Agathos, Eustathios, A., *Hoi Italoi En Cercyra*, p. 48.

The National Society and the War of 1897

The repeated inability of Europe to render justice to the enslaved Greeks of Crete, Macedonia and Epirus was not without its natural repercussions in both redeemed and unredeemed Greece. In 1894, a number of patriotic Greek officers and civilians, whose origin was representative of all parts of Hellas, founded the *Ethnike Hetaeria* or National Society. Modelled upon the principles of the Friendly Society of the Greek War of Independence, the National Society dedicated itself to the liberation of all parts of Greece still under Ottoman misrule.

The Northern Epirotes were an outstanding element in it. Almost every village elder, schoolmaster, priest and merchant of that tragic province took the hetaerist oath. In Constantinople, where Northern Epirotes were prominent in all strata of the city's great Greek merchant class, funds were raised by the organization's secret cells. These were used to equip Greek volunteer bands in Ottoman-held Greece and to build up the Greek Navy.

Cooler minds would have counseled patience, but the Greeks had had enough of fruitless waiting. The National Society was anxious, especially after the Cretan insurrection burst upon the already inflamed public mind, to terminate once and for all the Ottoman maladministration. It was in this state of mind that the Greeks entered their luckless war with the Turks in 1897.

Of Allies they had none. Serbia under Alexander Obrenovíc was Austrian-orientated and therefore neutral in Turkey's favor. Bulgaria had been bought out by an understanding respecting the spread of the exarchate in Macedonia at the expense of the older Christians. The Great Powers had shown themselves ready to crush the Cretan insurrection.

Alone in the fight, Greece had to wage a war in which the effectiveness of her navy was curtailed. Prohibited by the Great Powers from attacking the Turkish-held islands and afraid to bombard the coast of Asia Minor for fear of touching off a full-scale massacre of the native Greeks by the Turks, free Greece was able to bombard only Santi Quaranta and Preveza from the sea. Militarily, the war was a triumph for the Prussian officers who had taken over the training of the Ottoman Army.

Many Northern Epirotes went to Corfu for arms and returned to their homeland to fight the Turco-Albanians in the hills.

Corfu was the thriving arms market for the Epirote insurgent captains. Their forces, however, were impotent in the face of the Greek Army's retreat across Thessaly and Greece's subsequent defeat. Greece signed an uneasy peace with the Sultan's delegates on September 18, 1897.

The Greeks had learned the immensity of the task before them. They had to convert the defeat of 1897 into what was to be the victory of 1912. Greece would bide her time and win with arms what the Great Powers would take away from her by words.

Albanian "Nationalists" and their Movement

While the Northern Epirotes were maintaining their schools, contributing to the welfare of the free motherland and their own province and feverishly anticipating their great moment of liberation, where was the Albanian national awakening?

Among the Albanians themselves it was nonexistent. With certain Albanian leaders it continued to be largely a hothouse product of Ottoman policy. Thus, when the Sultan was undergoing pressure from the Great Powers for reform in Macedonia they organized the "League of Ipek" which was pledged against concessions to the Christians and the maintenance of Ottoman reaction. Four years after, in 1903, European demands for reform in Macedonia became more insistent and the Sultan had the "League of Ipek" revolt in Kossovo. The Russian consul at Mitrovica was murdered. As usual, Abdul Hamid told Europe of his willingness to effect reforms in Macedonia, but he could do nothing since the "spontaneous" revolt against change of his Albanian subjects. It was the old game of Armenian and Kurd played for European benefit in a new setting. Hamid promised to "mediate" with his unruly Gheg subjects and reform proposals in Macedonia went the same way as proposed reforms in Armenia. The "ogre of Yildiz" was using the Albanians to play a game he had often and successfully played before.

At no time did any Albanian leader consider Epirus with any seriousness in his schemes. The cleverest of them all, Ismail Kemal Vlora who had gone to Berlin in 1878, knew too much of the intrigues of Europe to believe that the Ottoman master he had served would win the final round in the Balkans. Just in case the Balkan nations became masters of their own house, or the Great Powers should step in, he embarked on a double game of his own. As spokesman for the Albanians he signed a secret agreement with Greek Premier Theotokis on Jan. 22, 1907 which embodied his conception of Albania's borders in the event Turkey in Europe was dismembered. He accepted the fact that:

> "The boundary-line between Albania and Epirus and Greek Macedonia shall be understood to be a line running from a point west of the town of Monastir to a point on the seaboard to the north of Corfu and its adjacent islands. This line shall be drawn in such a manner that the lands lying on either side of it, being separated by natural frontiers, shall correspond to the national aspirations of either race, through the annexation to Greece on one hand, of districts in which a majority of the inhabitants is, by language and national sentiment, Greek, and to Albania, on the other, of districts in which the majority is, by the same standards, Albanian."

This agreement, so honest in its approach to a solution, exists in Ismail Kemal's handwriting in the Foreign Ministry archives in Athens. A phototstat copy of the same is in the files of the Royal Hellenic Embassy in London.[36]

Ismail Kemal, the Ottoman diplomat, needed no crystal ball to tell him the empire's days were numbered. The bulk of the Albanian Moslems, however, were perfectly content with their Ottoman rulers. The idea of a free Albania provoked among them reactions ranging from derision to shock at the very idea. "The Sultan will never permit it," was the final Albanian word to any talk of independence. The Serbs, the Bulgars, the Rumanians and the Greeks had worked for and won the freedom of their national existence. Why not the Albanians, the most western geographically of all Ottoman subjects and thus the farthest from the Ottoman center? If the Albanians had been a nation instead of a geographic and racial designation they would have done so. As they saw it, before Albania was created by Europe's fiat, they had no need to do so. A tribal people with a limited self-rule that was actually no-rule, exempt from military service outside Europe, given opportunity to plunder as the scavangers of the Ottoman Army, they saw their best interests promoted by the wily Abdul Hamid and his empire.

Tribes of Albanians, from time to time, took to the hills in vendetta against each other or to hinder a local Pasha's enforcement of taxation, a thing Hamidian governors thought twice about in *Arnautistan*. In Constantinople, Hamid surrounded himself with Albanian Grand Viziers and Generals, the most loyal element in his empire. His bodyguards were Albanians

36 Cf. Pipinelis, M. P., *Europe and the Albanian Question*, p. 65.

dressed in their traditional costume. He looked after them as the flesh of his flesh and they, in turn, were ready to die for *Baba Hamit,* as they affectionately called the Red Sultan whose name was a curse to enlightened Europe.

The British Ambassador, wrote back to London in his annual report of 1908, on the eve of the Young Turk revolution:

> "This is the Albanian movement which, though known to exist as far back as the Congress of Berlin, had made little apparent progress up to the end of 1907 when it was still heard of only in connection with a few obscure newspapers, published in Bucharest, Sofia or elsewhere and one or two shady adventurers, who endeavoured to persuade the world they were at the head of it."[37]

In the Catholic areas of Ghegheria the Austrians were having no easy time spreading the gospel of Albanian nationalism in order to counter the expansion of Slavdom. The director of the Cultural and Political Office of the Austrian Foreign Ministry, Freiherr von Musulin, years after the breakup of the Hapsburg Empire, conceded that Austrian efforts in this direction were misplaced. "We wished," he confessed:

> "to strengthen the national spirit of the Albanians and to render them capable of offering successful resistance to a possible foreign invasion . . . Today (1924) it has become obvious that we were mistaken in our estimate of the Albanian people's capacity for development, and of the possibility that this people would, in the near future, create a national life of its own, transcending the opposition of North and South. The purpose at which we aimed could not be accomplished either by means of civilizing influences or by means of political counsels or material subsidies; it could be accomplished only by the establishment of a real protectorate. We failed, however, to decide in good time to take such a step, and at the period with which we are dealing it was too late."[38]

The Young Turks, after their revolution of 1909, went through a period of feeble attempts to keep the "Sick Man" from dying. This meant an attempt at the impossible consolidation of the empire already in its death throes. The Albanian chieftains at first supported the Young Turks as they had supported all Ottoman régimes, good, bad and indifferent.

The Young Turks, however, had other ideas not congenial to the "Arnaouts". They introduced forced military service and tax collecting in a region where the native Moslems had long had their own say. The reader remembers the disastrous attempt

[37] cf. *British Documents,* Vol. V, pp. 290 et seq.

[38] Musulin, Freiherr von, *Das Haus am Ballplatz,* p. 148.

of a local pasha to do just this in the days of Gjon Leka. The Albanians had not changed a bit since then. This was the case of the revolt of Iza Boletin in May, 1909, and of Hasan Slaku of Gjakova who removed the European-trained Turkish officers and declared that his district would continue to be administered exclusively by the "Sheriat Peygamberi" or sacred law of Mohammed. "Albanian nationalism" was, in short, a Hamidian reaction to any and all proposed reforms, whether inspired by Europe or by the Young Turks. In many cases, the Turkish soldiers had common causes with the Albanians and thus caused Young Turk reforms to go the frustrating way of similar past attempts.

Disturbances among the Moslems of Northern Epirus, such as the bandit raids of Çerçis Topulli and Demo Emini, were prompted by similar motivations. These annoyances to Turkish rule had as their source resentment of Young Turk bureaucracy, imported from Prussia, religious fanaticism against Europeanization, or just the common Albanian motive of pure and simple "placka" or plunder.

Albania remained a geographic expression not only to Europe, but to the Albanians themselves, save a few professional patriots abroad. The Albanian Moslems continued to live next to and lord over a Christian Greek people who scanned the southern horizon for a new dawn.

The Epirote century of hope was soon to near consummation. Ottoman rule had become a paleolithic fossil in an age of enlightenment. By the side of King George I of the Hellenes stood a Crown Prince whom a nation, in token of hopes yet unfulfilled, had named Constantine. A statesman from newly-redeemed Crete, Eleutherius Venizelos, was at the monarch's right hand as First Minister of the Kingdom. The year 1912 was born of the travail of 1898. The torch was ready, the fuse lit, and the First Balkan War burst upon a startled Europe.

Chapter V

THE GLORIOUS DAY

The Second Greek War of Independence

Greece stood alone in 1897 and was taught by her defeat the value of Balkan unity. The lesson was not lost on her neighbors. On March 13, 1912, the Serbs and Bulgars, ever ready to plunge the dagger into each other's throats, temporarily put aside their ancient enmity and came to terms with each other. On May 10, Greece threw caution to the winds and, forgetting the memory of the bloody Bulgarization of Eastern Roumelia and the Bulgarian Comitadji atrocities in Macedonia, joined Serbia in grasping Tsar Ferdinand's gory hand in alliance.

The cannons of Montenegro blasted their message of war on October 8. Greece, Serbia and Bulgaria had placed an ultimatum before the Ottomans on the 14th and on the 18th war had been declared between the Balkan allies and the Sultan. Every Balkan people, except the Albanians, had dreamed of that day and prepared for it through centuries of strife and servitude. The struggle which began on the dark day the Osmanlis crossed into Europe was now to reach its glorious consummation with the dawn of liberty.

All Europe knew that the time was at hand when the "Sick Man" would give up the ghost. On the obituary page of the Paris *Matin* of Nov. 1, 1912 appeared the following death notice:

"COME TO THE FUNERAL OF M. STATUS QUO
Died in Macedonia aged 459

"You are requested to attend the funeral ceremony and burial of Monsieur Status Quo, diplomatist, who departed this life on October 30, 1912, in Macedonia, aged 459 years. The ceremony will be held at an early date in the Christian Church of St. Sofia, Constantinople.

"Verses: 'Believe in Allah and in His Prophet and Thou Shalt reap in Paradise Eternal Caresses of Celestial Houris.'—Koran XXV.

"The mourners will meet at the ground.

"Sent on behalf of Turkey by his widow; Austria, his mother; Great Britain, his mother-in-law; Bulgaria, Serbia and Greece, his daughters;

Montenegro his grandson; Russia, his daughter-in-law; Germany, France, Italy, & C., his cousins and second cousins.
"The burial ceremony will take place in Asia Minor."

Greek enthusiasm everywhere was boundless. The whole nation was seized with the vision of this second Greek struggle for independence. Among the Greeks abroad, even in the Ottoman capital itself, the news was electrifying. A number of young Greeks from Constantinople, some of them sons of prominent Epirote merchants of that city, boarded a neutral vessel. When they had left Turkish waters, they threw their red fezes overboard and were among the first Greek Army volunteers upon landing at Piraeus. Another contingent arrived in Athens after slipping out of Constantinople in the disguise of Russian seamen.

In the United States, immigrants gave up their jobs and homes and recrossed the ocean. A Greek-American contingent, numbering 15,000, left from New York. Among their leaders was a pioneer Greek-American priest from Epirus, Father Bourazanis. A large number of Greeks, sons of Greeks and even great-grandsons of Greeks who could hardly speak the language, arrived in Greece from the earth's four corners to enlist in the ranks of the liberators.

The Greek Army took Preveza amidst the wild enthusiasm of the town's populace on Nov. 3. Macedonia, however, was the main theater of war and the best troops had accordingly been sent there. The troops on the Epirote front, led by General Sapountzakis, were as untrained as they were enthusiastic. Excepting a skeleton regular army, the forces consisted of the Greek-American contingent, Count Roma's Garibaldian volunteers and Cretan irregulars, the best trained of whom were commanded by Constantine Manos. Their lack of training was such a handicap that the Greek onslaught was slow. The overcautious policy of General Sapountzakis contributed to the loss of several tactical opportunities.

In addition to the regular Ottoman troops in Epirus there were also 12 battalions of Albanian reservists ("redifs") ranged against the Greeks. These fully demonstrated their capacity for murder and plunder. At Kamouzades, after an orderly Greek withdrawal, the Albanian reservists entered the village, rounded up the village priest and 25 unarmed civilians, and ordered them to shout cease fire to the Greek troops about 200 yards away. Then, in full view of the Greek soldiers, the Albanians shot all the 26 in the back. Two of them survived by playing dead. Escaping to the Greek lines they made it known that the Greek Army had not seen the worst. The Ottoman Albanians had previously locked all the women and girls in the village church and raped them before the altar. The Albanian irregulars were allowed a free hand, and 150 Epirote villages were put to the torch. Plunder was the Sultan's order of the day to the Shqyptars. The hardest hit were the villages of Zagoria, Jannina and Delvino.

During December the Greeks made an attempt to take Santi Quaranta. The Army of Macedonia had been swift and successful and Salonica had surrendered on Nov. 9. The heaviest fighting therefore took place in western Macedonia where the Greeks and Serbs continued their victorious march. Korytsa was taken on the 20th by Greek forces under General Damianos. It remained, therefore, for the Korytsa forces to move forward via the Korytsa-Delvinaki-Santi Quaranta route, effect a juncture at Delvinaki with an invading Greek force coming through Delvino from Santi Quaranta, and then attack Jannina in force from the north. The plan was abandoned because the Korytsa-Delvinaki route was snowbound and impassable and because supplies to Korytsa had to be made via Serbian-occupied Monastir, impossible because the Serbs had just reached an armistice with the Turks.

What had been originally a plan of attack was then, however unwisely, adopted as a diversion. A Northern Epirote contingent spearheaded a troop landing at Santi Quaranta. This force was necessarily small and led by the Liountziotes Captain John Poutetses or Tolios, a native of Stegopolis, and his lieutenant and nephew, Gregory Mantzaris from Kalezi. Poutetses was killed along with his nephew. Their severed heads were exhibited by the Albanians throughout the villages of Argyrocastron to terrify the Christian Greek populace. The remnants of the forces at Santi Quaranta returned to Corfu.

At the same time, Santi Quaranta and other points along the coast were evacuated by several thousand refugees from the villages of Delvino which had been destroyed by the Albanian bands. These men, women and children were taken to safety in Corfu where they were cared for by the Society of Panhellenic Charity.

Meanwhile, on Nov. 5, Chimarra rose in revolt under the leadership of Major Spyromelios and expelled the Ottomans from the district, holding them at bay until the arrival of the Greek Army.

The feudal lords of Albania realized, after Salonica surrendered and Korytsa was liberated, that Turkey had breathed her last in the western Balkans. Ismail Kemal Vlora, therefore, on Nov. 28, 1912, assembled a group of his followers at Valona and went through the motion of proclaiming the independence of Albania. Few Albanians then took this comedy at face value, and the Albanian "government", in consequence, was recognized outside Valona only by some local chiefs at Berati and Elbasan, and then only loosely.

One of the first acts of this Valona "government" was to send a blustering threat to the Northern Epirote defenders of Chimarra, signed by Eserem Bey of Valona and Shefket Gjoleka. It read in part:

> "Inhabitants of Chimarra: reflect once more, for the seven villages of Chimarra must become Albanian, otherwise they will all be destroyed as enemies of our race. You cannot continue to live beside Albania. On the contrary, come and fight with us against an infidel enemy. We give you three days wherein to make up your minds. Reflect! Life with us, or death with the Greeks,
>
> "After that period, cannons and Martinis (rifles) will speak.
>
> "As for you, you shall remember this letter."

Ninety years had passed since Ali Pasha had been buried, and though the hand was that of Eserem and Gjoleka, the voice was the voice of Ali, and the Epirotes knew it well. It was ever the language with which the Albanian Moslem has addressed his subjects. But 1912 was not 1798 for the Epirotes, and it was a different kind of reply Major Spyromelios made on Dec. 12, 1912.

> "You say that Italy and Austria will set up an Albanian principality: we are awaiting its erection and we shall rejoice at such an event, for even in that case we shall prove ourselves brothers toward that principality, for our noble sentiments are ever the same and will not alter, for we shall not forget that you are our brothers who have severed yourselves from us by denying your religion. Is it really necessary to remind the inhabitants of Koutsi that 90 years ago they were still Christians and that they have relatives among the inhabitants of Chimarra? The very name of Gjolekas shows the religion to which Shefket Bey's ancestors belonged.[39]
>
> "... As for your threats, I hope they are meant neither for Spyromelios nor for the inhabitants of Chimarra, for even the children of Gjolekas

39 Gjolekas or Gjon Leka, John Alexander or Lekas.

know that we are as much used to the Martini and Mauser rifles as they are. It is another who threatens while concealing himself behind Gjolekas, but that other has himself never fought, nor have his ancestors."[40]

Victory and Liberation

On Jan. 23, 1913, Crown Prince Constantine took over the troops in Epirus from General Sapountzakis. Seasoned troops from Salonica reinforced the Army of Epirus and on March 6 the beleaguered Ottoman garrison at Jannina, along with the main body of Ottoman troops in Epirus, surrendered to the triumphant Greeks.

The capital of Epirus in the long centuries of Ottoman domination, the hope and education of Hellas when Athens was but a fief of the Grand Eunuch of the Sultan's Seraglio, the seat of Ali the tyrant, had become Greek once more. Constantine entered the liberated city amidst an ovation that made it rock with sustained cries of "Zeto."

A part of the Ottoman forces under Djavid Pasha's command fled northward. Without wasting time, the Greeks took up pursuit and liberated the major part of Epirus. The forces of Hellas swept through Delvino, took Santi Quaranta and, after a four hour battle at Grapsi, near Argyrocastron, sent Djavid's broken forces fleeing northward in disorderly retreat.

The next day, March 17, the town of Argyrocastron opened its gates without contest to welcome the liberators. The Moslems, accepting their "kismet", joined in greeting the Hellenic Army. The official reception committee consisted of Metropolitan Basil of Dryinoupolis (himself a native of Upper Lambovo "of the Cross") and Mufti Hussein, the Moslem spiritual leader. Among the members of the committee of welcome were three members of the town council, the Christians Lioliomanes, merchant, and Panos Litos, former Aza (administrator) of Chimarra, and the Moslem Kamban Kadare, the town's most prominent merchant.

No sooner had the investiture of Argyrocastron become a reality when, the very next day, the tragic news came that George I, King of the Hellenes, was dead of an assassin's bullet in Salonica. Constantine, whom Europe would call the First and whom Hellenism named the Twelfth, left Jannina for Salonica at once. General Dangles, a brilliant Northern Epirote from the district of Premeti, was given charge of the military administra-

[40] Cf. Cassavetti, D. J., *Hellas and the Balkan Wars,* pp. 237-239.

tion in liberated Epirus. His own home district was the next to be freed.

Tepeleni, birthplace of Ali Pasha, was taken shortly thereafter. It would be impossible to reproduce on paper the feverish emotion which seized the Northern Epirotes upon the dawn of freedom. Everywhere there were the same wild ovations, the flaming patriotic speeches, the parades of Northern Epirote schoolchildren waving Greek flags. Yet the true spirit of the occasion, the deeper meaning of the liberation, was caught in a few words by the correspondent of the Paris *Temps*.

> "Before returning to France, after having heard the story of so much suffering, after having seen with my own eyes the admirable force of a patriotism which has never despaired, I can understand that son, who on the morning of the surrender of Bizani, the moment when the first Evzones appeared at St. John's, ran to the cemetery and, discharging his revolver over the grave of his father, from whom he had inherited the hope of liberation, cried out 'Father, the Greeks have arrived.' "[41]

[41] Puaux, René, *The Sorrows of Epirus*, pp. 119-120.

Chapter VI

THE DIPLOMATIC BETRAYAL

The London Conference

The armistice with Turkey proposed by the Great Powers was accepted by Serbia and Bulgaria on December 3, 1912. Practically all of Albania proper, including Durazzo, was in Serbian hands. In the south, Ismail Kemal held on to his shadowy government at Valona. Albania was in a thoroughly disorganized state as the Greeks prepared to take Jannina and liberate Epirus. Essad Pasha Toptani and his Gheg troops held out alone in the Sultan's name against the Montenegrin besiegers of Shkodra. Thus stood the situation when the belligerents came to the Conference of London presided over by British Foreign Secretary Sir Edward Grey. There they rediscovered that if small powers propose, it is always the Great Powers who dispose.

The interested Great Powers, i.e. Austria and Italy, came to the conference table with certain well-defined ideas about the Balkan settlement. Their views were substantially unaltered since the Congress of Berlin in 1878. Austria wanted to create an Albanian state to oppose a Serbian exit to the Adriatic. Italy wanted this and more. For her, it was the coastline opposite the Strait of Otranto that had to be included in the Albanian state so that the strategic coastline might eventually pass into Italian hands. That the province in question facing the Otranto strait was in no way a part of Albania troubled the Italians not at all. If Epirus was not Albanian, the Italians would see to it that it became so. The Italian flag in Valona was a part of long-range Italian objectives. For this reason, Italy had been exceptionally encouraging to Ismail Kemal who held one door open to negotiations with Rome and another to a possible reconciliation with the Porte.

Austria joined Italy in demanding Northern Epirus for Albania for quite another reason. The predominantly Albanian districts of Gjakova (Djakovica), Peja (Ipek), Prizren and Prishtina in the northwest were to be turned over to Serbia with Austrian acquiescence in order to bribe the Serbs into giving up their Adriatic outlet. The future Albanian state would be compensated for the loss of a purely Albanian district by the cession of an almost purely Greek district in the south, i.e. Northern Epirus. That Greece or the native Greek population of Northern Epirus might have something to say in the affair was a matter of little interest and even less concern.

The only hitch in Austro-Italian plans was that none of the other powers took the prospect of an independent Albania seriously. The most that could be done was to create an autonomous Albania which would be returned to the Porte to remain under the Sultan's nominal rule until such time as the Albanians might be better entitled to a place in civilized Europe. Even the German Emperor thought that the Austrian ambition to set up an independent Albania was merely an expensive Hapsburg whim. It is only in retrospect that, with the Austrian state papers no longer secret, we realize that for the Hapsburgs, "Albania was to solve everything. It was to save the prestige of the monarchy and atone for abandoning the Sandjak, while at the same time preventing any other great power from setting foot on the eastern side of the Adriatic."[42] Austrian and Italian policies, for perhaps diametrically opposed reasons, found themselves outwardly identical. It was just as clear to them, as it was clear even to Ismail Kemal himself, that Albania had far to go to reach truly independent status. So much the better for Austria and Italy who insisted more strongly upon an Albanian state. "This cooperation was important for it meant a united front on the part of the Triple Alliance."[43] Even Germany, much against the personal judgement of the Kaiser, was drawn into Austrian and Italian schemes to rearrange the Balkan map in their favor. The following declaration was therefore made by the Conference of Ambassadors in London on December 20, 1912: "The Ambassadors have recommended to their Governments, and the latter have in principle accepted, the granting of Albanian autonomy, together with a simultaneous decision guaranteeing to Serbia a commercial outlet to the Adriatic." Albanian autono-

[42] Helmreich, Ernst Christian, *The Diplomacy of the Balkan Wars*, 1912-13, pp. 189-190.

[43] *ibid.*, p. 212.

my, save for Austria and Italy, signified a system recognizing the Sultan's sovereignty and the continued occupation of the territory by a limited number of Ottoman troops. Neither this nor a Serbian outlet were ever realized because of the adamant insistence upon Albanian "independence" by Austria and Italy. The other Powers gave way and, "Since Austria-Hungary and Italy had taken the lead in proposing the establishment of an Albanian state, they were invited to draw up a general plan of its future government."[44] It was a foregone conclusion that, in spite of opposition, the Austrians and Italians would have their own way. As far as the boundaries were concerned, a meeting of Austrian diplomats at the Ballhausplatz had already decided on December 10th that almost all of Epirus, *including* Jannina, was to compensate the tribesmen of Albania for the loss of half their country to Serbia.

On February 3, 1913, the war between the Balkan allies and the Ottomans was resumed, continuing until April 15th. With the exception of desultory skirmishes, the fighting on the part of Greece, Serbia and Bulgaria on one hand and Turkey on the other had really finished. During this twilight war, talks in London between the Balkan representatives and the Porte were suspended, but the ambassadors of the Great Powers continued to meet informally. Meanwhile, the Montenegrin siege of Shkodra continued.

The Montenegrins, reinforced by Serbian troops, launched a grand attack on Shkodra on February 6th. In London every attempt was being made to persuade the Montenegrins to give up their siege. The only tangible result was that the civilians of Shkodra, on March 24th, were offered safe conduct by Montenegro to remove themselves from the doomed Albanian town. A naval demonstration by the Great Powers, blockading the coast from Antivari to the Drin on April 4th, was openly defied by the Black Mountain troops of King Nikita. Shkodra's garrison was in a state of starvation. Finally, Essad Pasha Toptani, military governor of Shkodra, entered into clandestine negotiations with Montenegrin King Nikita. A surrender settlement was reached between the two to the effect that, in return for Essad's surrender of Shkodra and the whole district as far as the river Drin, he would be allowed to leave Shkodra with full military honors, all his troops, arms and supplies, and, furthermore, receive Mon-

[44] *ibid.*, p. 252.

tenegrin recognition of himself as Prince of Albania under the Sultan's protection. To indicate his sincerity in terms the Albanians would understand, Nikita gave, and Essad accepted, the sum of 10,000 pounds sterling.[45] On April 22nd, Essad surrendered Shkodra and marched out as he had agreed. On April 26, Crown Prince Danilo made his entry with a short-lived triumphal flourish.

Essad moved down into Valona where he tried to negotiate with Ismail Kemal for control of the Albanian "government". Failing, he removed himself to Durazzo where he proclaimed a rival government with himself at the head. Albania, unable to recognize *one* government, now had two. It was soon to have a third when the International Control Commission set up business in Shkodra after Europe forced Nikita to get out.

The issue, ostensibly, of Essad's quarrel with Ismail Kemal was the former's insistence, with the support of the majority of the Moslem Ghegs, that the Turkish language be made Albania's second official language. Most Moslem Albanians, now that Great Turkey was dead for them, still hoped to create a "little Turkey" on the shores of the Adriatic. This sentiment for "little Turkey" was to remain a potent force for many years. It is still nostalgically evoked by many of the older generation of Albanian Moslems.

The actual issue was somewhat simpler—a struggle for power between Essad and Ismail Kemal. Anything that might embarrass the latter was eagerly pursued at Durazzo. Essad even initiated a secret correspondence with Turkish Vizier Izzet Pasha to have Ottoman troops dispatched to Valona to proclaim Izzet, with Essad's help, prince of Albania. Four hundred Ottomans actually landed near Valona to fulfil the bargain, but they were soon captured and killed by Ismail Kemal's police. Of course, Essad, from the first, had no intention of making the former Turkish War Minister king; he was still trying only to force Ismail Kemal to discuss his terms.

The Peace Treaty

Athens was understandably alarmed at the possibility that Epirus, in whole or in part, might be sacrificed to Austrian and Italian interests. The hope nevertheless persisted that the Triple

[45] Cf. *British Documents,* v. XIII, p. 734.

Entente, and Britain in particular, would back Greek insistence that the rights of 125,000-odd Greek Epirotes be considered. Sir Edward Grey gave the Greek Ambassador repeated verbal assurances that Greece's case would be heard. Ominously, however, the Greeks recalled that Italy, through Foreign Minister San Giuliano, had made the true state of affairs clear from the start. In December, 1912, he had bluntly told the Greek Chargé d'Affaires in Rome, "I recognize that Argyrocastron and Korytsa are Greek, but the rights of a small nation such as Greece cannot prevail over the interests of a Great Power like Italy."

The Greeks were informed by their supposed friends that the treaty of peace with Turkey should be hastened as quickly as possible. The exchange of views between Greece and the Great Powers over Epirus could wait until after that event. That the issue had already been prejudged by Austria and Italy, that their having their own way was the price Europe had to pay to forestall a general war, was discreetly left unmentioned. The Epirotes were to pay the price for an illusory peace that lasted hardly a year after the Peace Treaty was signed.

The Greeks were finally told by Sir Edward Grey to sign or leave. In such an atmosphere of tension and intrigue the Treaty of Peace between the Balkan nations and the Porte was signed at London on May 30, 1913. Article II of that treaty stated in part that, "His Imperial Majesty the Sultan cedes to Their Majesties, the Allied Sovereigns, all the territories of his Empire on the continent of Europe west of a line drawn from Enos on the Aegean Sea to Midia on the Black Sea, with the exception of Albania." Article III opened the door to Austro-Hungarian, Italian and German intrigues. It specified that, "His Imperial Majesty the Sultan and Their Majesties the Allied Sovereigns declare that they submit to His Majesty the Emperor of Germany, His Majesty the Emperor of Austria and King of Hungary, the President of the French Republic, His Majesty the King of Great Britain and Ireland and Emperor of India, His Majesty the King of Italy and His Majesty the Emperor of All the Russias the matter of arranging the delimitation of the frontiers of Albania and all the other questions concerning Albania."

The Boundary Commission and the Protocol of Florence

It was on September 8, 1913 that the Greek Government was informed that an International Commission of the Great

Powers would draw up the boundary between Greece and Albania. It was predecided by the Great Powers under Austro-Italian pressure that, in any event, the Northern Epirote seacoast from Phtelia Bay and Cape Stylus (opposite Corfu) to Cape Glossa, including the Island of Sasson (Saseno) which had been Greek since 1864, was to be ceded to Albania. The Austrians and Italians, pursuing their intention, caused the Boundary Commission to be given a fantastic condition in defining the Greco-Albanian border on ostensibly ethnographic grounds—*they were expressly forbidden to consider a single criterion save that of language.* In view of the by no means usual linguistic history of Northern Epirus, this meant that it was to be turned over to a foreign state organized by its oppressors of the day before.

The Commission was given no authority to consider national sentiment, though pro-Greek sentiment might commonly be expressed by the Northern Epirotes in Albanian. The common tongue of the Northern Epirote majority, regardless of what was said in it, was to be used to condemn them to the same Albanians who had been the Sultan's storm troopers. Moreover, the investigators were ordered to ignore the Epirote language of learning, the language that served as the literary and commercial medium and which, under the Ottoman oppression, the Northern Epirotes had once risked their very lives to study. This would have been disturbing proof of the true ethnic character of the province, and the Austro-Italian cabal would have none of that. Instead, instructions were to ascertain the language most frequently used in the family circle.

One of the persons who accompanied the Boundary Commission was the British Colonel Murray. He gave an excellent account of the Commission's absurd investigations in a lecture given at Morley Hall on January 7, 1914. He related that, "England was represented by Lieutenant-Colonel Doughty-Wylie, C.N.G., lately Consul at Adana, and now holding the same position at Addis Ababa. He was assisted by Captain King, R.E., for topographical work. Lieutenant-Colonel Lallemand, of the French Artillery, and M. Krayer, Vice-Consul at Volo, were the French delegates. Colonel Gouten, Russian military attaché at Athens, represented the Russian Government. The German delegate was Lieutenant-Colonel Tierry, of the General Staff, Austria-Hungary being represented by Herr Bilinski, and Herr Buchberger, who held the posts respectively of Consul-General and Vice-Consul at Jannina until the capture of that place by

H.M. King Constantine. Signor Labia, late Italian Consul at Jannina, was the Italian representative, and was assisted by Captain Castoldi, who had formerly been in the Turkish service as a gendarme officer, or something similar.

"There is not a great deal to be said about these gentlemen or their work, and if there were it would be only wasting your time to talk about it. For they began to disagree among themselves almost from the first day they met together at Monastir . . . Their instructions were to go over the country lying between the frontier claimed by Greece, and the frontier proposed by Italy . . . and find out whether the inhabitants were Greeks or Albanians. But they were forbidden to receive any addresses or deputations, or to make any inquiries, except about the language spoken by the people. And, as everyone knows what language the Epirotes speak—an Albanian patois at home and the Greek language outside home—the Commissioners' inquiries were useless and had no determining effect one way or another in regard to the nationality of the people. What added to the absurdity of the position was that only two members of the Commission could speak Greek or Albanian, and one of these, Herr Bilinski, was too ill to leave his house, while the other, Captain Castoldi, made so many mistakes in translating answers that the Commissioners lost all faith in him as an interpreter . . ."[46]

Upon its arrival at Korytsa, the Commission was courteously received by the Greek military administrator Colonel Contoules. As soon as their presence became known, the Commissioners witnessed over 2,500 Greek schoolchildren who paraded before them their national sentiment. We turn once more to Colonel Murray's eye-witness account:

"I shall never forget standing at Korytsa, side by side with one of the International Commissioners, who shall be nameless, and who was watching the scene passing in the street below us. A procession was going by the house in the midst of which were the girls of the school, waving their flags and singing national songs of liberty, when one girl stopped before the house and held up a scroll on which she had embroidered with great labour in letters of gold the words, 'Enosis e Thanatos', Union or Death. She just held up the scroll for us to see, and I never can forget the sweet, gentle, upturned face, majestic in its childishness, and beautiful in its innocence, and yet expressive of her brave determination to suffer, if required to do so, for hearth and home and nationality and faith. I could see the tears stand in the diplomatist's eyes as he turned away with the words, 'I can stand this no longer. If I look any more I shall break down and be accused of being a philhellene.' Even diplomacy has its human side."

Immediately after the above incident, the Austrian and Italian members of the Commission left for Erseka, the center

[46] Cf. Cassavetes, Nicholas J., *The Question of Northern Epirus at the Peace Conference,* 1919, pp. 135 et seq.

of the Colonia district in which the investigations were to begin. The other Commissioners that evening visited the Metropolitan of Korytsa, the Most Reverend Germanus. During the entire night parades and demonstrations took place before the residence of the Commission. A Northern Epirote Committee formed by the intelligentsia of the province came to make known to the Commissioners the native sentiments of the Northern Epirotes. Seven of its delegates including John Mamopoulos, former representative of Argyrocastron in the first Young Turk Parliament, came from Argyrocastron to place their memorandum before the Commissioners at Korytsa. Colonel Doughty-Wylie, as President of the Commission, could not receive them at the Commission's place of residence, but came down to the courtyard where, deeply impressed, he heard their case, answering them, "I have received my orders which I likewise have to carry out. Because of this it is impossible for me to receive your memorandum. Nonetheless, as an Englishman, I shall report what I see where I must."

The next day, October 28, 1913, the Commission left for Erseka where it began its investigations. From the first it was clear to the British and French Commissioners that, if the Commission was to function properly, it should have taken a course of action which would have permitted it to investigate the educational, religious and national sentiments of the Northern Epirotes. As it was, even the linguistic criterion was eventually suspended and the boundary fixed with no consideration beyond Austro-Italian interests.

At Erseka, they were received by the then Greek administrator and later cabinet minister Constantine Rentes. During their stay in the Colonia district they visited only six villages in twenty-two days. The Austrian and Italian Commissioners, so eager to start out, began to invent all sorts of delays. Much to the annoyance of the Austrians and Italians, who promptly cried that the deputations were coerced, even the Moslems came forward to declare themselves in favor of the Greek regime that had given them the first period of peace and security in their lives. At Erseka, the Moslems presented the following address to the Commission, to which were appended the signatures of forty Moslem leaders from twenty-five Moslem villages of Colonia:

"The undersigned representatives of the Moslem community of the Caza of Colonia take the opportunity of the International Commission's presence in their district to convey to the Commissioners their recognition of the freedom which they enjoy under the new régime in all that concerns their religion and their customs, as well as the absolute security which they now have for life and property. They have the honor to declare that they are now in possession of full liberty, that the Greek Army behaves toward the population in a brotherly manner, and that their interests are firmly bound up with Greece, with which country they desire to be united."

Colonel Murray cites the above document as well as a profusion of Moslem notables who told him the same thing personally. Ahmet Efendi, Moslem Mayor of Korytsa admitted to him quite frankly, "We Moslems of Korytsa come from the same original stock as our Christian townsmen, and we intend to stand alongside of them now in this crisis. I am quite sincere, and speak from my heart, when I say that all the Moslems of this district are perfectly content with Greek rule, and wish to see it permanently established here." The same sentiments were forthcoming from Hajdar Bey Rusi, the likewise Moslem Mayor of Leskoviki. He told the British Colonel, "The Moslems and Christians of Leskoviki live like brothers together, and we are all quite happy now under Greek rule. I am on the town committee of defence and, if necessary, I and my sons will fight along with our Christian townsmen for union with Greece."

Whence came this sudden and unlooked-for pro-Greek sentiment? Of course, it was not the opinion of all the Moslems of Epirus. The unruly Moslem elements wanted license, not liberty. They were not to give up so easily their Ottoman privileges of feuding and plunder. Two facts, however, should be kept constantly in mind. One is the opportunism that is almost a national characteristic. Among the Moslem educated class there was a considerable loss of faith in moribund Ottoman Turkey without any corresponding faith in the practicability, let alone permanence, of an Albanian state. Greece offered them the right to conduct their own affairs and practice their religion. For the first time bandits ceased to infest the land and a degree of order reigned in the province. They therefore saw in Greek rule a stable and benevolent order. If Greece were even today to become the ruler of the province we should not be surprised at the ease with which today's fanatically Moslem Albanians would become philhellenes. Another factor had its effect upon a different segment of the Moslem minority of the province. This was the then prevailing feudal system. Another contemporary British observer put it this way: "The Beys naturally welcome the pleasing prospect (of an Albanian state), for there will be fat years of rich bribes from Italy and Austria, there will be priceless opportunities of looting the Greek and Serbian homes within their boundaries, and it is not the Beys who will have to do the fighting but their retainers. The *bona fide* Albanian peasants and such few traders as exist do not welcome the prospect. The rule of one Albanian Bey is bad enough, but that of an oligarchy of Beys is something that hardly bears contemplation. The Beys are not likely to be content with extorting a lesser revenue than heretofore out of their luckless tenants, whilst in addition there will be the taxes to the state and the Beys' own taxes to the State. The Albanian peasant will have to pay all these."[47] The example of Greek land reforms in Thessaly was not lost on Moslem tenant-farmers in Northern Epirus. Thus the second reason for a growing acceptance of Greece.

It soon became apparent to the Northern Epirotes themselves that the International Commission was really investigating nothing and that the luckless province had in fact been condemned by Austro-Italian intrigues long before the farcical Commission set foot on Epirote soil. But they had waited too long and sacrified too much for their freedom to be so summarily condemned to Albanian misrule. If Greece yielded on the matter, the Northern Epirotes were one and all determined to give even their lives in the struggle for "Union or Death". Arms which had been issued by the Greek Government to the Epirote villagers during the course of the war were not returned. The Epirotes wisely prepared for an evil hour when they might use them again. In order to insure against any eventuality, every male capable of bearing arms, which included grandfathers and schoolboys barely fifteen and often younger, enlisted themselves in voluntary village militias called *Hierolochoi* or Sacred Legions.

After its stay at Erseka, the Commission went to Leskoviki where it stayed thirty-two days without examining a single soul. It then made its way to Argyrocastron where it likewise did nothing for four days. It then became known that during the fifty-eight days of its supposedly serious investigations in Northern Epirus, it had examined exactly *fourteen* individuals and had met only *twelve* times. During that time it had been extended every opportunity possible to investigate the character of the province thoroughly. The entire populace had made every effort to make known its Greek patriotism. Yet, only fourteen people, mostly aged Albanophone Greek women, were examined

[47] Trapmann, *op. cit.*, p. 132.

and these were asked not what nationality they claimed but what language they spoke most often. Captain Trapmann relates:

> "In November 1913, I was, on behalf of the *Daily Telegraph,* undertaking a tour through Epirus at the time that the International Boundary Commission were executing their labours. I had planned to motor from Yannina to Arghyrocastro, a distance of fifty-six miles, but the weather broke in such a deluge of rain that at the last moment I altered my mind and postponed my trip to the following day. I had, however, mentioned my proposed journey, and news of it got abroad, and the Epirots of the Arghyrocastro valley determined that I at least should learn whether their sentiments were Greek or Albanian, wherefore they planned to leave their villages *en masse* and to line the roadway which I must pass. I of course was in ignorance of their intentions, nor ever thought my movements could be of interest, so I failed to notify anybody of the change in my plans.
>
> "The following afternoon, when the weather had abated, I left Yannina, and so soon as I entered the Arghyrocastro valley I found the roadway lined with two endless walls of Epirot peasantry. They had stood thus ever since the morning of the previous day all through that dreadful night of rain without food or shelter, *men, women and children,* determined that I should see them and judge for myself the sincerity of their cry 'Union or Death'. For twenty miles and more I motored through this living avenue of rain-sodden peasantry, but not one reproached me for having kept them so long waiting. To one old woman of ninety years, indeed, I offered my apology. 'Nay!' she said, 'it is nothing! So we should stand, if it would serve, until Union with Greece or death!' And in all that vast concourse of humanity there was not one human being but held a modern rifle. Is it a wonder that I am impressed with the determination of the Epirot to make good his boast of Union or death? If it were not for their wonderful physique and endurance, that thirty hours of waiting in the deluge alone would cost many a score of lives."[48]

As the possible danger of Albanian rule in the event of the Great Powers' unfavorable decision became more apparent, the local village committees of defense who had organized themselves into "hierolochoi" drew together in a common organization. A "Pan-Epirotic Assembly of National Defense" met at Argyrocastron. Its president, chosen by unanimous acclaim, was none other than George Christaki Zographos, son of the Northern Epirote Christaki Zographos whose multitude of benefactions were blessed from one end of the Greek world to the other.

George Zographos had not rested upon his father's justly deserved reputation. He had been both Minister of Foreign Affairs in the Rallis cabinet and, for a brief period immediately following the liberation, had served as Governor-General of

[48] *ibid.,* pp. 130-131.

Epirus. As a native of the district of Argyrocastron, he heard the call of his desperate Epirote countrymen and accepted the presidency of the Northern Epirote National Defense.

At the Convention, the Northern Epirotes reiterated their decision to fight if turned over to Albania. A protest was sent to every one of the European Powers in which the assembled delegates from every part of Greek Northern Epirus again made it clear they would never tolerate the return of Albanian tyranny. The protest closed with the hope that civilized Christian Europe would take steps to prevent such a blot on its conscience. Europe's failure to do so is the reason the free world today is faced with the Reds looking out across the very mouth of the Adriatic. Mussolini's occupation of Albania and Communism's tenacious control over that country owe not a little to the follies committed before World War I.

The Ambassadorial Conference at Florence on December 25, 1913, severed Epirus in half and created the question of Northern Epirus. From that day to this, crisis upon crisis has kept Europe uneasy. The near-sighted politicians around a green table had done their work. The line of Florence was substantially the line proposed by Italy at London. It marks the present uneasy frontier between our Greek ally and Red Albania.

The Greeks Depart

Meanwhile, things were taking their course in Albania. After a long period of indecision, the Great Powers on November 23, 1913, chose a Prussian army captain as King of Albania who happened to be the nephew of Queen Elizabeth of Rumania. The name of this aristocratic nobody was Prince Wilhelm of Wied. He was to rule for ten years jointly with an "International Commission of Control" consisting of delegates from each of the Great Powers and one Albanian representative. This was to be Albania's real government for, as everyone realized, a completely self-governing Albania was a ridiculous impossibility. It might be remarked in passing that Mehdi Frashëri, the Albanian representative on the Commission, was made a regent of Mussolini's puppet Albania many years later.

Ismail Kemal immediately accepted the Great Powers' proposal, but Essad took his time to decide. He too finally gave up his pretensions for a time and went to head the Albanian delegation which arrived in Germany to offer the crown to the Prussian princeling.

The implementation of the Protocol of Florence was delayed for over a month. During this time, Greece tried feverishly through diplomatic channels to save Epirus from dismemberment and the Northern Epirotes from Albanian occupation. Greece had no course but to pull out her troops and leave if the Great Powers pressed their decision. It became evident that the issue was shortly to come to such an end. The Great Powers had yielded to the terrific pressure of Vienna and Rome. A European War hung over the heads of Entente leaders and Northern Epirus could not be permitted to become an issue. The British now advised the Greek victims of Europe not to raise difficulties. Sir Edward Grey was later to recall in his memoirs, "As the (Greek) Minister continued to press the question of Albania, saying that it was the interests of Italy and Austria that were being considered, I observed that even Great Powers must sometimes be allowed to have interests as well as the smaller Powers."

At 5:30 P.M. on February 13, 1914, British Ambassador Elliot handed Greek Foreign Minister Streit a note from the Great Powers jointly ordering Greece to hand over Northern Epirus to Albania. It warned Greece of the dire consequences of a Greek Government-supported uprising in that province.

The Greek Government had to yield, but serious problems still confronted them. How could Greece disarm the Northern Epirote populace before withdrawing and deliver thousands of Greeks to certain massacre? If the means of resistance were left in Epirote hands there was certain to be a Northern Epirote resistance to Albania in which the Greek Government would be accused of conspiracy. Moreover, a part of the Greek Army in Epirus was composed of volunteer natives and some of the officers as well, including Staff Generals, were Northern Epirotes who might defy Athens' orders. In this case a considerable portion of the Army in Northern Epirus, including non-Epirote Greeks who would stand with their local brethren, might mutiny. The best that Greece could hope for was an orderly withdrawal of the whole of the Army, leaving the population to do as it would after the evacuation.

What that course would be every Greek unofficially knew—the Northern Epirotes intended to defend themselves unto death. There was no other course open as the Albanian Moslem rabble prepared to plunder and massacre the Christian Greeks.

Law and order were leaving. The clock was being turned back to the long years of Ottoman occupation. Moslem urchins were no longer careful about taunting the Christian Epirotes openly in the streets and markets with the following doggerel:

"Kozstandino i mier	"Oh wretched Constantine,
Erdhe për një copë her'	For a little while you came.
Ikën me robën te çierr	In tattered clothes you go.
Na lé morat në der'.	You leave us lice upon the doorstep.
T'erdhi vahti për remull	Your time for seizure has arrived
O moj Dropulli me vull."	Oh thou renowned Dropolis."

On the 24th, the Greek Press Office issued the following bulletin: "The Government and the King are in agreement regarding questions of foreign policy. Hard necessity compels the evacuation of Northern Epirus." Major-General Papoulas arrived the same day in Korytsa to take charge of the evacuation which was to begin in four days. The representatives of the Northern Epirote National Defense refused to accept General Papoulas' assurances of guarantees of their civil and religious liberties and walked out indignantly when told of the impending evacuation. Papoulas' answer was to repeat the empty assurances and order the National Defense dissolved. The police at Korytsa were to take the proper steps to see that this was done. The Northern Epirotes decided to ignore it. It was bad enough to have to defend themselves against the Albanians, but would they have to do likewise in Greece's name against the Greek Government itself?

The first clarion call to arms came from Argyrocastron. Zographos, now head of the National Defense, arrived in Argyrocastron from Athens on the 27th. An air of expectancy hung over the mountain town. Zographos remained closeted with National Defense leaders from every part of Greek Northern Epirus to prepare the step from which there could be no turning back.

The Greek military evacuation began on the 28th as planned. On March 2, 1914, at three in the afternoon, a vast assembly of Northern Epirotes, all well armed, gathered by the edge of the Drynus River at the foot of Argyrocastron.

There were tears in every eye as the crowd made way for George Zographos, Alexius Carapanos, Metropolitan Basil of Dryinoupolis and the then Metropolitan of Velas and Konitsa, later of Jannina, Metropolitan Spyridon, who still later became Primate of Greece. Donning their ceremonial vestments, the bishops began the blessing. With the uttering of "Blessed art Thou our God," the murmuring mass fell reverently silent.

When the deacon voiced the customary petition in the litany for the King of the Hellenes, the entire body knelt in still devotion by the water's edge. Then, the deacon voiced a petition for "The President of Northern Epirus, George Zographos," and seven thousand men fired their rifles into the air. "Long live the Autonomy," went up from every throat.

The Metropolitans came forward. Slowly and sadly the national flag of Greece, symbol of every Epirote dream, was lowered. Another flag, blessed with the water of the Drynus was smartly run up. It was the Greek standard, with its white cross centered upon the solid sky-blue background. At its center, however, with large wings outstretched, it bore the imperial double-eagle of Byzantium. Metropolitan Basil spoke:

> "By reason of overwhelming national necessity, we have lowered thee, oh divine dream, thou blue and white national banner of ours and of our fathers. But in thy place we raise not a foreign flag, but thy daughter, the Epirote colors, dedicated to triumph against the Albanian Crescent."

This was the Epirote way of proclaiming before Europe and the world that the province which had stood guard through the ages in Greece's northwest would again defend its birthright against the barbarians.

Chapter VII

FOR CROSS AND FLAG

The Struggle Begins

Europe had suspected that the Northern Epirotes would fight. Greece had known it and had sought to avoid it by every means possible. Now that it had come to this, Greece was determined to uphold Europe's decision lest the very nation be put in jeopardy. Beyond doubt, there was a difference between official Greece which had to condemn and the Greek common man who not only condoned but applauded the daring of the Northern Epirotes. The British journalist C. S. Butler told the facts as he observed them:

"That the Greek army, officers and soldiers, are to a man in keen sympathy with the Epirotes is a well known fact. It is also well known that a small number of Greek officers (not exceeding 30), most of them natives of Northern Epirus, have deserted to the Epirote camp with perhaps a couple of hundred of the rank and file. In one case a half-battery of machine guns, commanded by a lieutenant of Epirote origin, when the evacuation of Leskoviki was ordered by the Greek Government, bolted into the nearest mountains and joined the Epirote insurgents. It is also true that Cretan volunteers, to a total of about 300, found their way to Northern Epirus, mostly in small sailing vessels. A small band of Greek 'Garibaldians' was also equipped by the late Count Roma and took part in the fighting on the Argyrocastron frontier. This is the sum total of outside help that the Epirotes have received from any part of Greece, and that in direct defiance of the orders and well defined policy of the Greek Government, which proceeded to extremes that no Greek Government has ever yet dared to apply in opposing what was unmistakably the popular will. To begin with, the Greek troops, in evacuating Northern Epirus, were careful to take with them all the army stores, guns, ammunition, etc. Even the Turkish guns captured at Korytsa and Argyrocastron during the Balkan War, which could easily have been 'overlooked' were carried away; and at Georgoutsates, the junction of the Argyrocastron-Delvino-Jannina routes, the Greek troops actually fired upon a party of Epirotes who attempted to prevent the transfer of the military stores thence, and killed seven and wounded thirty, including two women. That does not look much like connivance; and yet the firing party were distinctly in sympathy with the Epirotes and only obeyed orders. The Greek officers and privates who deserted to the

Epirotes have been proclaimed deserters and stricken from the roster; a company of Evzones, who with their captain and non-coms, broke away and started to join the Epirotes, were rounded up and sentenced to six months' imprisonment.

"More than this, Mr. Venizelos, with his characteristic vehemence, did all he could to discourage and browbeat the Epirote insurrection against Europe's fiat; and in the Greek Chamber publicly predicted disaster for their undertaking—a prediction which has proved utterly mistaken. He even went so far as to lay hands upon and turn to the use of the Greek Government a donation of £10,000 sent by a rich Epirote of America for the insurgent cause—a thing that, strictly speaking, the Greek Premier had no right to do—and the writer, in the Greek Foreign Office, was an unwitting auditor of a violent altercation between Mr. Venizelos and Mr. Zographos, in which the latter was told in so many words that official Greece considered him well nigh a traitor to the interests of Greece because he had placed himself at the head of the Epirote insurrection."[49]

Official Greece notwithstanding, the Northern Epirotes refused to yield to Europe's wishes and become Albanians after they had remained Greeks through hundreds of years of successive persecutions. Wrote the correspondent of the London *Daily Telegraph:*

"If Europe imagines for one moment that the Epirot is attempting to play a game of bluff, she is giving proof of incredible ignorance of the aspirations and character of this sturdy, simple-minded people. Many people and nations have from time to time in the height of their power attempted to denationalise the Epirot. Rome, Venice, Serbia, Bulgaria, Turkey, Skander Bey and Ali Pasha—each in turn has spent his strength and treasure, enjoyed the questionable advantages of a military occupation of the country, but none has ever succeeded in making a single Epirot change his nationality. It is not likely that the Marquis di San Giuliano and Sir Edward Grey will succeed where these have failed, even when backed by the Prince de Wied and the Kingdom of autonomous Albania. If it were not so infinitely sad it would be infinitely ridiculous."[50]

The Provisional Government

The Northern Epirotes were fortunate in possessing all the prerequisites for local self-government. Under the Ottoman Empire they were used to managing their own affairs in the absence of responsible government. It was also true that a province which had given its native sons to the highest offices in the government of free Greece could hardly lack political and military leadership in its hour of need. George Christaki

[49] Cf. *Manchester Guardian,* Sept. 30, 1914.

[50] Trapmann, op. cit., p. 129.

Zographos became his native province's provisional President and Prime Minister. Alexius Carapanos, an Epirote with fifteen years experience in the Greek diplomatic service as well as the Greek Parliament, brother of an internationally-known archeologist, assumed the post of Foreign Minister. Metropolitan Basil of Dryinoupolis, Bishop of Argyrocastron and a native of the district, became Minister of Justice and Religion. Metropolitan Spyridon of Velas and Konitsa, the late head of the Church of Greece, headed the Ministry of the Interior.

It was decided that the all important post of Minister of War and Commander-in-Chief of the Epirote forces was to be offered to Colonel Demetrius Doulis, a native of the Chimarriote village of Nivitsa near Santi Quaranta. Doulis was still on the active list of the Greek Army and was stationed in Argyrocastron. He had transmitted his acceptance of the post to the Pan-Epirotic Assembly. When this became public, the Greek General Staff was furious. General Papoulas telephoned Colonel Doulis on March 3rd to verify this apparent disobedience of orders. The following is a transcript of that conversation:

Papoulas: " Is it true that your countrymen have declared you chief of the autonomous state's army?"

Doulis: "My countrymen have given me a hearty, universal and armed reception upon my arrival here yesterday."

Papoulas: "I'm asking you if you've accepted the command."

Doulis: "Not yet. However, should matters call for it, I shall accept."

Papoulas: "Then you will inform me."

That same afternoon, at 2:00 P.M., Papoulas put in a second call from Jannina to Doulis in Argyrocastron. Papoulas curtly informed the Colonel that the Greek ranks had to continue to function in an orderly fashion. Doulis answered, "The Government of Autonomous Epirus has offered me the administration of its military establishment." Papoulas blew up and demanded that Doulis hand over the regiment to Major Grivas and return at once to Jannina. The rest of the conversation ran as follows:

Doulis: "I find myself upon the territory of the Autonomous State of Epirus as Minister of the armies of its Government."

Papoulas: "The Greek Army has given its oath which it is obliged to keep, which means to execute the orders of the Royal Government and H.M. King Constantine and wishes to hear from Doulis and not from the Minister that the army must keep its place and wishes Mr. Doulis to advise the officers to remove themselves."

Doulis: "The struggle of Epirus is a national cause since the Epirotes ask to remain faithful subjects of the glorious Commander-in-Chief King Constantine XII."

Papoulas: "But the Greek Army has given an oath."

Doulis: "H.M. our King, nevertheless, in his message to the Army and people after the Bulgarian war, expected us to be ready always to preserve what we've acquired with so much blood and that we must not permit anyone to think of taking from us even one inch of ground. This is exactly what we're doing today in forbidding a part of land to be removed in disputed regions we've gotten with so much blood."

Papoulas: "Your Government has assumed this responsibility, but the Greek Army is obliged to get out in time."

Doulis: "But Epirus will struggle to be thus in complete accord with H.M. our King's orders."

Papoulas: "As the Government wishes, I lead the Greek Army."

Doulis: "But since the Government does not so wish, I lead as a Greek Epirote."

Papoulas: "I communicate to you the cipher telegram just received this moment from H.M. the King and await the reply:

"Major-General Papoulas, Jannina.

'Inform as final in my name Colonel Doulis, that the first obligation of a soldier is obedience to the orders of his King and preservation of his oath. Unless he carries out his duty he will be considered a deserter. I do not consider his act justifiable under conditions of which he is unable to be the judge.'

'Constantine, Rex.' "

Doulis: Reply:

"Major-General Papoulas, Jannina.

'Until today, according to my knowledge, I performed faithfully and true to my oath my duty. Now, as one born and bred in the condemned regions of Epirus, I have a further duty to struggle for my massacred brethren, damned to a more tyrannical yoke than that of the Turk. I regret from the depths of my heart that, after my long military service, I now find myself unavoidably obliged to deviate from my idolized King's commands.

'Doulis.' "

One more name among hundreds was stricken from the military list. One more Epirote had become an outlaw for defying Greece in her own name. The Epirotes defied Europe and Greece as they defied Albania—because they remained faithful to Hellas when Greece was forced to be unfaithful to herself.

To the outside world the Austro-Italians, their Albanian sycophants and their friends said that Greece had encouraged an armed rebellion led by a Greek minority and fought by non-Epirotes against the Albanians who, of course, were the people of Argyrocastron and Korytsa. The facts given here show the extent of the Albanian perjury. The ultimate defiance of Greece itself by the Northern Epirotes stands as the best possible proof of the true nature of the situation.

Wied and the Northern Epirotes

On March 7, 1914, Prince Wilhelm of Wied arrived at Durazzo. He found a government riddled with rivalries, an Ottoman-minded tribal population on the verge of mutiny and a Greek southern province that had already seceded from his makeshift kingdom. If he did not know then how doomed to failure he was, he discovered the truth soon enough.

In the sectors of Argyrocastron, Chimarra, Santi Quaranta and Delvino, the insurgent Epirotes were in full power despite all attempts to dislodge them. In these attempts even Greece participated with a blockade of Santi Quaranta by the Greek warships *Alpheius* and *Eurotas.* This Greek blockade was carried out despite the bitter opposition of a large section of the Greek Parliament.

In view of the disquieting situation among the Moslem Ghegs of northern Albania, it was thought prudent by Wied to come to some understanding with the Northern Epirotes. On March 11, Colonel Thompson, the Dutch head of Wied's gendarmerie, arrived in Corfu with plenipotentiary powers to discuss the situation with Northern Epirote Foreign Minister Carapanos. His offer was one of limited local government for the province. This was rejected by the Northern Epirote Government in favor of nothing less than complete autonomy.

Everywhere, save in Korytsa, for reasons we shall see shortly, the armies of the Autonomy successfully engaged the Dutch-commanded Albanian gendarmerie and such ragged and ill-organized irregulars as Wied could send against them.

The Greek Government, true to its pledge to the Great Powers, had been able to hand Korytsa over to Albania. This was due to the zealous suppression of the Northern Epirote autonomists there by the Greek Colonel Contoules. After conferring with the Greek authorities in Jannina, he had returned to Korytsa with General Papoulas to begin the evacuation. A meeting of Papoulas with the leaders of the National Defense at Korytsa convinced the local Epirote leaders that Greece really meant to pull out. The next day, Papoulas left once more for Jannina. On the same day, news of the proclamation of the autonomy in Argyrocastron reached Korytsa. Contoules ordered martial law to be observed rigidly and threatened to shoot the first citizen who dared raise the Northern Epirote flag in Korytsa. When Metropolitan Spyridon appeared in Erseka to proclaim the Autonomy there, Contoules immediately had him arrested.

On the day scheduled for the delivery of Korytsa to Albania, the entire Greek population was confined to its homes to avoid bloodshed. With the new administrator, Mustafa Bey, the straggling force of 150 Albanian ex-deserters from the Turkish Army, dragging with them one mortar, invested the city in the name of Albania. They were led by gendarmerie lieutenant Ghilardi, a Croat in the Austrian service and much later a Zogist general (assassinated at Fieri, August 1935). Contoules turned the city over to this force and left to do the same at Erseka.

While the Albanians were laying siege to Korytsa, a Northern Epirote fighting force from the National Defense units of the Korytsa district had rallied to nearby Viglista. There, under the leadership of Epaminondas Charisiades, they prepared to move on Korytsa as soon as the Greek forces left.

Korytsa's Five Day Revolt

On Thursday, March 22, the Hierolochites at Viglista sent a body of troops toward Korytsa. The communications between Korytsa-Pogradets-Colonia were cut. As soon as word that these guerillas had taken up positions near the city reached the underground National Defense members in Korytsa, they immediately donned uniforms and assaulted the Albanian gendarmerie within the city. Alarmed and thinking the city already in Northern Epirote hands, Abdyl Bey Ypi, Mustafa Bey's successor, abandoned Korytsa. The Dutch Major Schneller and the local Albanian police under Themistocles Germeni (a spy and traitor we shall meet again) remained to hold off the Northern Epirotes. A street battle raged furiously, with both the leader of the Greeks and Schneller being rendered *hors de combat.* For a brief while, and with as much ceremony as the desperate situation would permit, the Northern Epirote flag flew over the town.

On Saturday, the guerillas who had taken up positions on nearby Mt. St. Elias began a steady mortar fire upon the Albanians, but their position was worse than that of the Epirotes within the town. The guerillas' ammunition was getting low and reinforcements from Viglista failed to arrive. Realizing this, Abdyl Bey returned with reinforcements from the nearby Moslem villages.

Finally, five days after the operation had begun, their ammunition exhausted and their escape cut off, the guerrillas on Mt. St. Elias surrendered to the Albanians who took them in custody. Most of them were shot in the back and only a remnant was led to prison. After the town was once more securely under its Albanian masters, Metropolitan Germanus and twenty members of the town council were arrested for conspiracy and moved during the following night north to Elbasan via Pogradets. They were later freed by the Essadists under Qamil Musa and Haxhi Fejza. It was not until July 8th that Korytsa, after several days' battle, was finally freed by the Autonomists.

The Protocol of Corfu

Essad had broken with Wied. The all-powerful Minister of War now made his own war upon Prince Wied's melting forces, identifying himself with the Moslem tribesmen of central and northern Albania. The International Commission of Control left Durazzo for Tirana which was in Essadist hands. Upon their arrival, they were stunned to see armed throngs greet them with "Padishahmiz chok yasha!" (Long live our Sultan!). The insurgent flag was the Star and Crescent. Somewhat nonplussed, the delegates wired home to their governments the extraordinary demands of the tribesmen: an Osmanli prince for ruler, a return to limited autonomy under the Ottoman Sultan, the supremacy of the *Sheriat,* etc. Having created and sweated to bring the exotic flower of Albanian nationalism to bloom, they had ventured forth to be met by the specter of Abdul Hamid! Petriaew, the Russian delegate, wired his Tsar what had happened. Before filing the telegram away, Nicholas the Last added his own terse comment: "Delightful country . . . . ."[51]

Under such circumstances, the Commission redoubled its efforts to effect a Wied-Northern Epirote agreement. On May 6, 1914, Zographos received a communication from the Commission.

"Upon the request of the Albanian Government, the International Control Commission is willing to communicate to you the text of the concessions dependent upon the guaranteed condition of an immediate ceasing of all hostility and advance, which will likewise be done by the Albanian forces. The Commission will arrive in Santi Quaranta where, upon the acceptance of this condition, it will proceed to announce to you the concessions, the putting into effect of which it will supervise itself in the event

[51] *Red Documents,* Vol. I, 3, Tel. No. 112,15544.

they are accepted, guaranteeing likewise their observance. We await reply. Telegraph at once.

(s) "Mehdi
"Winchei
"Krall
"Krajewski
"Lamb
"Leoni
"Petriaew"

An urgent telegram was sent by Zographos from Argyrocastron accepting the proposal and requesting the Commission to name the date of its arrival at Santi Quaranta. An armistice was ordered for noon the next day. This was observed everywhere save at Korytsa where, by reason of faulty communications with Argyrocastron, the Epirote forces under Autonomist General George Tsontos-Vardas continued to advance. When the cease-fire order was finally received, he had broken the Albanian defenses and commanded the heights of Mt. Morava.

Upon arrival at Santi Quaranta, Zographos requested the Commission to adjourn to neutral Corfu to begin discussions. With the members of the Commission, Zographos arrived in Corfu aboard the motor launch *Puglia*. The discussions then began at the *Hotel Bella Venezia* where agreement was finally reached. Naturally, Northern Epirote union with Greece was not going to be acceded to by the Powers, but the force of Northern Epirote arms and European anxiety over the anarchy in northern Albania had brought the Albanians to terms and made Europe bow to the demands of Northern Epirus. The Epirotes won a completely autonomous existence as a *corpus separatum* under the purely nominal hegemony of Prince Wied. This was embodied in a now historic document that deserves reprinting in full. It became known as the Protocol of Corfu and is prefaced by a signed statement of the Commission:

"The International Commission of Control, in order to avoid the resumption of hostilities, believes it to be its duty to reconcile as much as possible the point of view of the Epirote populations with regard to the special dispositions which they ask for, and that of the Albanian Government. It is with this idea in mind that the Commission has agreed to submit to the Powers which it represents, as well as to the Albanian Government, the enclosed text, which is the result of discussions between the members of this Commission and the Epirote delegates:

"Corfu, May 17, 1914"

(s) "Winchei, A. Leoni, Krall, Mehdi Frashëri, Harry H. Lamb, Leon Krajewski, A. Petriaew.

"Signed subject to the approval of our Principals:
"G. Christaki Zographos, Al. C. Carapanos."

"PROVISIONS CONCERNING THE TERRITORIES EVACUATED BY THE GREEK TROOPS AND FORMING THE PROVINCES OF ARGYROCASTRO AND CORYTZA"

"I. ORGANIZATION: The execution and maintenance of the provisions laid down for the organization of the two southern provinces are now entrusted to the C.I.C. (Commission Internationale de Cõntrolé). The Commission will organize the department of administration and that of justice and finance. The Albanian Government, by agreement with the C.I.C., will appoint and dismiss the governors and high officials, taking into account, as much as possible, the numerical importance of the adherents of each religion.

"II. LOCAL COUNCILS: The number of elective members in the administrative councils shall be at least three times the number of the *de jure* members.

"III. ADMINISTRATIVE DELIMITATION AND SUBDIVISION: The C.I.C. will supervise both the administrative delimitation and subdivision of the two provinces, and this when once settled cannot be further modified without the consent of the Powers.

"IV. TERRITORY: All the provisions in question shall apply to the populations of the territories previously occupied by Greece and annexed to Albania.

"V. GENDARMERIE: For the maintenance of order in the southern provinces there shall be created, with officers, non-commissioned officers, and gendarmes, a local gendarmerie composed of representatives of each of the different religious faiths, in proportion to the number of members of each sect in these provinces. This gendarmerie may serve outside the limits of these provinces only for a fixed period and then only in the case of *force majeure* as recognized by the C.I.C. The same restrictions shall apply to employment in these southern provinces of corps of gendarmerie composed of men who are not natives. Officers commanding gendarmerie are recommended to employ in the various localities only detachments of men who belong to the same religious faith as the inhabitants of the locality.

"In cases where the local element proves insufficient to furnish the proportional component part of the gendarmerie, recourse will be had to natives of other Albanian provinces. In conformity with the principles set forth above, the Dutch officers will immediately proceed with the work of enrollment. It is understood that the foregoing provisions will not impair the unity of the Albanian gendarmerie as laid down by the Conference of London.

"VI. ARMED FORCES: Except in the case of war or revolution in the southern provinces, non-native military units shall not be transferred to or employed in these provinces.

"VII. ORTHODOX COMMUNITIES: The Orthodox Christian communities are recognized as juridical persons, like the others. They will enjoy the possession of their property, and be free to dispose of it as they please. The relations of the Orthodox communities with their spiritual chiefs will be as in the past. The ancient rights and hierarchical organization of the said communities shall not be impaired except under agreement between the Albanian Government and the Oecumenical Patriarchate of Constantinople.

"VIII. SCHOOLS: Education shall be free. In the schools of the Orthodox communities the instruction shall be in Greek. In the three elementary classes Albanian will be taught concurrently with Greek. Nevertheless, religious education shall be exclusively in Greek.

"IX. LIBERTY OF LANGUAGE: In virtue of the principle laid down in the Note of the Powers to Greece, dated April 11/24, 1914, the permission to use both Albanian and Greek shall be assured in the southern provinces before all the authorities, including the Courts, as well as the elective councils.

"X. OCCUPATION: The C.I.C. will take possession of the territory in question, in the name of the Albanian Government, by proceeding to the place. The officers of the Dutch Mission will at once begin the organization of the local gendarmerie. Provisionally, and until the formation of this local gendarmerie, the Dutch officers, with the help of the local elements, will make themselves responsible for public security.

"The C.I.C. will also proceed to the constitution of mixed commissions, composed of Christians and Moslems, in the respective numerical importance of these elements. For the time being, and until the organization of the local authorities, these commissions will assume administrative functions under the effective surveillance of the C.I.C., of which surveillance the latter will determine the extent. Before the arrival of the Dutch officers, the necessary steps will be taken by the Provisional Government of Argyrocastro for the removal from the country of all armed foreign elements. These provisions will not only be applied in that part of the province of Corytza now occupied militarily by Albania, but also in the other southern regions.

"XI. RELIEF: The Albanian Government, in agreement with the C.I.C., will take the necessary measures to relieve the population which has suffered from the events of recent years.

"XII. AMNESTY: A full and complete amnesty is granted to the Epirotes for all acts prior to the occupation of these provinces by the representatives of the Albanian Government. No person not of Epirote origin shall be prosecuted in respect of the period above mentioned except for non-political offenses.

"XIII. GUARANTEE: The Powers who, by the Conference of London, have guaranteed the institution of Albania and established the C.I.C. guarantee the execution and maintenance of the foregoing provisions."

On the 25th of June, the Albanian Government, through the Chairman of the C.I.C., accepted the Protocol in its entirety. The Autonomy gave its final approval after the Protocol was discussed at length at a special Constituent Assembly convoked at Delvino.The Great Powers likewise signified their ratification in a communication to the Greek Government on July 1st.

Meanwhile, the C.I.C. was having its hands full with the

Albanians. Prince Wied found himself and the International Commission bottled up in Durazzo. Most of central Albania was now in Essadist hands. Sensing the hopelessness of the situation, the Commission went to Sh'Jak on August 31st to negotiate with the insurgents. While there, they received a communication that made it imperative for them to return to Durazzo at once. The Albanian gendarmerie within Durazzo had mutinied. "The men belonging to this corps were opposing the departure of the Prince before he had paid their wages and threatened to make use of their weapons."[52]

The next day, in fear of life and limb, modern Albania's first ruler boarded the Italian warship *Misurata* in Durazzo harbor. On September 3rd, accompanied by his wife Sophie, Prime Minister Turhan Pasha and several aides, he sailed for Venice never to return.

> "With Prince William of Wied and the international corps of occupation gone, the Albanians were left to themselves. At Durazzo, a body of notables calling themselves the Senate, adopted resolutions restoring the Ottoman flag and the suzerainty of the Sultan, invited Prince Burhaneddin Efendi, a son of Abdul Hamid, to become their ruler, and solemnly decreed that hereafter the Turkish language should be restored to its former position as the official language of the country."[53]

While no Osmanli prince ever came forward to take the proffered sceptre, the incident is illuminating as regards the Gheg temperament in post-Wied Albania.

Essad Pasha, with a force of 10,000 followers in Durazzo, had no trouble persuading the self-constituted "Senate" to recognize him on October 4th as "President and Premier" of Albania. The C.I.C. likewise gave him its recognition.

Essad held Durazzo and was trying to hold all of central Albania. The Northern Epirotes, despite skirmishes with bandits and Essadists, were secure behind their now recognized frontier. The Catholic Mirdites under Prenk Bib Doda recognized no government but their own. In Valona, Ismail Kemal and a "Committee of Public Safety" composed of his followers stood alone until the Italian occupation. "For the rest there were as many rulers in Albania as there were tribes."[54] So ended the tragic-comic debut of Albania as a modern European state.

[52] cf. *Corriere della Sera,* Milan, Italy, 3 September 1914.

[53] Gibbons, Herbert Adams, *New Map of Europe,* p. 364.

[54] Marriott, John A. R., *The Eastern Question,* p. 472.

The Final Reunion with Greece

On June 28, 1914, a shot fired by a Serbian student in the Bosnian town of Sarajevo struck down Archduke Francis Ferdinand, heir to the Hapsburg crowns. Touching off a series of progressively greater explosions, it had, by August 4, plunged Serbia, Austria-Hungary, Russia, Germany, France, Belgium and Great Britain into the raging inferno of World War I. Eventually it was to engulf the United States. Greece, exhausted by her sustained efforts during two Balkan Wars and Italy, nominally tied to the Central Powers but coveting Austrian-held territory, elected to remain neutral for a while.

Without any effective government in Albania, matters there had gone back to what they were in early 1913. Italy, still a neutral, indicated that she wished to step into Valona "to guarantee Albanian neutrality in accordance with the provisions of the Conference of London." In view of this, Greece requested the Great Powers to permit her to reenter Northern Epirus. Having finally given up all hopes for an Albanian state, all the Great Powers now no longer saw a reason for not countenancing, indeed urging, Greece to take the step they had vociferously denounced in 1913. On October 26, 1914, the Autonomous Republic of Northern Epirus joyfully lowered its colors to give way to those of the Hellenic motherland. Very shortly, Europe gave its blessing.

> REUTERS—"Following are the replies of the great powers to the Greek note announcing the intention of Greece to reoccupy Epirus:
> "France declared that she saw no objection to the course proposed by M. Venizelos's note.
> "Russia intimated that she would gladly accept whatever decision in the matter was reached by Great Britain and France.
> "The British Government accepted M. Venizelos's note.
> "Germany and Austria-Hungary replied that they accepted the declaration of the Greek Government that the occupation would not be contrary to the decisions of the London Conference.
> "Italy declared that she, for the same purpose as set forth in the Greek note, namely the maintenance of order and security, was taking similar steps at Valona, and that she had adopted this course while fully respecting the decisions of the powers. She raised no objections to M. Venizelos's proposal."[55]

Amid exuberant demonstrations of a nightmare ended and a dream come true, the populace of Northern Epirus greeted

[55] Cf. *London Morning Post*, 30 October 1914

the return of the Greek Army. For the second time within a year the Greek flag was flying from Korytsa to the Adriatic, and for a little while Epirus was free again.

Note: Some material not otherwise credited will be found in the valuable historical contributions regarding the Autonomist movement by Constantine Skenderes, former Greek M.P. from Korytsa. Most of the material from Skenderes is not readily available in English.

Chapter VIII

FROM FALSE DAWN TO MIDNIGHT

The False Daybreak

In spite of their ordeal which showed how little fate was to be trusted, the Epirotes were highly optimistic that a better day had dawned at last. Union with Greece had become, as far as they could see, a permanent actuality. It was at this point that a thousand years of martyrdom and desperate struggle could have been ended on a triumphant note. In greeting the Greek forces back to Korytsa, Metropolitan Jacob gave voice to the universal Epirote thanksgiving. He assured his flock that, "After commotion comes quiet, after a flood follows peace. And we, after the shock we have suffered, after the terrible evils which descended upon our heads, after the terrible floods we have survived, are now beholding Divine Grace as we enter the harbor of salvation."

Throughout Epirus complete order was restored. The Moslems as well as the Christians were made to put aside the sword for the plough. The assimilation of Northern Epirus into the general administration of the Greek state gradually replaced the military administration.

After the Protocol of Corfu elections had taken place in the then Autonomous Republic. The M.P.s elected sought entrance now to the Greek Parliament. Since these had been elected according to the Ottoman electoral system and in the absence of election rolls, the Greek Government nullified the results and called for new elections. It was not until December 20, 1915 that these were held and the following Deputies were elected to Parliament: from Argyrocastron 8—Demetrius Doulis, Spyros Spyromelios, P. Zappas, Kyriakos Kyritsis, Ch. Gioscas, D. Papoulas, Themistocles Adamides, Basil Soteriades; from Korytsa 6—J. Adamides, C. Polenas, S. Charisiades, Constantine Skenderes, Euclid Somos, Demetrius Zecos.

The Italians in Valona

At the same time that Northern Epirus was reunited to Greece, the Italians officially planted the flag of their kingdom on a Balkan beachhead. On October 30, 1914, Italy occupied the former Greek Island of Sason (Saseno) in Valona harbor. On December 26, the Italians landed and took over in Valona. Their commander issued the following declaration:

> "The grave disorders that became apparent from time to time in this country have paralyzed commerce, work and are endangering the life and property of the inhabitants.
>
> "The Italian Government, a watchful guardian of Albanian fortunes, desires that your tranquility, so cruelly tried, shall be assured. Invoked by your wishes the marines of Italy are disembarking from the ships to establish order and defend you."
>
> "(s) Admiral Patris"

Not yet a member of the Entente, Italy had already assumed the self-bestowed title of "guardian of Albanian fortunes." Austria-Hungary no longer being seriously involved in Albania, the time had come to realize the dreams of Italy's empire-makers. For the time being they were confined to Valona, but not for long. The difference between Greek reunited to Greece in Northern Epirus and Albanian "protected" by Italy in Valona is a clue to the sinister acts that were to follow.

Italy, the Allies and Northern Epirus

Greece, having achieved the reunion of Northern Epirus, had attained the limit of her objectives in that area. Italy, in occupying Valona, had only embarked on the first step to realizing hers. In Greece, Allied pressure was brought to bear to force the Greeks to abandon neutrality.

A heavy haze of Venizelist and Constantinist propaganda still covers the actual issues between the King and Premier. Venizelos, placing his faith in the victory of the Allies, argued that Greece had to commit herself unconditionally and uncritically to their dictates in order to secure for herself an honored place at the peace table. The worst that can be said of his opponents was that, noting carefully the bait dangled before Italy to abandon neutrality, they could see little reason to lay Greece open to devastation without similar Allied concessions.

The wisdom or folly of either side, the mudslinging epithets hurled by both and the party passions that only now appear to be healed are not germane to the issue discussed here. Suffice it to say that after Venizelos' resignation, the new premier, Gounaris, indicated his willingness to continue negotiations with the Allies.

A document brought to light after the Bolshevik Revolution in the Russian Foreign Ministry Archives sheds some light on a complicated issue. "On April 1 (14) M. Gounaris declared the willingness of Greece to enter (the war) if the Allies would guarantee her territorial integrity, together with North Epirus and the islands for the period of the war and a certain period after it, while the question of territorial acquisitions in Asiatic Turkey was to be a matter for later discussion. No reply was given to this, and on May 1 (14) the Greek Minister declared that since the Allies had apparently no intention to guarantee the territorial integrity of Greece the latter had decided to remain neutral."[56]

The bait dangled before Italy by the Allies was finally embodied formally in the secret treaty of London concluded on April 26, 1915. The following articles of that treaty formed the basis for Italy's renewed intrigues in Albania:

> "Article 6. Italy shall receive full sovereignty over Valona, the island of Saseno and surrounding territory of sufficient extent to assure defence of these points (from Voiussa to the north and east, approximately to the northern boundary of the district of Chimara on the south).
> "Article 7. Should Italy obtain the Trentino and Istria in accordance with the provisions of Article 4, together with Dalmatia and the Adriatic islands within the limits specified in Article 5, and the Bay of Valona (Article 6), and if the central portion of Albania is reserved for the establishment of a small autonomous neutralized State, Italy shall not oppose the division of Northern and Southern Albania between Montenegro, Serbia and Greece, should France, Great Britain and Russia so desire. The coast from the southern boundary of the Italian territory of Valona (see Article 6) up to Cape Stylos shall be neutralized.
>
> "Italy shall be charged with the representation of the State of Albania in its relations with foreign Powers.
>
> "Italy agrees, moreover, to leave sufficient territory in any event to the east of Albania to ensure the existence of a frontier line between Greece and Serbia to the west of Lake Ochrida."

In view of the fact that Northern Epirus was now Greek, Italy was in Valona and the Essadists were now under Italian patronage, the above merely confirmed the *status quo* internationally. What the Allies would not guarantee for little Greece

[56] Cf. *Manchester Guardian,* 7 December 1917.

they were more than willing to bestow upon Great Power Italy. The Italians were now able to enter the war on the Allied side with everything to gain from an Allied victory. They further realized that, tempting as the Allied guarantee of Valona might be, still more tempting would be a reconstituted Albania within the boundaries of 1913 in which Italy could play the role of sole protecting power. To achieve this Italy had to use the framework of the Treaty of London to destroy its sense and displace Greece and Serbia from any territory or claims to territory in the Albania of the Protocol of Florence. Where to begin?

At this point, it should be remembered that Serbia and Montenegro were then locked in mortal combat with Austria-Hungary. At the same time they had been stabbed in the back by Bulgaria's declaration of war against the Allies. While Italian troops sent to Durazzo and northern Albania would have had the effect of strengthening the Serbians it would have been contrary to Italian interests to do so. The Italians had no desire to expend their army in the difficult mountain terrain of northern Albania, least of all for their brother cobelligerent Serbs. There remained but one direction for Italian policies—southward toward Epirus.

The French and British, desirous of wooing and winning Italy, supported her in raising all kinds of diplomatic issues with Athens over Northern Epirus. From their point of view this was done as much to embarrass Greece into joining the Allied camp actively as it was to please the Italians. "On February 14 (27), 1915, the Allied Ambassadors in Athens protested against the Greek seizure of territory in Albania. The latter replied they had no such intentions."[57]

During the period that followed, the Allied armies under French General Sarrail occupied Salonica in spite of Greek neutrality. Later, supported by his partisans and the Allies, Venizelos was to establish a rebel government in Salonica which finally replaced that of King Constantine in Athens. His associates in the "triumvirate" heading the rebels were Admiral Koundouriotes (scion of the Albanophone Hydran hero of 1821) and General Dangles (from Premeti, Northern Epirus). But let's not get ahead of our story.

After the battle of Mt. Lovchen, Montenegro was overrun by the Austrians. The Serbian Army fell back of Shkodra and began a retreat through Albania to Durazzo where it expected

[57] Manchester Guardian, *ibid.*

Italian reinforcements. The Austrians crossed over in pursuit on January 25, 1916. On February 26, more dead than alive, King Peter I and 100,000 Serbs reached Durazzo. They found no reinforcements, but Italian ships which had been ordered to evacuate them to Bari. They asked to go to Salonica instead and were taken there after regrouping at Allied-held Corfu. On the way to Durazzo they had had to fight plundering tribes of Albanians as well as Austrians. Hundreds had fallen into Gheg hands to be robbed and tortured. Others were looted and shot as they lay dying in the snow of the Albanian highlands. D'Annunzio wrote poems extolling their bravery, but Italy was too busy with intrigue for Northern Epirus to send the Serbs more than poetic effusions. Besides, if the Italians had helped the Serbs to fight their way through northern Albania again, the Serbs might have been in a position to occupy their slice of Albania under the Treaty of London. No, it was better that the Austrian enemy occupy northern Albania temporarily. The day after the Serbian evacuation the Austrians entered Durazzo.

The Italian-inspired squeezeplay on Northern Epirus continued with new Allied protests, the meaning of which were only too clear. "On March 7 (20), 1916, the Greek Premier Skouloudis declared in the Chamber that North Epirus was part of Greece, and that the Government had appointed two prefects in these regions."[58]

The very next day the rumor was circulated that a Royal Decree had been issued by King Constantine calling for withdrawal of Greece from Northern Epirus. The reason for this false rumor became all too plain when Italian troops moved hastily from Valona into the territory between Paliassa (Chimarra) and the town of Chimarra. They were stopped by the commander of the local Greek force at Phagea who requested the Italians courteously but firmly to leave. The Italians appeared puzzled and asked for twenty-four hours' leave to obtain further orders from Valona. After that period of time they quietly returned to their point of origin. The same day (March 22), after the departure of the mysterious Italian troops, a discussion of the incident ensued in the Greek Parliament. In replies from the Chimarriote M.P. from Argyrocastron (former Major) Spyros Spyromelios, Premier Skouloudis assured the Chamber that he had the word of Italian Ambassador Count Bosdari that there

[58] Manchester Guardian, *ibid.*

would be no repetitions of the most regrettable incident. Shortly thereafter, "On March 13 (26) the Allied Ambassadors in Athens protested against the union of North Epirus to Greece as a breach of the undertaking given in October, 1914."[59]

During the course of 1916 Greece was riven more and more by external pressures and internal anarchy. Greek Macedonia was the battleground of the French, Serbs and Venizelists against invading forces of Bulgarians and Austrians. The rest of Greece was in a state of semi-starvation due to the Allied blockade. Athens was the scene of riots and street fights between the two Greek factions. There were now in fact two Greeces, Constantinist and Venizelist. General Sarrail, to protect his exposed flank in carrying out operations in the Florina sector, ordered the French troops to walk into the district of Korytsa. Italy, never failing to use a golden opportunity, used the excuse of the unreliability of the forces of the Athens Government and strategic necessity to move her strongly reinforced troops in Valona and duly occupied the district of Argyrocastron. Bewildered and bedeviled, the Greek forces lowered their flags and silently stole away. They were not to return until 1940, this time in hot pursuit of the Italian Army. What had passed for Epirote daybreak had fast become twilight. All of a sudden, black midnight descended. With infinite care and patience, Italy had spun the web of doom over Northern Epirus.

The Italians in Argyrocastron

The Italian Government, as member of the International Control Commission, had been made to accept the Greek nationality of the Northern Epirotes. As one of the powers that had approved the second Greek occupation and confirmed it through the secret Treaty of London she had tacitly permitted Northern Epirote union with Greece. Now all this was reversed and Baron Sonnino's government could sail under its true colors. They said that they never really recognized Northern Epirus, nay, "Southern Albania" as Greek. General Ferrero and his occupation force were the instruments chosen to reattempt the task which had frustrated every conqueror in ages past—to uproot Hellenic civilization and to drive it from the province that had been Hellas' cradle first and Holy of Holies afterwards.

59 Manchester Guardian, *ibid.*

Almost the first action of the Italians was to close forceably the Greek schools and to expel the staunchly patriotic Metropolitan Basil from Argyrocastron. "As a matter of fact," the exiled Bishop protested later to Venizelos in Athens, "these unfortunate Greek people have been deprived even of their spiritual leadership by my violent expulsion on 22nd September 1916 from Argyrocastron, escorted by an Italian guard of fifteen soldiers with bayonets fixed as if I were a criminal. In fact, I was told that I was pernicious to public safety because I protested against the occupation of our towns by Italian troops who came to promote the albanification of Northern Epirus."[60]

After closing the Greek schools, the Italians brought in Italian instructors and textbooks and very generously offered to defray all the expenses for those schoolchildren who attended. Guarantees of employment by Italian firms for the graduates were likewise extended. To all this, the Northern Epirotes turned their backs and thousands of schoolchildren stayed home rather than receive the openhanded beneficence of Italian education. This, of course, infuriated the Italians. "Unsuccessful in these attempts, the Italians made the lives of the Epirotes who resisted them a burden. Hundreds were exiled for such causes as the refusal to raise an Albanian flag. The gendarmerie was almost exclusively recruited among Muhammedans. The command of the detachments was entrusted to leaders of Albanian bands who were previously known for their persecution of Christians; they ground down the Christian peasants without mercy; they committed outrages without name. There is a long list of Christians who have been victims of the extortions, beatings and massacres committed by the Albanian units, armed and regularly incorporated by the Italians. When it was a question of sending these fine Albanian troops to the front, however, the numerous deserters formed themselves into bands of brigands who, a fresh scourge to the Christian population, devastated the country. The administration of justice, which was assured by Italian or Italo-Albanian courts, had to contend with local committees composed after the best methods of Albanian propaganda. All of the Christians who were possessed of any substantial means had to pay blackmail to their Muhammedan accusers, in order to

[60] Translation of the text in full in Cassavetes, Nicholas J., *The Question of Northern Epirus At the Peace Conference,* 1919, pp. 104-105.

avoid judicial proceedings. There is no known case of judgment having gone against one sole Muhammedan . . . ."[60]

Upon the very face of it, the old Ottoman system of administration, amplified and expanded, had now returned to Epirus thinly disguised behind the Christian shield of the House of Savoy.

Among the victims of this new reign of terror were the Chimarriotes. In October, 1916, ninety Chimarriote leaders, including the mayor of Chimarra and the captain of Porto Palermo, were deported by the Italians to the desert island of Favignana off the coast of Tripolitania. Examples of imprisonment, torture, arson, brigandage, extortion and sacrilege can be cited as regular occurrences throughout the length of the province. Almost from the first, the Italians made it mandatory for the Albanian flag to be flown alongside the Italian. The many Greek Epirote refusals to do so were met with the most barbaric reprisals. A fairly accurate catalogue of some of these Italo-Albanian atrocities may be found in the work of Mr. N. J. Cassavetes cited above. (See especially pp. 98-109).

The Italians went even further. On June 3, 1917, General Ferrero at Argyrocastron, well supported by the Italian bayonets of his occupation troops, proclaimed Albanian "independence". This was all "in accordance with the orders of His Majesty King Victor Emmanuel" who would uphold "the unity and independence of the whole of Albania, under the shield and protection of the Kingdom of Italy."

At the same time, the Italian forces moved from Northern Epirus into free Epirus, occupying temporarily Jannina and the Pindus strongholds of Metsovo and Mega Peristeri overlooking Thessaly. Innumerable ancient and mediaeval conquerors had preceded them along this route. They themselves were to try to use it again in 1940. The Communists used it in their recent attempts to conquer Greece, and still masters of Albania and Northern Epirus, will be prepared to use it tomorrow.

The French in Korytsa

France's World War I Premier, Georges Clémenceau had, in 1913, condemned bitterly the Italian duplicity of falsifying the ethnic character of Northern Epirus. "If we desire," he wrote, "to form a good opinion of the state of mind of the Italian diplomats, we must consult the ethnographic maps of southern

Albania which are circulated in Italy. Everything is falsified at will. The district of Korytsa, where over half the population is Greek, is indicated in these Italian maps as exclusively Albanian; the districts of Jannina and Delvino, where the Greeks represent 80% of the total population, are indicated with here and there groups of Greeks."[61]

These opinions of the liberal French Premier, however, did not reflect upon the actions of Colonel Descoins who was sent by the French command at Salonica to undertake the military administration of Korytsa. The good Colonel, it seems, had acquired a very choleric attitude against the Greeks *in toto*. He soon found ample opportunity to vent his spleen at the expense of the Greeks of Korytsa. In November, 1916, Descoins proclaimed an Albanian republic at Korytsa. The administration of this "republic" was entrusted to Themistocles Germeni, whose activities in the struggle between the Albanians and the Hierolochites of Korytsa we remember. Before becoming a civil servant in Albania he had been an innkeeper at Monastir. He had, after the fall of Wied, made himself everywhere suspected as an Austrian agent and not without good reason. Now Descoins and Germeni proceeded about a business that was entirely without the sanction of the French Government. "A friend of Colonel Descoins, he (Germeni) proceeded to close the Greek schools and to open Albanian ones, which, however, were visited by not more than a hundred children. Thereupon the grecophils, who were the great majority of the Christian population, opened their own schools in several empty houses that were without tables or benches. The Chief of Police, a Frenchman named Dru, was requested by them to furnish these necessities, and he agreed to do so; but within a month Descoins ordered him to be sent away to Salonika. 'I have laboured that your little republic,' wrote Colonel Descoins to Harizi, the general secretary of the Korytza council of administration, 'I have labored that it should be a model State, a living proof of all that could be done in free and autonomous Albania.' One of the chief activities of Themistokles and his friends was, under the eyes of the French, to gather money in every possible way, and, above all, by their methods of distributing corn and maize to the people."[62]

[61] Cf. Baerlein, *op. cit.*, pp. 48-50.

[62] *L'Homme Libre,* **Paris, 15 May, 1913.**

After fourteen months of this, France got around to registering disapproval of Descoins' methods and, especially, his friends. Colonel Descoins was recalled to Salonica. Germeni, with his protector gone, his treasonable activities with Austria uncovered and his influence nil, was courtmartialed by the new French administrator. "...having been convicted of being an Austrian spy, he was taken out by the French and hanged. Several of his friends suffered the same fate; . . . and one of them paid tribute to his leader's volubility, for, on being asked if he objected to a set speech by Themistokles, 'By no means,' he answered, 'but hang me first. . .' "[63]

The French thereafter permitted the reopening of the Greek schools and their 2,000 pupils went back. The Albanian school at Korytsa was not closed, but such was the fanatically Greek attitude of the majority of the inhabitants that not more than 200 pupils could be persuaded to go. One of the achievements of this "model state" was the full reenactment of the burning of Moschopolis. After it was thoroughly gutted, the Moslem bands fell to their pleasant task of raping, looting and massacring.

The End of the War

The termination of the "war to end wars" radically altered the composition of the European Powers. Imperial Russia passed into history. Poland and the Baltic states was raised from the dead. The most important single factor in the Balkans was liquidation of Austria-Hungary and the resultant rise of a "greater Serbia", Yugoslavia, which entered immediately upon a protracted struggle with Italy over the Hapsburg inheritance which is still not resolved. In place of the Dual Monarchy there was now a Slav state that covered Serbia, Montenegro, Bosnia, Herzogovina, Kossovo, Serbian Macedonia, Croatia, Slovenia, not to speak of Dalmatia and a slice of what had been Hungary proper. The Serbs of Belgrade, wronged for centuries and helpless amidst diplomatic tugs of war between the mighty, had succeeded to an imperial inheritance that made them overnight the mightiest state in the Balkans. The future of Albania was to be one of the pawns in the new power struggle.

The end of hostilities found France out of Korytsa and the Italians, masters of Valona, controlling an Albanian protectorate

[63] Baerlein, op. cit. pp. 50-51.

that had settled very nearly behind the boundaries of 1913. All the Greek schools were closed and remained closed. The Italian policy, one admirably suited to the Albanian conception of political life, remained in force. The innumerable evils visited upon the Christian Northern Epirotes were well designed to set back the state of the inhabitants to what it had been in the early eighteenth century.

Albania still remained a principality in theory, though now without a prince. A regency, nominated by an Albanian "congress" at Lushnja (and subsequently removed to Tirana) was the nominal sovereign of the country. It was maintained in power by the allegiance of the most backward tribe in all Albania, that of Mati. Its chieftain, who occupied the posts of Minister of War, the Interior, and Governor of Shkodra, had been an Austrian mercenary before the Austro-Hungarian collapse. In December, 1916, a colonel then in Austria's Albanian contingents, he had gone to Vienna as part of an Albanian military delegation after first proving himself and his tribesmen in the awful massacre of the retreating Serbs in 1915-1916. Before the war he had been an Ottoman officer and a personal protegé of Abdul Hamid himself. His name?—Ahmed Zogolli, the future King Zog I of Albania.

The Withdrawal of Italy and Reestablishment of Albania

In Italy itself the war-weariness of the people and the prevailing economic conditions were reflected in a wave of Socialist-inspired strikes. The metal workers of Torino and Milan seized the factories and established Soviets. The dockworkers refused to load shipments of supplies and provisions destined for Valona. Meanwhile the Italian Government was having its hands full with Yugoslavia over the issues of Trieste, Fiume and Dalmatia. The Albanian venture, however justified it might have been thought by the Italian Foreign Ministry, did not pay for itself. Added to the feeling of the Italian troops in Albania who wanted to go home, a reflection of conditions in Italy was the Italian Government's realization, as Nitti afterwards confessed, that schemes to colonize parts of Albania with Italian settlers were then impractical. Taken into consideration was the prohibitive expenditure of capital necessary to drain the marshes. Added to the Italian troubles was the opposition of Yugoslavia and, naturally, of those Albanians who now orientated themselves to Belgrade.

So, in 1919, Italy turned over Albania, lock, stock and barrel, to that Albanian government she could be reasonably sure of dominating, and pulled out of Valona, but kept the island of Saseno just in case.

On behalf of that Albanian government, Mehdi Frashëri headed a delegation to the Paris Peace Conference. Essad Pasha Toptani, to the embarrassment of all concerned, likewise showed up as head of an Albanian government that no longer existed. He did, however, possess high nuisance value so, while in Paris, he was assassinated at the alleged instigation of Italy. The two other perennial troublemakers likewise were no more, Mirdite chieftain Prenk Bib Doda having met the same fate as Essad and Ismail Kemal, having died in Italy in 1918. Fan Noli also appeared in Paris representing, he claimed, the Albanians in America.

The now mighty Serbs, paying back with interest their shabby treatment at Albanian hands during the great retreat to the sea, encroached upon Albanian territory in the north and visited upon the Albanians the horrors which the Albanians had so long been accustomed to practice upon others. Italy, however, was more concerned with combating Greek aspirations to Northern Epirus to care much. The representatives of the Albanian government reflected this Italian disinterest on one hand and passionate involvement on the other. The testimony of Mr. Clive Day, Chief of the U.S. Peace Negotiation Commission's Balkan Division bears witness to this conduct before the Allied "Council of Ten":

> "Much of the business which occupied the attention of the Council was formal in character. The smaller states, excluded from its deliberations, demanded at least the opportunity to present to it their claims, and many hearings were granted to their representatives . . . To illustrate the artificiality of these proceedings may be cited the occasion on which the claims of Albania to national independence were put before the Council. The Albanians are a people apart, who for centuries have lived a free life in their wild country, and to the present day have preserved the virtues and defects of a primitive population. Their spokesman before the Council was a broken-down old Turk who had no interest in Albania, who enjoyed no respect or following there, who got his place at Paris because he was willing to sacrifice the aspirations of the Albanians to the ambitions of Italy to extend her power across the Adriatic. He read from a manuscript which had doubtless been prepared for him, and with the contents of which he was certainly not familiar, for he stopped long at every page until he could find the continuation of his sentence on the next. The reading was lifeless, it seemed interminable. 'How much longer is this going on?' asked one of

the American plenipotentiaries, very audibly, of the interpreter. And all this took place while almost hourly reports were coming in of war, famine, and pestilence in stricken Europe, and while the people of northern Albania itself were fighting a desperate struggle against the harsh Serbs. Surely no greater contrast is conceivable than that between the idle words which filled M. Pichon's luxurious study in the palace on the Quai d'Orsay and the grim reality of life in the mountains of High Albania, where people were being massacred by thousands."[64]

Meanwhile, Albanians in the south terrorized all of Northern Epirus. Here is a typical example from several villages between Argyrocastron and Libochoven:

"Upper Lambovon—The Memos family paid 500 (gold) napoleons. The Albanian band also murdered one in-law of the family.

"Soukha—The Tiaras family paid 500 napoleons, Constantine Litses paid 500 napoleons, Basil Meros paid 100 napoleons.

"Stegopolis—Spyridon Bogas paid 150 napoleons.

"Sarakinista—Spyridon Rembes, 300 napoleons; Philip Bogas, 150 napoleons, and his brother, George Bogas, 150 napoleons; John Notes, 100 napoleons.

"Doxati—Christos B. Kyros, while travelling to Argyrocastron, was kidnapped on the road by Moslem Albanians and released after the payment of 300 napoleons ransom.

"Erinti—Here was murdered Cosmas Tsitses.

"In Zagoria and its environs the situation is described as intolerable . . .

"All of the above villages are a few hours away from Argyrocastron."

Many Northern Epirotes, unable to stand the prevailing conditions, migrated to Corfu, Athens and elsewhere. Albanian priests, most of them barely literate, seized the Greek communities and proceeded to say mass in Albanian to the great disgust of the Greek population which refused to attend. The experience of the Italians with the stubborn Northern Epirotes was repeated a hundredfold. In Argyrocastron in 1917 they had imported a Father Panos who said the Easter service in Albanian, whereupon the entire congregation in a body got up and walked out.

Fan Noli, the "Albanian" saint and sage from Adrianople, was to have his hands full when he seized the Archdiocese of Korytsa and proceeded to celebrate Divine Liturgy in the historic Cathedral of St. George. The Albanian authorities later hustled the legitimate Metropolitan, Jacob, into a car and transported him to Greece. Noli's attempt resulted in a riot on Easter Sunday, 1921, and the Albanian gendarmerie had merry

[64] Day, Clive, "The Atmosphere and Organization of the Peace Conference" in Seymour and House, eds., *What Really Happened at Paris,* 1921, p. 18.

work in bashing Greek skulls. In the course of the riot, "the priests were hustled and Fan Noli's beard was pulled—some say it came off; that is, the artificial beard he is alleged to wear to supplement his meagre one and make him more imposing. But whatever be the truth of this, Fan Noli's party had the civil and the military power behind them, and they triumphed."[65]

It is significant that this occurred after Fan Noli himself, as Albanian delegate to the League of Nations, had been the signer of the Minorities Declaration solemnly promising to respect the Greek churches and schools of Northern Epirus. That however is another story which we will come to during the course of this history.

In answer to Fan Noli, the people who could do so attended church in nearby villages where the Greek language had not yet been banned. Typical of the methods used to put an end to this practice was the following. The priest of one of these villages was for a time unmolested and he continued to hold services in Greek. "And on January 7, St. John's Day, there was a pilgrimage of about 3,000 people to his village and another. On the way they were met by gendarmes and a pitched battle took place; afterwards a thousand persons came into the courtyard of the Serbian Consulate and the wide street opposite. They besought the Consul to protect them; his advice was that until the League of Nations had decided what was to be done in Church affairs, they should remain at home and pray to God from there.

"A few elderly women were charged by the police with having made a riot, and the police thrashed them. So they brought their case before the judge, for which they secured the assistance of Albanian lawyers.

"When the case came into court the judge did his utmost to make it appear that these old pious women—who had only wished to satisfy their religious sentiments—were against the State. In his eyes it was simply a political move. And in the midst of the proceedings he burst out: 'What were you doing at the Serbian Consulate? Did you sleep with the Consul?' This gentleman is regarded by the Albanian Government as one of their best judges. He used to be a Turkish judge at Ochrida before the Balkan War, and now—having learned rather less

65 Baerlein, *op. cit.*, p. 131.

than 200 words of Albanian—he adorns the bench of that country."[66]

At the same time the villages of Korytsa were victims of the Albanian Government they were also terrified by the depredations of Albanian brigands. Many of the villagers vainly demanded that the Albanian Government either protect them or allow them to emigrate.

At Argyrocastron the atrocities committed by the Albanians had the sanction of the new prefect, a creature of Fan Noli's named, appropriately enough, Kol Tromara ('Nick the Terror'), who had graduated to this post by selling bananas in the United States.

But even those Christians who, in some cases in the United States, had swallowed the Albanian ideology, began to feel revulsion at the methods used by their bishop's Moslem accomplices to crush the Northern Epirote people. At Tirana three of the Christian M.P.s from Korytsa and Argyrocastron (who had, incidently, been elected by the Moslems as window-dressing since the majority of the people of Northern Epirus had boycotted the elections) issued the following communiqué to the press:

"Tirana, 22 December 1921

"The undersigned Deputies of the Christians of Gjinokastra and Korça, in the name of the Christian people of these provinces, denounce and protest against the measures of Mr. Fan Noli against the sacred Christian institutions.

"These measures of Fan Noli constitute from a religious viewpoint a sacrilege of the sacred institutions of the Christians and from the political viewpoint an unforgivable proceeding of dissension between the elements.

"We assure the Christian people that repeated steps will be taken in Parliament toward the return of the former ecclesiastical régime.

"With all respect:
"Koço Tasi
"Sotir Peçi
"Agathoklli Xhitoni"

The significance of the above is greater because it comes from three renegades, one of whom is the self-same Soterios Petsis (Sotir Peçi) who founded the first Albanian-language newspaper in America. The above protest was published in the Argyrocastron *Konkordia* which was edited in both Albanian and Greek. Shortly afterwards the authorities suppressed the newspaper.

66 Baerlein, *op. cit.*, p. 132-133

Save for the short-lived Chimarriote revolt in 1920, there was no resistance possible to the now disarmed population. Greece, as we shall show below, did what she could diplomatically to cancel out Italian intrigues and obtain the freedom of the Northern Epirotes. Mocking these Greek efforts could be heard the voice of the old European diplomacy of 1913 that the interests of a small nation were as nothing before the aspirations of a greater one. The injustice to Greece at the Peace Conference and the League of Nations was not unrelated to the injustices later suffered by helpless Ethiopia and war-torn China. Soon the world was to know the ineffectuality of the League as an instrument of peace and a guardian of justice.

The Peace Conference and the League

Oral and written memoranda were submitted by Premier Venizelos to the Council of Ten at Paris in 1919. Northern Epirus was chief among the claims made by Greece's Prime Minister who, as he confessed, had suffered the evils of war and civil strife to be visited upon Greece so that his nation might fight on the Allied side and share in the common victory.[67]

> "The extension of the Greek frontier into Southern Albania is based upon ethnic considerations. About Korytsa there is a strong native Moslem (Albanian) element, but exclusion of this portion would be economically injurious, and would block the Greeks from the only good road uniting the northern territories and running from Kastoria to Jannina.
>
> "Only on the basis of a united Albania (which we do not recommend) should southern Albania be withheld from Greece. Southern Albania's strong Hellenic inclinations and culture, and the success with which Greece has in the past assimilated Albanian elements, indicate that this territory should be ceded to Greece with full sovereignty.
>
> "The area in question is estimated to include 2,400 square miles and about 250,000 inhabitants, of whom approximately one-half are Christian."[68]

On the first of March, 1919, the Committee on Greek and Albanian Affairs, after considering the divergent points of view on the subject, rendered its formal report. This showed that the views of the British, French, American and Italian delegations were considerably at variance. The British and French, eager on one hand to be fair and on the other to placate Italy,

67 Cf. *Greece Before the Peace Conference, 1919, submitted by E. K. Venizelos.*

68 *Outline of a Tentative Report, Doc. 246,* p. 249.

proposed a line differing from the Venizelos claim only in the following respects: From Chimarra it ran further to the south of Tepeleni, then passed north of Premeti and then north to Lake Ochrida, leaving, for no good reason, Moschopolis to Albania. The British and French fully upheld the viewpoint that the 1913 boundaries which pretended to take only language into consideration were unacceptable to the population. They recommended that Northern Epirus up to the line they proposed be ceded to Greece.

The American delegation, more willing to compromise because not directly involved, proposed a boundary that would unite that part of Epirus to Greece that lay southeast of the Aous (Viossa) River and leave Korytsa and Premeti to Albania, notwithstanding Venizelos' willingness to propose a plebescite for those districts.

The Italian delegation went out on a limb with its intransigent position that the 1913 boundary (Protocol of Florence) was final. This attitude forced the Council to postpone a final decision. One of the participants was later to note that:

". . . The attitude of Italy toward this problem was illogical, irritating and strange. The Italians, since April, 1915, had come to dislike the Albanian section of the Treaty of London. They still wanted a protectorate over the future Albanian State. They still, as always, wanted the Treaty of London. They were no longer prepared, however, to fulfill the remaining conditions of that section of the Treaty and to hand over to Serbia and Greece the northern and southern portions of Albania. The former cession would represent an accession of territory to Yugoslavia. The latter cession would place Greece in strategic command of the Corfu channel. And in any case, if Italy were to be given a protectorate over Albania, it seemed fitting to her that Albania should be as large, both north and south, as possible.

"The result was that, although on all other matters (except Fiume) the Italians clamored, on the basis of the 'Sanctity of Treaties', for the integral fulfilment of the Treaty of London, they argued that in respect to Albania this Treaty was not fully in accord with the principles of self-determination. When it was pointed out to them that the retention of Valona might also be regarded as a violation of that principle, they contended that in such retention 'the honor of Italy' was involved.

"Day after day were we obliged to listen patiently to this exegesis of our Italian colleagues upon the doctrine of Wilsonism, without being permitted to express the distaste, and indeed the blind fury, which such sophistry evoked. Upon myself the tolerance displayed by the Americans and the Conference generally in face of such distortion of doctrine had a most demoralizing effect. The courtesy of international conduct forbade us to express our righteous indignation by anything but a pained silence. Yet at any moment it would have been open to the United States representatives to explode as follows: 'You have just appealed in this matter to the doctrine of self-determination as overriding the Treaty of London. May I inform my President that Italy will apply this principle to every question in which Italian interests are involved?' There would have been no answer to such a question. Yet it was never asked. We endured in silence . . ."[69]

These Italian dialectic somersaults look rather uncomfortably familiar in retrospect. As a matter of fact the nearest parallel would be found in the Soviet diplomatic tactics following Yalta and Potsdam. The same parallel can also be drawn between American naiveté in both instances.

The growing desire of the Italian public to be rid of the Albanian white elephant and the succession of the more moderate Tittoni to imperialist diehard Sonnino's post persuaded Venizelos, however unwisely, to propose a desperate horse-trade with Italy. On July 29, 1919 he signed the Tittoni-Venizelos Agreement. Articles 1 and 2 pledged Italy to support at the Peace Conference Greece's Thracian and Northern Epirote claims. In addition, Greek sovereignty over the Dodecanese (with the exception of Rhodes) was recognized. In return, Greece relinquished a part of her Asia Minor claims in return for the above Italian support. At Italian insistence a seventh and final article was inserted guaranteeing Italy full freedom of action in respect to the above should she not receive the stipulated areas of Asia Minor. This clause was to prove a joker and eventually invalidated the agreement. Italian interests in Valona were also taken into account.

When the matter finally came up again before the Council the Tittoni-Venizelos Agreement had already been signed by the two principals. A meeting of the Council on January 13, 1920 gave its unanimous assent to the decision reached by Greece and Italy respecting Northern Epirus.

In actuality, the Tittoni-Venizelos Agreement was not due to be implemented. As it happened, and in spite of a United States Senate resolution expressing that august body's sentiment in favor of Greek claims, Wilson, in conflict with Congress over the general issue of American foreign policy, came out against any territorial alterations respecting Albania. The clue to this attitude will be found in Wilson's stand respecting Fiume and Dalmatia. After having infuriated the Italians by supporting Yugoslavia in these explosive issues, Wilson felt obliged to

[69] Nicolson, Harold, *Peacemaking 1919*.

balance the account by supporting Italy's ambitions to retain Albania within the 1913 frontiers. This was to have a telling effect after the Italian policy reversal repudiating the Tittoni-Venizelos Agreement.

Quite frankly, be it said to his credit, the late Count Sforza admitted the Machiavellian motives in his renunciation of his predecessor's agreement with Venizelos. In his book, *The Makers of Modern Europe,* he admitted:

> "When I came to power in Italy in July, 1920, and took cognizance of this arrangement (with Venizelos), which Tittoni had kept secret, I absolutely failed to see how it could be of any use to Italy. With undue breach of modesty, I considered that it was not for a Great Power like Italy to have written agreements that Greece should 'support' any essential point of Italian interests in Albania . . . Albania, to my mind, was to come under the sphere of Italian influence, but not as a result of a juridical situation wounding Albanian pride and working against the very force of Italian expansion in Albania. This being so—and bent on setting Italian policy toward ways which seemed to me more in conformity with our interests—I denounced the Tittoni-Venizelos agreement that meant for us nothing but a series of burdens with no compensatory counterpart."[70]

As a result, Italy gave Greece due notification of her repudiation of the Tittoni-Venizelos Agreement in a Note to the Greek Government dated July 22, 1920. In September, at the adamant insistence of Italy, Albania was admitted into the League of Nations.

In order to ease their conscience, the other member states of the League required Albania, as a condition of membership, to sign a minorities declaration providing, among other things, that, "within six months from the date of the present Declaration detailed information will be presented to the Council of the League of Nations with regard to the legal status of the religious communities, churches, convents, schools, voluntary establishments, and associations of racial, religious, and linguistic minorities. The Albanian Government will take into account any advice it may receive from the League of Nations with regard to this question."

With tongue in cheek, and already contemplating further measures in violation of the Northern Epirote Hellenic population's ancient rights, Albania's new League delegate, Fan Noli, signed the Declaration. Needless to say it was a mere "scrap of paper" from its inception.

[70] Sforza, *The Makers of Modern Europe,* p. 170.

The entire matter of the Albanian boundaries was then cast into the laps of the delegates to the Ambassadorial Conference of Great Britain, France and Italy which took place in London during the summer of 1921. Greece and Yugoslavia, as the principal interested parties, vainly sought admission. Here even the old diplomatic adage that the small powers propose and the Great Powers dispose was violated at Italy's insistence. These small powers, though they were the most interested parties in the matter, were barred from even appearing before that body to bring out their points of view. At a subsequent Ambassadorial Conference held in Paris on November 9th, Italian pressure proved too great even for those Powers not especially warm to the Italian viewpoint. It was therefore thought prudent to give in almost entirely to Italy's contention respecting the finality of the 1913 borders and, "The Conference, taking into account that the southern frontier of Albania was fixed on the spot by the boundary commission, which drew up the Protocol of Florence of the 17th December, 1913", accepted that line with the reservation that a new boundary commission was to undertake a final on the spot delimitation.

At the same time the League of Nations Secretariat sent a commission of inquiry to Northern Epirus to obtain a better picture of the existing ethnic situation there. The delegation, presided over by Mr. J. J. Sederholm, a Finnish geologist, was made up of Mr. Sederholm, Major J. C. Meinich, a Norwegian, and Comte de Pourtales, a Swiss.

The Commission of Inquiry

The procedure of this League commission was hardly an improvement over that of the Great Powers in 1913. The terror-stricken population might have been willing to give the Commission the facts it required had not, according to the Commission's own report, "in all these villages" the inquiry taken place publicly, "in the presence of the Prefect of the district, of the Albanian military commandant, of the Serbian (sic!) interpreter and of all the inhabitants, who thus had the opportunity to lay their complaints before the Commission and the competent authorities."

If the Commission regarded as "competent authorities" the Albanian Prefect and military commandant (to say nothing of a Serbian interpreter) they were travelling in Alice's Wonderland. Frankness was at a premium when the Albanian officials mentioned had previously explained the fate of the "Grecomane" villagers who dared whisper their "treasonable" sentiments to the commission. A comparable situation today would be a commission to investigate complaints of the inmates of the Soviet slave labor camps in full presence of the MVD administrator and the district commissar of the Communist Party.

The Commission was "accompanied by Captain Veaute, a former French officer extremely well acquainted with the country, whom the Commission has considered useful to attach to itself as an observer." Can we insult the intelligence of the three disinterested gentlemen (who were, after all, two Scandinavians and a Swiss) by believing they had no idea of Captain Veaute's past? Yet not a word of Veaute's official position was breathed in their reports. A former non-com in the French Zouaves before the war and a rough soldier of fortune, he had been Chief of the Secret Police of Descoin's ill-starred "Republic" of Korytsa. After the war he served the Albanians so well that Tirana appointed him Albania's Inspector of Police. And now, with this worthy prominently attached to the Commission, Sederholm and his associates intended to ascertain the Northern Epirote people's real sentiments!

The Commission excused the superficiality of its inquiries by claiming to be pressed for time. Of the three, the Swiss member felt most uneasily suspicious that there was more to the story than they were getting. However so, the farce ended and the report was rendered to the Secretariat of the League in due course. Somehow, in spite of their evident credulity, the members of the Commission balked at swallowing entirely the fish story served up to them by the Albanians. Mr. Sederholm's report to the first Assembly of the League (December 16, 1922) ever so lightly hinted that all was not quite according to Hoyle.

"Many people speak two languages, Albanian and Greek, but at home they usually employ only one language . . .

"The number of inhabitants of the region of Argyrocastron who speak Greek is much more considerable than has generally been admitted. The Albanian authorities have, on many occasions, indicated the number of 16,000, but only in the under-prefacture of Delvino, there are, according to an authorized source, 15,500 persons of the Greek language; moreover, almost all the villages situated along the Greek frontier between Libohovo and Psilotera on the East, and those which are on the western part of the valley of Argyrocastron, at the south of this city, are of Greek language, namely that Greek is the language spoken by the inhabitants in their homes. According to the census of May, 1921, in view of the elections, there are 33,000 persons in the prefacture of Argyrocastron of the Greek language . . . The question of teaching in the region of Korytsa does not present itself under the same aspect as in the west. In that country there are no minorities of language. As has already been remarked, all of the inhabitants, even the most ardent Hellenophiles, speak Albanian in their homes . . ."

The Boundary Commission and the Corfu Incident

Italy's disturbances coupled with the imperialistic outlook of the ruling class led directly to the ascendency of a totalitarian system that soon found imitators elsewhere. In October 1922, Il Duce Benito Mussolini and his black-shirted hoodlums marched on Rome. Like a building rotten in its foundations the parliamentary government collapsed and the King appointed Mussolini Premier after the apparently bloodless march. "Fascismo" had come into its own in the land that spawned it. It soon reached out to claim its first victim, Greece.

The Hellenic nation had undergone upheaval after upheaval. In an election held by Venizelos the Monarchists had come to power. Venizelos left the country and Constantine returned. Greece's attempts to claim territory in Asia Minor ran smack into the rising young force of Kemalism. The Greeks overreached their supplies. What then began as an orderly withdrawal from the interior of Asia Minor turned into a rout. One million Asia Minor Greeks were killed as they fled before the Turkish force. Another million reached Smyrna and were evacuated after which the Turks burned all of "infidel Smyrna" to the ground. The surviving million were dumped into Greece's lap. A revolution in Greece followed the Asia Minor war and the King's ministers were executed. Constantine fled, the Venizelists returned and Greece was proclaimed a republic. All these events must be taken into account in understanding what Mussolini was soon to do to a Greece exhausted beyond human endurance. The Boundary Commission sent to implement the decision of the Ambassadorial Conference gave him his opportunity.

On August 27, 1923, near the Greek border post of Kakavia, a mysterious crime took place. A car was speeding across the border along the road from Jannina to Argyrocastron. In it was the entire Italian delegation of the Boundary Commission, consisting of General Tellini, Major Corti, Lieutenant Bonaccini, the chauffeur Farnetti and an Albanian interpreter. A dark forest was on either side of the road. About nine in the morning the Italian automobile had to stop because a tree was blocking the road. The occupants at once realized it was a trap. They were then quite cold-bloodedly shot down either in their car or attempting to flee into the woods. The assassins escaped.

The authorities in Epirus took immediate but fruitless measures to apprehend the murderers. A high official of the Greek Foreign Ministry at once conveyed to the Italian Ambassador in Athens the Greek Government's condolences. The next day, Italian Ambassador Montagna visited the Greek Foreign Ministry to register his protests. The Minister conveyed to the Italian Ambassador Greece's official grief and made known to him the extraordinary measures taken by the authorities in Epirus to uncover the culprits. A short while later the Foreign Minister himself went to the Italian Embassy to deliver his personal regrets that such a crime had been committed on Greek soil. Two days after the crime, Mussolini's government handed Greece a note with a 24 hour time limit. It contained the following terms:

"1) The Greek Government, in the fullest and most official manner, is to request forgiveness of the Italian Government. This forgiveness will be requested of the Italian Ambassador here on the part of the Greek military command.

"2) The Greek Government will hold a memorial service in honor of the victims in the Catholic church of Athens, which all the Cabinet members will be obliged to attend.

"3) Honors will be paid the Italian flag on the same day as the requiem in the following manner:

"After 8:00 A.M. an Italian flotilla will approach Phaleron. When it anchors, a number of Greek warships (completely excluding light torpedo boats, which are obliged to remain anchored within the Gulf of Salamis or the bay of Peiraeus), will first drop anchor near the place where the flotilla will be stationed, rendering honors to the Italian flag with a 21 cannon salute, which flag will be flown from the masts of all the Greek craft.

"During the course of the requiem the Greek as well as the Italian ships will fly their colors at half mast. That evening, before the sun sets, the Italian flotilla will leave Phaleron and, at the time of its departure, will be given a farewell by the appropriate cannon salutes.

"4) The Greek authorities are obliged to institute a strict investigation on the scene of the murder in collaboration with Italian Embassy military attaché Colonel Perone di San Martino.

"The Greek Government will be responsible for the personal safety of Colonel Perone and will assist him in every way in the execution of his appointed mission.

"The investigation must be completed within five days of the receipt of these demands.

"5) All the guilty will be condemned to death.

"6) The Greek Government is obliged to pay the Italian Government 50 million lire in reparations, the sum of which is to be handed over within five days of the day this notification is delivered.

"7) Military honors will be given to the bodies of the victims at Preveza the moment they are carried aboard the Italian vessel."

Such an ultimatum from one sovereign nation to another had not been given since Austria-Hungary's 1914 demands on Serbia which had precipitated World War I. Even if it were granted that the Greek Government was guilty, this piece of Mussolinian affrontry went far beyond the boundaries of diplomatic exchange. But was the Greek Government guilty?

These were the facts brought out by the investigation. The chief instigators of the murders appear to have been none other than the Albanian Chief of Police at Argyrocastron, Hysni Lepenica, his nephew, who was a Major of the Albanian gendarmerie, and a professional bandit named Memo. Spyros Kyrouses, a native of Kakavia, testified that he witnessed a strange sight on the eve of the murder. He saw coming from the direction of Georgoutsates in Northern Epirus an automobile which stopped by the bridge at Kakavia. He noted that the occupants, as they came out of the vehicle, were armed with Mauser rifles. He had no trouble recognizing three of them. They were Major Lepenica, Nevruz Belo and Xhellaledin Aqif Feta, alias Daut Hoxha. The latter was to attain a certain fame later on when his death provided the excuse for Mussolini's invasion of Greece in 1940.

They then slipped across the border through a path in the forest of Arinista, thus avoiding the nearby frontier post of Hagios Nikolaos. Greek intelligence filled in the missing details. The Albanian assassins completed their arrangements at the local inn at Georgoutsates. The Albanian frontier guards allowed them to pass unhindered and they remained hidden in the Arinista forest until the time of the murder. The spot where they threw the tree barrier was the center of an S curve in the road about 54 kilometres before the inn at Arinista.

The crime was a godsend to the Albanians who were able to accuse the Greek Government of the crime. To Mussolini it was a choice opportunity to give the world a show of Fascist strength. It remains, however, forever a mystery whether the Italian general and his aides were really the intended victims.

In setting out from Jannina, the automobile of the Albanian delegation left first, followed by the Greek and then the Italian. There was considerable distance between them. The Greek vehicle ran into some engine trouble and was hauled to Kalpaki for repairs. Thus, the order in which the Greek and Italian vehicles had been proceeding was actually reversed. Whether the assassins had known this or not is the final mystery and so it remains.

The day after the receipt of the Italian note, the Greek Government replied that it accepted those parts of the demands that did not infringe upon Greece's sovereign rights as defined in accepted international usage. Before the Greek reply was sent the Fascisti struck.

On August 31, 1923, Italian warships entered the unfortified harbor of Corfu and demanded the immediate surrender of the island to Italian occupation forces. Realizing their plight, the authorities requested time to consult Athens. The Italian Admiral refused and the Greeks made ready to post a proclamation requesting the islanders to submit quietly to the Italians. At that instant the Italian warships gave the world the first international example of Fascist frightfulness. For twenty-five minutes the warships kept up a vicious bombardment of the harbor with their cannons until they had the satisfaction of seeing the white flag raised by the Greek harbor authorities. Near the ruined Venetian walls by the sea was a camp of Asia Minor refugees consisting largely of orphan children and aged. It had been the special target of Mussolini's heroes and the fifteen dead included a six year-old Armenian child and a sixty-five year-old Greek refugee woman.

Of course, the authors of the initial crime, safely back in Argyrocastron, could not be found. Greece paid the full indemnity Mussolini demanded and, on September 27, Mussolini's forces evacuated Corfu.

The New Protocol of Florence

On January 27, 1925, the French, British and Italians signed a new protocol at Florence. The new Greco-Albanian frontier, with one seemingly unimportant modification, was that of the old Protocol of Florence. The modification consisted of fourteen villages of Greek Macedonia which were now included formally within the Albanian state. They had been occupied some years earlier by the Albanians in the absence of an opposing Greek force and forceably incorporated into Albania. Their geographic location along Lake Prespa was later to give the Albanian-aided Greek Communist guerillas a position astride Greek territory which Zachariades called the "guerilla Gibraltar"—the so-called "triangle" formed by the extension of Albania was only broken by the Greek Army after the hardest fighting in the Greek "civil war". The Albanian flanks of the "triangle" still remain an easy Red vantage point from which a Communist force from Korytsa can strike at the Greek border town of Florina.

The Greek representative, Colonel Avramides, attached the following to the new Florence protocol:

> "The Greek representative considers that a declaration in regard to the question at issue is superfluous, seeing that the Greek Government duly notified the Conference of Ambassadors of its objections, which were, however, not taken into account, and that thereafter the Greek Government submitted to the decisions of the Conference."

A definitive protocol was signed by the delegates of France, Britain, Italy and Japan and countersigned by the Greek, Yugoslav and Albanian representatives at the Ambassadorial Conference of July 30, 1926.

The "gravediggers of modern Europe" had hopes that this would bury forever the issue of Greek Northern Epirus, just as they were to think later that the betrayal of Czechoslovakia had brought them "peace in our time". Nevertheless, the issue was not one that could remain buried and their successors will continue to be haunted by it until justice is done to Greece and the martyred Greeks of Northern Epirus.

Chapter IX

BETWEEN TWO WARS

The Northern Epirotes in the Interregnum

Deprived of the elementary ethnic rights to which they had held fast through centuries of foreign oppression, the Northern Epirotes now seemed tied permanently to a state that made it its first task to destroy their heritage. What if there had been a time when even the Moslems had recognized the force of this Greek nationalism? What if the Albanians, in the so-called "Agreement of Kapestitsa" (May 15, 1920), had recognized the Greek ethnic character of Northern Epirus? No matter that the Albanians had given their word to the League, or that their premier, Sylejman Bey Delvina, had been proud once to show his guest, Crown Prince (later King) George of Greece a Greek church maintained on his own *chiflik* at Delvino. "Autres temps, autres moeurs!"

Liberal opinion in western Europe had deplored the Prussian "kulturkampf" against the Kaiser's Polish subjects. Bismarck had been attacked because he tried to replace Polish schools with the undoubtedly excellent, even superior, but abhorently alien Prussian educational system. If this were a crime, what can one say of Albanian efforts to replace Epirus' native Greek schools with those in which the uncouth and no less hateful Albanian tongue would be crammed down the pupils' throats?

As it was impossible for the Albanians to maintain that there were no Greeks in Northern Epirus, outside opinion forced them to recognize at least a Greek "minority" consisting of the forty-odd thousand exclusively Grecophones in the Prefecture of Argyrocastron. For this fraction of the total Greek population a few schools were tolerated. The rest, the Albanian-speaking Greek majority of Northern Epirus, were forced to send their children to Albanian schools.

Considering that the founders, contributors and supporters of the Greek schools in Ottoman times had been the largely

Albanophone Epirotes, this condemned to slow extinction the few Greek schools permitted. At the same time, careful not to arouse too much international indignation, the Albanians did everything to eliminate even these few remaining schools. From 70 in 1925 they shrank to 60 in 1926, 43 in 1931, 10 in 1933 and these were finally shut by the authorities at one stroke in 1934.

Typical of the teachers imposed upon the Northern Epirote majority to convert it to Albanism were Moslem mullahs, ex-manual laborers who had learned their ABC's from Fan Noli in America, street-peddlers, ex-innkeepers, etc. The travesty of imposing such instructors upon a people who had led modern Greece in education, whose kin occupied chairs in Greece's greatest universities, who were the founders and professors of the great Greek institutions of Constantinople, Asia Minor, Alexandria, Rumania, Trieste and Imperial Russia was irony indeed.

Having imposed this policy of albanization upon the Albanian-speaking Northern Epirotes, the Albanians determined to rid themselves of the linguistic minority by such means as would induce its members to flee to southern Epirus. This policy, continuing throughout the period between the two World Wars, was initiated at the very inception of the Albanian régime in 1919. Between 1919 and May, 1922, 403 families comprising 1,352 persons were compelled to seek refuge in Greece. Their numbers continued to grow through the years.

The more prosperous Albanophones found means to send their children to Corfu, Jannina, Salonica and Athens to study. This, however, was not very practical for those who lacked the means. Thus in time, in the twenty years of direct Albanian rule, Albanophone Northern Epirote children reluctantly found themselves in Albanian schools. Having been worn down by false hopes and real disappointments, some even came to accept the gratuitous scholarships offered by fascist Italy. They could not dream that Greece would again march in to set Epirus free.

Circumstances divided the Albanophone Greek Epirotes into three groups, one of which was larger than the other two combined. They could be considered thus: 1) the handful of renegades who identified themselves with the régime and for whom there was no way to return to the fold; 2) the few courageous souls who suffered prison, torture, death and exile to resist the Albanian tyrants and 3) the many who, while driven by threats and despair into appearing to serve their persecutors, proclaimed their true Greek allegiance secretly among their own. This third group, whose kin abroad suffer no such compulsion to hide their Greek sentiments, comprise a far larger group than an outsider might suspect. They gave demonstrative proof of their true allegiance when the third Greek liberation of Epirus took place in 1940-1941. We shall refer to them again because they are our secret friends and unacknowledged allies in Albania today.

Albania and Her "Protectors"

Albanian politics in the period between wars were a tangled skein of Italian and Yugoslav intrigue. At no time did there appear a movement in Albania that might be considered as anything beyond an extension of the foreign policies of Rome and Belgrade. In outstanding instances the leaders of the Albanian groups traded sides depending on the ascendency of one of these two outside powers. In this respect the Albanians played the game consistent with their policy of selling their services to the highest bidder. This traditional cornerstone of Albanian thinking survived Byzantium, Ottoman Turkey, Fascist Italy, and bids fair to survive the present Communist régime.

A general history of Albania would doubtlessly include the Italo-Yugoslav intrigues in detail. Here only a sketch can be given to provide the indispensable background against which the course of events in Northern Epirus can be interpreted.

The most powerful figure to arise in the early twenties was the ex-Ottoman officer, Austrian mercenary and chief of the approximately 24,000 Moslem tribesmen of Mati in central Albania, Ahmed Bey Zogu. As Minister of War and the Interior in 1920 he was backed by Italy. Soon he changed sides and placed himself under Yugoslav tutelage. He then became premier. In 1923 he resigned the premiership in favor of his supporter and prospective father-in-law Shevket Vërlaci—the same Vërlaci who was to help sell out Albania to Mussolini in 1939.

At no time during this period in the early twenties was the government installed in Tirana absolute master of Ghegheria. Uprisings of the tribesmen of one or another of the *bajraktars* assumed the aspect of a chronic disorder of the Albanian body politic. On several instances the Tirana government was forced to abandon its seat, returning only when the opposition could be bribed into changing sides or diplomatic pressure of one sponsoring government was brought to bear on the other.

> ". . . the rival nations vied with one another to secure the friendship or compel the obedience of the Albanians; and they, owning no common allegiance, took sides and changed in accordance with the dictates of interest and the counsels of opportunity. Thus the situation in Albania came to reflect, as in a mirror, the true relations between the Powers, obscured to the general view by the smoke of battle blown before the wind of words."[71]

In 1924 Zogu and Vërlaci were sent fleeing the country to Belgrade and Rome respectively. With Zogu the two Moslem regents also left who were part of the nominal executive of the country. The victorious successors to the Zogist clique were Fan Noli (who became Premier) and his newfound co-conspirators who included at that time Ali Klisura, Mustafa Kruja and their followers. Italy's hopes for this régime, which in its six-month span of life turned over Albania's fisheries, among other things, to Italian exploitation, were frustrated by Zog's return.

Upon taking over again, Zog made himself president of the "Albanian Republic." Kruja fled to Italy, living mostly on a pension thoughtfully provided by Mussolini's government on the Italian-held Dalmatian island of Zara. With the republic established in January of 1925, Zogu had Albania, but Yugoslavia was far from sure that she had Zogu.

While Zogu had been giving the Yugoslavs evidences of good faith, Vërlaci in Rome had been busy paving the way for an about face should King Alexander of Yugoslavia become more parsimonious in dispensing the necessary emoluments to the Zogists. Yugoslavia being quite limited in gold to be expended in holding Albania, it was in the nature of things that Italy would take advantage of the surreptitious siren call of Zogu *cum* Vërlaci. The time had come for Italy to bind Albania economically, with the very willing acquiescence of Zogu and his followers, to the new Roman imperium.

The Italian Credit Trust which was owned by the Italian government controlled the Albanian National Bank. The first step was for the Albanian National Bank to organize the "Societá per lo Sviluppo Economico dell'Albania" (SVEA). During 1925-26 the newly formed SVEA floated an Albanian loan of fifty million gold francs at 13% interest. Due to Albania's

71 Amery, Julian, *Sons of the Eagle; a study in guerilla warfare*, p. 5.

recognized inability to meet the payments regularly it was agreed that she was to grant most of her forestry and mineral resources to Italy as security. In addition, Albania was prevented from granting any concessions to other interests for forty years without Italy's express approval. In July, 1926, Mussolini made a bid for actual political control of Albania.

That month, Italian Minister to Albania, Baron Aloisi approached the Zogu government with a demand that it formally recognize Italy's "right" to protect Albania. The authority for this demand was a 1921 agreement between the Great Powers recognizing Italian preeminence in Albania. The Italians, knowing well that demands unaccompanied by "baksheesh" are seldom listened to in Albania, coolly offered about fifteen million lire to Zogu personally for his approval.

At about that time Zogu granted exploitation rights to the Fieri oil fields to the Anglo-Iranian Oil Company, a concession which that concern later saw fit to abandon to the Italians. This may explain why British Minister to Albania Reilly energetically advised Zog to refuse the demands. The Foreign Office followed this up by requesting Mussolini to clarify Aloisi's action. Mussolini settled everything by maintaining that Aloisi had exceeded his instructions. Needless to say, Aloisi was not recalled. The British Minister to Tirana subsequently was. His replacement did not try to urge Zogu to defy Aloisi's demands. These demands, now more subtly put so as not to offend British sensibilities, reappeared after the Italians gave Zogu a good scare to show him who was now master. In November, 1926, certain Gheg chieftains with their followers marched on Shkodra in revolt. It has since been claimed that the entire affair was bought and paid for by Italy.

The leaders of this revolt were the *bajraktars* Loro Caka and Hasan Bey Prishtina. Zogu was able to put this down with the use of twelve thousand troops. His new administrator in Shkodra, Galo Bey Bushati, and Minister of the Interior Musa Juka, dealt with the situation in time-honored Albanian fashion. After driving the rebels out they burned a few villages, executed and imprisoned captured rebels and hanged a Roman Catholic priest in the Shkodra marketplace for his part in the affair. Afterwards Zogu had no trouble from that quarter for a long time. Nevertheless, he had learned his lesson. From then on he who paid the piper also called the tune.

The result was a treaty with Italy protecting Zogu against

any further threats to his régime in return for his assurance that Yugoslavia would be frozen out of any arrangements in Albania (Article II). The main portion of the treaty is given below:

"Article I. Italy and Albania recognize that any disturbance directed against the political, juridical, and territorial *status quo* of Albania is opposed to their reciprocal political interest.

"Article II. To safeguard the above-mentioned interest, the High Contracting Parties undertake to give their mutual support and cordial collaboration; they likewise undertake not to conclude with other Powers political or military agreements prejudicial to the interests of the other Party as defined in the present pact.

"Article III. The High Contracting Parties undertake to submit to a special procedure of conciliation and of arbitration questions which may arise between them and which cannot be settled through regular diplomatic channels.

"The conditions of this procedure of peaceful settlement will be the object of special convention to be concluded as soon as possible.

"Article IV. The present pact shall remain in force for five years, and may be denounced or renewed one year before the expiration.

"Article V. The present pact shall be ratified and afterwards registered with the League of Nations. The ratification shall be exchanged at Rome.

"Done at Tirana, 27 November 1926.

(s) "Pompeo Aloisi
"H. Vrioni"

The Pact was ratified by Albania on December 9. Though Yugoslavia stormed and railed, and though Yugoslav-Albanian relations were strained almost to the breaking point, Zogu's government continued to steer Albania along the gold-paved road that led to Rome. Whatever the Yugoslavs might think, the Albanians had sold out again and Belgrade, as far as Albania was concerned, was definitely *ausgespielt*.

All but the last touches were necessary to consider Albania a full Italian colony after 1927. On November 22nd of that year a new Treaty of Tirana was signed by Italy and Albania. This pledged either party to come to the other's aid if one of them were attacked. In that event, the joint armies of the two states were to be commanded by a general of the country attacked. Inasmuch as Italian advisors, military organizers etc. had now moved into commanding Albanian positions, this was interpreted to mean, Albanian uniform or not, an Italian in either case.

On September 2, 1928, Ahmed Bey Zogu of Mati, dictator "president" of Albania, went through the farce of accepting a crown from his people, figuratively, for no actual coronation took place. He was now King Zog I of Albania. Actually nothing was changed as it mattered little what Zog chose to call himself, except to make the throne hereditary if ever an Albanian ruler's heirs could manage to live long enough to succeed him. Not a few Gheg chieftains aspired to replace Zog. Some were bought, others sent to the other world. These included such opponents of Zog as Zija Dibra, Cena Bey Kryeziu, Hasan Prishtina and a number of lesser tribal sachems. Doubtless they would have done the same if the shoe had been on the other foot.

Zog's policy toward Italy consisted of keeping the gold flowing while at the same time preserving what little internal freedom of action his government possessed. As matters stood, Albania could not have any foreign policy save that mapped out by Mussolini. The Italians, as time went on, naturally tried to increase their internal control of Albania in proportion to the money they poured into the country. Zog found himself in the unenviable position of having no other Power of Italy's magnitude interested in Albania. There being no Power capable of being played off by him against Italy, Yugoslavia now having retired from the game, Zog was now in a corner. Along with the money came the demands.

When on several occasions Zog was inclined to balk, there were always ways to bring him back in line. These included the June, 1934 Italian naval demonstration at Durazzo and the abortive Fieri "uprising" in August, 1935. Italy's tool in the latter affair was Shevket Vërlaci.

He had not, after all, become the King's father-in-law and his daughter married Xhemil Dino, later the Nazi butcher of Thesprotia, instead. Since it was the King who had broken the engagement, Vërlaci felt he had been made a fool. Since 1932, as Deputy for Elbasan, he stood at the head of the opposition. As Albania's wealthiest landlord with high connections in Italy he was hard to get rid of. His behind-the-scenes role in the Fieri affair finally gave Zog sufficient grounds to add him to the growing catalogue of ex-colleagues. Vërlaci fled to Mussolini's open arms to be kept in reserve should Zog not behave. In 1939 he was to return as Mussolini's chief Albanian stooge.

Albania thus had been bought and paid for by Italy. Between the Fieri incident and the Italian annexation of Albania there remained about four years of nominal independence. The farce of Albania's second venture as a sovereign state sped on to its inglorious end.

Zog and the Northern Epirotes

Despite a paper show of impartiality toward the different religious establishments in the Albanian state, Zog's government gave ample internal evidence of maintaining the Ottoman double standard of justice. There was, as always, a written law supposedly working in behalf of the whole country and an unwritten one working for the exclusive benefit of the Moslems. A non-political crime committed by one Moslem against another or by a non-Moslem against a follower of the Prophet was promptly redressed, especially in the latter case, with all the severity of the law. Crimes in which the criminal was a Moslem and the victim a Christian were often passed over or dismissed. One example will suffice:

On May 28, 1931, a well-known brigand and murderer named Idriz Jaho, a Moslem from Koutsi, slew the Orthodox priest Demetrius Eleutheriou of Nokovon (district of Argyrocastron) in the presence of witnesses who included the wife of the victim. Jaho had two other convictions for murder hanging over him, having been sentenced previously for a crime committed in the village of Nivitsa and another of life imprisonment for a murder in Koutsi. For both those crimes against fellow Moslems he had been sentenced but not caught. He had, however, the good fortune to kill a Christian priest before final capture—and in consequence walked out of the Argyrocastron courtroom a free man, for want of evidence!

What can an Albanian nationalist reply to a fanatical hater of the Greeks, the Albanian Orthodox usurper of the See of Durazzo Vissarion? Though an instrument of nationalist extremists, even *he* could no longer ignore the injustice to the Orthodox, irrespective of national sympathies. He had to admit publicly:

> "The Royal officials continue to persecute systematically the Orthodox Church both at Tirana and throughout the rest of Albania. In the State schools, especially at Elbassan, the teachers set an example of disrespect for religion and insubordination to the parents. The local government authorities appropriate church properties and assets. The judiciaries and agents of the Ministry of Justice as well as the police scandalously support foreign propaganda acting against Albanian interests."[72]

[72] Cf. daily *Proïa*, Athens, Greece, 16 February 1935.

We have spoken of Fan Noli's solemn "Declaration on Minorities" of October 2, 1921 in the League of Nations. It is not true that the Albanians violated this agreement because they had never honored it. The Declaration, like the Hamidian reform proposals of yore, was so much eyewash for infidel consumption. The Greeks at the time of the declaration had sought to have conditions attached because they knew how little value could be placed upon the Albanian word of honor. They knew, as Lord Cecil never could, the true mettle of the Shqiptars. The Europeans, never having the dubious privilege of observing the Albanian highlander in his native habitat, could easily be charmed by Fan Noli's cultivated speech. Albania's neighbors, however, were under no illusions that their next-door neighbors were Harvard gentlemen. They had had a little more experience with the "noble Albanians".

It was not until 1934 that the matter of "minority" schools came to a head. It was then that the last Greek school in the Grecophone Northern Epirote villages was closed. Another general school strike was called in Northern Epirus and the Greek parents swore they would rather see their children dead than in Albanian schools. Many of the inhabitants were exiled after clashes with Albanian gendarmes who tried to force the villagers to comply with the government's edict. The resultant protest against these methods stirred the Northern Epirote organizations abroad to appeal to the Greek Government to take the case to the League of Nations.

The League Council, in turn, referred the matter to the Permanent Court of International Justice (Hague Tribunal). It specifically asked that Court to decide whether Articles 206 and 207 of the 1933 Albanian Constitution were in violation of Albania's international obligation assumed on October 2, 1921. These articles stated:

> "The instruction and education of Albanian subjects are reserved to the State and will be given in State schools. Primary education is compulsory for all Albanian nationals and will be given free of charge. Private schools of all categories at present in operation will be closed."

The Tribunal at its 34th session on April 6, 1935, rendered its opinion by a vote of eight to three:

> "... the plea of the Albanian Government that, as the abolition of private schools in Albania constitutes a general measure applicable to the majority as well as to the minority, it is in conformity with the letter and spirit

of the stipulations laid down in Article 5, first paragraph of the Declaration of October 2nd, 1921, is not well founded."[73]

In simpler language, Albania could not insist that because non-Greek (i.e. purely Albanian) institutions *might* be affected by its edict the government was absolved from its obligations toward the Greek minority. Albania did not have a legal leg to stand on.

On May 23, 1935, Madariaga laid before the League Council the Hague Tribunal's opinion which was accepted. Mehdi Frashëri, the Albanian representative, assured the League that Albania would rectify the wrong done to the Grecophones of Northern Epirus. To do so, he claimed, it was necessary to call a Constituent Assembly to revise the offending constitutional provisions. As the constitution was an instrument dictated by the Crown, a stall was obviously implied. In deference to Albanian sensibilities the League chose to ignore this fact and refer the matter to the September session of the Council for final consideration.

This gave the Albanians three months to find ways and means not only to avoid their obligation to the League but to rid themselves of the source of the obligation as well. The Albanian Government called together all the feudal Beys and Agas of Argyrocastron, Delvino and Libochovo and proposed to them the expulsion of the Grecophone peasants from the Moslem *chifliks.* After they were driven to Greece or into exile in the interior of Albania, Yugoslavia could be persuaded to decrease her own Albania population by allowing Ghegs from Kossovo to settle in Northern Epirus as workers on the Moslem *latifundiae*.

This proposal was turned down for reasons that plainly indicate the fundamentally Ottoman outlook of the Moslem feudarchs. It was explained to the Albanian Government that the removal of the Christian *rayas* would be an economic catastrophe, inasmuch as a Moslem Bey had no means of terrorizing into submission or extorting usurous returns from a still more savage Gheg tribesman from Moslem Kossovo. It was possible for the Beys to force the frightened Greek peasants to carry the Beys' entire economic burden and then some while the Beys, living off the yield, spent their time idling in the market-places of

[73] International Justice, Permanent Court of, The Hague, *Fascicule No. 64 Series A./B., Minority Schools in Albania, XXXIV Session, April 6, 1935.*

Argyrocastron as they had done in the days of the old and (by them) much lamented Ottoman Empire. Should Moslem Ghegs replace these Greeks the Beys might even be faced with the calamity of having to soil their own hands to earn a living. The argument was not new. When, before the Greek Revolution, a proposal to massacre all the Greeks in the Empire was put before the Ottoman Divan, the Christians were saved only by one Vizier's sobering question, "If we kill the Christians who shall pay the capitation tax?"

Upon receiving the Hague Tribunal's judgement the Albanian authorities tried to compel the Grecophones to send Zog their thanks for having reopened their schools. The schools, of course, had not been reopened, but proof to the contrary had to be shown the League Council. Not for nothing had the rulers of Albania been taught their tricks in the Hamidian civil and military service.

Many of the villagers, feeling that the weight of civilized international opinion was with them, tried to take matters into their own hands and demonstrated for the reopening of the schools. There were armed clashes between the gendarmerie and the populace. One such took place at Vouliarates, a village near Argyrocastron, on June 17, 1935. Several villagers and gendarmes were wounded and the usual reprisals followed the restoration of order.

Having reached an impasse the government restored the school records to the village communes. At the same time the Ministry of Education sent officials headed by Inspector-General Xhafer Ypi to force the communes to hand over the records to it. Refusal again was met with reprisal and the Albanian Government issued an edict forbidding all public discussion of the school issue.

Later about twelve schools were reopened in the villages of Delvino and the Dropolis valley. The plan to oust the Greek peasants and introduce Ghegs was dropped at the point when the Beys began to be more favorably inclined to it. To effect its aim, the Albanian Government offered the Beys a good price for their lands and superior lands in the Myzeqe valley in central Albania which they and their Christian peasants could resettle. Upon the Beys' acceptance the Albanian Government opened negotiations with Belgrade to resettle Kossovars in Northern Epirus. To this Albania's master, Mussolini, objected because he had staked out the Myzeqe valley for colonization by 10,000 Italian settlers. It was there that matters stood in 1939 when the curtain fell on Zog's Albania and a new and painful chapter in Balkan history began.

Chapter X

ITALY MOVES IN

Preparation for Conquest

Zog was entangled in Italy's snare beyond the point where he could act in any way contrary to Mussolini's dictates. He was incapable of reorientation favorable to the other Balkan nations. This went beyond mere passiveness to increased Italian influence. When, for instance, the League of Nations slapped a sanction on Italian imports during the Ethiopian campaign, Albania and Austria were the only two countries to issue official refusals to go along with the League.

It was largely to hold Zog a captive to Italian demands that loan after loan had been poured into the country. Mussolini knew that much of this was going into the pockets of the clique around Zog. Unfortunately for these Albanian sycophants there was a point at which Italian liberality had to cease and some substantial economic return was to be realized. It was at this point that Mussolini realized that nothing short of annexation of Albania would do. Moreover, Albania was to fit into the new scheme of things contemplated by Mussolini with his new partner in Berlin. It would be entirely within the scope of Nazi foreign policy to regard Mussolini's contemplated annexation of Albania as added insurance against Yugoslav defection to the Allies.

The European Powers were once more caught up in a struggle between two rival blocs. Munich solved nothing except Czechoslovakia's betrayal. The realignment of Balkan power through adherence to the Axis by Yugoslavia's Regent Paul and Greece's eventual submission would clear the way for the joint Hitler-Mussolini conquest of the British and French dominated Middle East. For both strategic and economic reasons Zog was a King whose days on the throne were numbered.

Italy's reasons for subsidizing Zog's political opponents abroad became clearer. These leaders, organized in the fascist "Bashkimi Kombëtar" or National Union, were led by Ali Klisura (Këlçyra) from his exile in Grenoble, France. In 1938 he issued two resolutions which bore the signatures of Klisura, Mustafa Kruja and Qazim Koçuli. They have since been cited by the Tirana Communist organ *Bashkkimi,* by the Greeks ("La Participation de l'Albanie dans la guerre mondiale", Edition "Paix par la Justice") and by the anti-NCFA Balli Kombëtar organ *Flamuri* (October 31, 1953, No. 45-46). The first resolution declared boldly:

"We the undersigned,

"Believing that we represent the will of the great majority of the Albanian people and considering ourselves morally responsible for its fate;

"Having decided not to spare any effort and sacrifice in order to save them from the dangers that threaten their political, economic and moral life, and from the misfortunes that have befallen them;

"Convinced that the root and source of all these dangers and misfortunes is the régime of terror, misery, shame and treason which Ahmet Zogu installed more than 14 years ago;

"Convinced also, by the experience of the last 15 years and by the international situation at present, as well as by our country's geographical position, that only by relying on the Fascist Government's support can we save our people from Zog's régime which is the source and always remains the cause of all misfortunes; that only with the help of Italy, which is the sole Great Power directly interested in Albania, can be secured the economic recovery and the civilized progress of our country; that only a close and loyal friendship with Fascist Italy will favor our national aspirations in accord with the new spirit of the Munich Conference and the policy of the Rome-Berlin Axis; that only by following the line of this policy through a close and loyal friendship with the Italians shall our small nation, which has no other real and powerful support, be able to safeguard its independence and territorial integrity;

"We decide to ask for a prince of the blood of Savoy as King of the Albanians and founder of the future dynasty of our Monarchy.

(s) "Mustafa Kruja
"Qazim Koçuli
"Ali Këlçyra"

The second resolution was even bolder and went on record as demanding a fully totalitarian régime for Albania. The triumvirate at the head of the "National Union" resolved:

"Taking into consideration the indispensable need of the Albanian people for a strong government that will be just to the entire people as well as toward the elements which compose it and individuals without elemental or class privileges;

"Taking into consideration likewise the previous experience of our country under the various régimes and the example of other peoples around and above us;

"We have decided to found an authoritarian régime based on a single national popular party which will gather in its folds all honest Albanians who accept this system of government.

(s) "Mustafa Kruja
"Qazim Koçuli
"Ali Këlçyra"

Within Albania many who seemed closest to Zog regarded him as indispensable only as long as he was the medium through which Italian subsidies were distributed. When this ceased to be the case they had no trouble preparing themselves to accept Italian occupation of the country. One of these was Zog's Foreign Minister (Ekrem Libohova) at the moment when Italy occupied the country. He shifted his allegiance and became Axis puppet premier of Albania in 1943. This shows how truly alone Zog was, for few Albanians will follow a leader unable to hold their loyalty with hard cash.

Good Friday, 1939

At the beginning of 1939 vague rumors from Belgrade warned Zog of an approaching reckoning with Italy. The latter did all it could to reassure Zog publicly while laying plans to seize the country. Secretly the pot was boiling. Mussolini was anxious that it should not boil over until the Italians wound up their business in Spain where Mussolini had intervened on the side of Franco.

Italian Foreign Minister Ciano was all for a swift move on Albania. On February 6, 1939 he wrote in his diary:

" . . . I gave the Duce my point of view in the Albanian matter: we must work faster. He agreed with me. We shall intensify local revolutionary preparations. The date of the action: Easter week."[74]

The coming showdown had been decided and its date set. Nothing more remained to be done. Albania was finished.

Franz von Papen, in his recent memoirs, claims that Italy's move was "apparently unexpected" and that the Germans had not been properly consulted. It is more probable that, given the personal relations between Ribbentrop and Papen, he was unaware of the Italo-German consultations on this matter. Ciano's diary entry of February 10th shows us that the Wilhelmstrasse regarded Albania ripe for the picking and looked forward

[74] *The Ciano Diaries, 1939-1943,* Gibson, Hugh, ed., p. 23.

to obtaining a lion's share of the Albanian oil. This drew forth from Ciano, "I called Mackensen and informed him that we considered Albania just like another Italian province . . . ." The next day Germany hastened to assure Ciano that Hitler would do nothing against Italian interests in Albania.[75]

The Italians reasoned and the Germans agreed that if Hitler could take Czechoslovakia it was only natural that Mussolini should move on Albania. For one thing, Mussolini felt strongly that Italian imperial expansion was not keeping up with that of his Berlin partner. Ciano's diary entry for March 15th reads:

> "It is useless to deny that all this concerns and humiliates the Italian people. It is necessary to give them a satisfaction and compensation: Albania."[76]

Two days later the Italian Foreign Office was grinding out denials of its obvious intentions:

> "An official Italian declaration emphasizes the fact that the rumors circulated abroad of an impending Italian intervention in Albania are malignant falsehoods propagated with the object of disturbing the peace in the Adriatic."[77]

The Italians had decided on the concrete steps to be taken. They were to annex Albania officially and Zog could remain as a figurehead if he so desired. If not, Ciano wrote,

> "We shall undertake the military seizure of the country. To this end we are already mobilizing and concentrating in Puglia four regiments of Bersaglieri, an infantry division, air force detachments, and all of the first naval squadron."[78]

In command of the forces being readied were Army General Guzzoni, Admiral Riccardi and Air Force General Paricolo.

Zog was handed an ultimatum to which he tried to delay an answer as long as possible. On April 2 the Italians were ready to move. Orders for the evacuation of Italian civilians from Albania were given. Refusing a straight-forward yes or no to the Italians, Zog proposed a convocation of the Albanian Cabinet and let his ministers take the responsibility for the fatal deci-

[75] Ciano, *Ibid.* p. 26.

[76] *Ibid,* pp. 42-43.

[77] *Greek White Book, Diplomatic Documents Relating to Italy's Aggression Against Greece,* no. 2, p. 23.

[78] Ciano, *op. cit.*, p. 51.

sion. The Italians demanded immediate Albanian capitulations while the Albanians tried to dicker some more.

Meanwhile Zog's wife, the Hungarian Geraldine, née Áp-ponyi, delivered an heir to the throne. Ciano noted,

> "At dawn Zog's son was born. How long will he be the heir to the Albanian throne?"[79]

It no longer mattered what Zog might decide. His doom was sealed. A final ultimatum was delivered by Italy on April 5 giving Zog until the 6th midnight to capitulate. At the end of the time limit Zog was still attempting to negotiate. The Italians, however, were no longer interested in what he had to say.

As the haze cleared on the morning of Good Friday, April 7, 1939, the Italian fleet was lying off the harbors of St. John Medua, Durazzo, Valona and Santi Quaranta. The San Marco Battalion and a body of Italian Marines were landed without difficulty except for a minor battle at Durazzo. They were surprised with the ease with which the mountainous country, ideal for guerilla warfare, surrendered. The Durazzo column reached Tirana and occupied it on the 8th, then marched through Albania occupying Elbasan and Korytsa. There it was met by the Valona column which came by way of Berati and the Devoli valley. The forces from Santi Quaranta occupied Delvino, Argyrocastron and Tepeleni. Mussolini had taken Albania at the official cost of 12 Italians dead and 53 wounded.

With scarcely a shot fired in his name Zog had been dispossessed. He arrived on April 8th with his wife and new-born son at Florina, Greece, where he asked for asylum. Italian flags flew from the windows of his Tirana palace and Black Shirts, who were by no means all Italians, paraded through the streets of Albanian towns. Ciano made a dramatic appearance the next day at Tirana and scattered lire from the palace balcony to the Tirana crowds as the colorfully attired Ghegs below shouted "Rrnoft Duce, Rrnoft mbret Italis!" (Long live Il Duce, Long live the King of Italy!) The same day the Greek Minister to Albania reported an ominous sign of things to come. "The Commander of the first battalion to enter Tirana declared that Italy is coming to create a greater Albania."[80]

[79] Ciano, *ibid.*, p. 60.

[80] *Greek White Book,* Doc. No. 18, p. 26.

A Great Italy and a Greater Albania

Almost from the first moment the Italians began to encourage the Albanians with talk about Albanian expansion—talk that soon became action. The Ghegs could not fail to be attracted by promises of Kossovo in Yugoslavia where, indeed, the Albanians had (and have) a perfectly valid ethnic claim. At the same time the beys of Northern Epirus were reassured that Greek Paramythia (in free Epirus), where there was a pre-World War II minority of 18,109 Moslems out of a total population of 65,074, would likewise speedily be added to Albania. Mussolini was, in effect, raising the old Turco-Albanian cry of 1878. "Albania", the League of Prizren had proclaimed, "is five vilayets."

Hostility to Greece was manifested the first day of the Italian occupation. Upon taking Santi Quaranta the Italians shelled the Greek Consulate there for forty-five minutes, at the end of which time they entered the building with fixed bayonets and turned one of the rooms into an Italian ammunition dump. One Greek consular employee was wounded. The ammunition was removed only after many protests to the Italian commandant.

On April 16th the Albanian delegation, headed by Shefket Vërlaci, went through the ceremony at the Quirinal Palace in Rome of handing Albania's Crown to the "King of Italy and Emperor of Ethiopia" who thereby became also king of Albania. Afterward Mussolini sent them back to Albania with reassurances that their country soon would be enlarged.

Italy assured Greece that there was no reason to regard her occupation as a threat, but the Greeks (and the world) knew by then what value could be placed on the Fascist word of honor. The Greek Minister in Tirana informed his Government that no less a personage than one of the ministers had confided to a Greek Legation employee that Italy had set her sights on all of Epirus as far as Preveza. The Italian Minister of Education on June 14th, in a speech at Korytsa, dropped thinly veiled hints about Albanian expansion. Even more explicit were Marshal Badoglio and the Italian King's personal envoy to Albania, Visconti Prasca. The Italian Army embarked on grand maneuvres in Northern Epirus close to the Greek border. Rumors of impending Italian aggression aimed at Corfu and Salonica were in the air. Public speeches of Italian official spokesmen were full of persistent variations on the theme of Albanian territorial expansion.

The Italian Government could reassure Athens of Italy's purity of intention, but the strident song of Fascism's army, "Sbarcheremo al Pireo e conquisteremo tutto l'Egeo," was loud in Greek ears. Italy's occupation of Albania had once more made Northern Epirus the loaded gun levelled at the head of Greece. The Greeks, quietly and prudently, began to reinforce their army in free Epirus and Macedonia.

Northern Epirus in the Crisis

When the Italian annexation of Albania took place Greece feared the possibility of Northern Epirote demonstrations and sought to calm her compatriots who had been unwilling subjects of Albania and who had become equally unwilling slaves of the Fascist empire. The day before Italy's final ultimatum to Zog, the Permanent Greek Undersecretary for Foreign Affairs Mavroudis had instructed the Hellenic Vice-Consul at Argyrocastron to, "recommend to the Greeks to refrain from any anti-Italian demonstrations."[81]

After the occupation the Italians began to organize Albanian units to be incorporated into the Italian Army. Among them were units of Kossovars and Tsams (Moslem natives of Paramythia who had migrated across the border). Particularly outstanding were the "Tarabosh" and "Tomori" regiments. The former was Kossovar, the latter was commanded by Spiro Moisi who later became a Partisan "General" in the army of Enver Hoxha.

Italy made one miscalculation that was to affect the coming struggle. She too was deluded into thinking that the Northern Epirote Christians, albanophone and subject to twenty years of Albanian and fascist indoctrination, had been won over to her side. Mussolini's planners did not realize until it was too late that only hopelessness kept down these Greeks. When bodies of Northern Epirotes, drafted by Italy into the Albanian army, were to meet their brother Greeks in combat, it would be with devastating results—for the Italians. Given one ray of hope hundreds were to desert to the triumphant troops of their Greek motherland. While the Italians were to be continually badly informed on Greek troop movements the Greeks had the most efficient and trustworthy native intelligence spotting every move

[81] *Greek White Book, ibid.,* Doc. Nos. 8, 9, p. 24.

the Italians made. This was to be the practical basis for what the world was to call the "Greek miracle". The Northern Epirotes were to pay highly for this later on.

The fascisti went up and down the country Italianizing. Santi Quaranta was renamed Porto Edda in honor of Ciano's wife (Mussolini's daughter). Albanian-speaking Italian teachers and priests, drawn from the old albanophone colonies in Sicily and Calabria, were introduced into the country to preach Mussolini's doctrines. The Italian Uniat clergy met with a resounding failure except in Gheg Elbasan where a uniate congregation already existed. In Argyrocastron where they attempted to set up a Papist Oriental rite church to oppose the Orthodox Metropolis they were able to attract only a few gypsies who were given a dole as an inducement to attend.

A newspaper in both an Italian and an Albanian-language edition, *Tomori,* was set up in Tirana under the Albanian Hilmi Leka's dummy editorship. A disproportionate amount of articles and "news" was devoted to anti-Greek propaganda coupled with paeans to the Duce. It was in that newspaper that the Italians initiated a press campaign to create "incidents" with Greece. The most important of these was an affair concerning the death of an Albanian brigand and professional assassin whose name the reader has met before in these pages, Daut Hoxha.

The Affair of Daut Hoxha

Mussolini confided to his closest henchmen that what he was after was Corfu and Paramythia (Tsamouria). It was either this or the whole of Greece. Ciano's diary speaks of these plans and of a news dispatch specially doctored by Mussolini.

> "Mussolini still speaks of the Greek question and wants particulars on Tsamouria. He has prepared a Stefani Despatch, which will start agitation on the question. He has had Jacomoni and Visconti Prasca come to Rome and intends to confer with them. He speaks of a surprise attack against Greece toward the end of September. If he has decided this, I feel that he must work fast. It is dangerous to give the Greeks time to prepare."[82]

The heart of this Stefani Agency dispatch edited by Mussolini and given to the world on August 11, 1940, concerned a rather obscure individual.

[82] Ciano, *op. cit.,* p. 283.

"The great Albanian patriot Daut Hoxha, born in the unredeemed region of Tsamouria, has been savagely murdered on Albanian territory close to the frontier . . . Daut Hoxha had been compelled some time ago to leave Tsamouria secretly in order to escape persecution by the Greek authorities who could not forgive his untiring propaganda among his compatriots for the annexation of Tsamouria to the Mother-country."[83]

Who was this "great Albanian patriot" and what caused him to be so savagely murdered? The answer to the first part of this question is to be found in this excerpt from the files of the Criminal Division of the Greek Police:

"1. By decision No. 36 of October 9, 1919, of the Preveza Assize-Court, Hoxha and his two accomplices Basil Cotzias (Christian), Malo Osman (Moslem), and Takis Nicomanes (Christian) were sentenced by default to penal servitude for life for the premeditated murder of Vehip Cimo (Moslem) and Zeqir Rehip (Moslem).

"2. By decision No. 14 of November 14, 1919, of the Jannina Assize-Court, Hoxha was condemned by default to twenty years' penal servitude for murdering, with the aid of an accomplice, Zeqir Zeko (Moslem) and Rahip Habib Bey (Moslem).

"3. By decision No. 30 of June 10, 1921, of the Preveza Assize-Court, Hoxha and his accomplices Takis Nicomanes (Christian), Constantine Souliotis (Christian) and Malo Bushi (Moslem) were sentenced by default to seventeen years' penal servitude for robbing Ahmet Hasin (Moslem), Balluk Mehmet (Moslem), and Ismail Çorçi (Moslem), for cattle thieving and attempted murder of Husejn Jakup (Moslem) and Basil Tourvalis (Christian), and for illegally carrying weapons.

"4. By decision No. 14 of December 1921 of the Preveza Assize-Court, Hoxha was sentenced by default to four years' imprisonment for attempted blackmail.

"5. By decision No. 22 of the year 1923 of the Jannina Assize-Court, Hoxha, together with his accomplices Takis Pliatsikas (Christian) and Takis Zoghas (Christian), was sentenced by default to eighteen years' penal servitude for attempted murder. The brigand Zoghas was arrested a short while afterwards and beheaded.

"6. By decision No. 9 of May 6, 1925, of the Jannina Assize-Court, Hoxha and his accomplices Christos Soulas (Christian) and Anastasius Georgious (Christian) were condemned to death by default for kidnapping, blackmail, and illegally carrying weapons.

"7. By decision No. 23 of October 8, 1925, of the Jannina Assize-Court, Hoxha and his accomplice Takis Nicomanes (Christian) were sentenced to death for brigandage."[84]

Here we have the classic picture of an Albanian highwayman. The one crime that does not figure here is his no doubt well-paid services in the 1923 assassination of the Italians at Kakavia.

[83] *Greek White Book,* Doc. No. 111, p. 77.

[84] *ibid.,* Doc. No. 115, pp. 81-82.

There was nothing he had not done. His ingrained "faith" permitted him to slit the throat or shoot a Christian Greek and an Albanian Moslem with equal facility. His companions were drawn from the scum of both races. He had led the Greek Police a merry chase along the border, but his final escape in 1925 convinced him that the time had come for him to retire from the profession.

Accordingly, Daut Hoxha made an excellent steward of an Albanian Bey's *chiflik* at Saronia, Vourkon (Delvino). There he acquired a new reputation for brutality toward the shepherds and Greek tenant-farmers. It was therefore to nobody's surprise that his headless corpse was discovered one day near the border, on the Albanian side, of course. The killers of the 50 year-old ex-brigand were two local Greek shepherds, Albanian subjects, 17 year-old Pilios Kotsos and 24 year-old Elias Photos. They crossed over into Greece after the murder, since the Greeks would hardly prosecute them for killing the bandit they had condemned to death. This, then, was the *cause celèbre* Mussolini chose to trumpet around the world to justify the move he was soon to make.

On the Eve of War

On August 15, 1940, hundreds of pilgrims were worshipping at the famous shrine of the Virgin at Tenos Island on the traditional date of the Assumption of the Virgin Mary. This Greek Orthodox day of prayer, marked with great official solemnity, was marred by an incident that left no doubt of Italian intentions. A submarine, which at the time the Greeks found prudent to pretend was of unknown nationality, entered Tenos harbor and sank the Greek cruiser *Helle*.

Soon afterwards the Duce alerted his forces for a new war. The date set provisionally was October 26. It fell two days short of the actual date his Ambassador delivered the ultimatum. As the Ciano diaries show, the Italian General Staff had forebodings about the outcome of their master's new adventure, but were afraid to voice their fears before the almighty Duce.

Italian preparations in Northern Epirus included raising irregular Moslem Albanian bands to strike terror along the Greek frontier. Stories emanated from Rome accusing Greece of persecuting the Tsams and found their way to the front pages of the dummy press in Albania. A systematic arrest of Northern

Epirotes who had not been careful enough to hide their feelings was carried out with fascist *squadrista* thoroughness. There were continued concentrations of Italian troops poised along the border.

"Incidents" were created along the frontier and the Greek Government wanted explanations. On the very eve of war the Greek commandant of the sector in which the incidents occurred arrived at a border post to receive some explanation. He was met there by only an Italian warrant officer who had no comment to make. Northern Epirus was again the ground upon which an alien horde stood ready to pour into Greece. Only a melodramatic Italian gesture was necessary.

On October 26, Italian Major-General Zannini in Korytsa issued an order of the day to his *Ferrara* Division:

> "It is now nineteen months since we have been tempering our weapons and our hearts in this well-defended and rugged country of Albania, straining toward the goal which is now in sight.
>
> "With wills and energies bound together tightly in one, infantry, blackshirts, gunners, engineers, all, Italians and Albanians, let us turn our eyes toward Epirus."

Chapter XI

GREECE'S FINEST HOUR

The Day of the Immortal "NO"

On the 28th day of October, 1940, at 2:55 in the morning, Greek Premier John Metaxas was awakened by one of the gendarmes guarding his Athens home. He was told the French Ambassador was waiting to see him. Metaxas ordered the guard to show him up. In a few minutes, instead of the Ambassador of France, there stood before him Ambassador Grazzi of Italy who curtly handed him an ultimatum. When Ciano had drawn it up six days before he had fixed the exact hour of delivery. It was "a document that allows no way out for Greece. Either she accepts occupation or she will be attacked."[85]

Attached to it was a *three hour* time limit! The Italians knew it would take all of three hours at 3 A.M. to summon the Cabinet even to look at the document. After reading it and learning the fantastic time limit attached, Metaxas looked at the Italian envoy squarely and told him "We understand, then, this is war." Thereupon he rose and showed Grazzi to the door. The Second World War had come to Greece.

The Greeks knew well what forces the enemy could summon and what means the Axis would use. It is no exaggeration to say that this was the moment the Greek people rose at the call of three thousand years of history and spoke through their Premier's mouth an answer simple and naked as a Doric column, "OXI!—NO!"

To the minds of great and humble came the proud recollection of how another despot's demands had been met when the King of Kings of Persia had demanded earth and water as tokens of craven submission. *That* emperor's envoys had been thrown into a well where they were told to help themselves to plenty of both.

85 Ciano, *op. cit.*, p. 304.

In the Mountains of Epirus

On the morning of the historic 28th of October the Greek General Staff issued its first laconic war communique:

> "Since 5:30 this morning Italian military forces have been attacking our advanced units on the Greco-Albanian frontier.
> "Our forces are defending the national soil."

From Argyrocastron and Korytsa the Italians advanced on Greece. The Italian General Ubaldo Soddu had, all told, approximately 300,000 men, excellent artillery, tanks, and about two thousand planes. Each Italian division had attached to it a regiment of Albanians such as the *Dajti, Drini, Tomori, Tarabosh,* etc. In addition there were blackshirted units of the Albanian Fascist Militia and 3,500 Albanian volunteer irregulars led by their chiefs in the traditional search for plunder.

The Italian left flank advanced by way of Viglista from Korytsa to Florina. The center, spearheaded by the *Giulia* Division of Alpine troops and Albanian units was first to advance toward the Pindus Mountains from which it hoped to overrun Thessaly. The right flank prepared to follow the Epirote coastline to Preveza.

Against this force were ranged a little over 35,000 Greek troops who had been gathered at the frontier with great difficulty and caution since August. These had to hold the front until the arrival of reinforcements.

The *Giulia* Division advanced through the heavily wooded Smolika and Grammos Mountains, took Samarina and Distrotos and arrived twenty kilometres outside of its objective, Metsovo, which stands in the heart of the Pindus halfway between Epirus and Thessaly. It was there that the tide first turned against the undefeated Axis war machine.

The Greek troops, without even a constant supply line, were ordered to turn their defense into an attack. Their supply problem was solved by the unexampled sacrifice of the hardy mountaineer women of the Pindus. Without misgivings for the dangerous task they elected to undertake, these modern Amazons became human pack-animals, carrying food and ammunition to their soldiers in the snowy hills. In magnificent defiance of the odds their army proved itself worthy of the sacrifice. The Greeks attacked.

To this day, military historians stand amazed at this apparent reversal of every rule of logic in modern warfare. The Italians broke and ran, with the Greeks relentlessly pursuing. Reinforcements from Valona met the fleeing Italians and joined them in flight. A mere handful of Greeks had not only turned a horde but were pursuing it back to its base!

The miracle had its counterpart elsewhere on the front. By the first of November the Italians who had advanced from Korytsa expecting to sweep on to Salonica had been beaten back and the Greeks stood five kilometres within Albanian territory. Thus, after twenty-four painful years the Greek Army stood once more upon the unredeemed soil of Northern Epirus.

Mussolini's army continued to show its back to the oncoming Evzones who advanced with fixed bayonets to their mountaineer cry of "Aera!." Their bravery was building a bridge that spanned centuries and the world beheld them as the reincarnation of their forebears.

The Italian advance down the coast was routed between the Acheron and Calamas (Thyamis) Rivers. The Italians followed this by a blunder which sent the armored *Centaur* division inland toward Jannina. The Greeks sprung a trap and crushed the *Centaur,* the remnants of which were pursued and obliterated.

By the 18th of November not a single armed Italian remained on the soil of the national state of Greece. The Greeks continued into Northern Epirus to liberate the major portion of the province. Greek resistance became the miracle of victory. The whole world sat up and took notice. The Allies and the United States stood up and cheered.

Even the microscopic Greek airforce, reinforced by about 18 old British and French planes, claimed its own victories. On the ninth day of the war it went into action over Korytsa and Argyrocastron and demolished the Italian aircraft before they had a chance to get off the ground. The Greeks were transported with their own ecstatic vision of a holy war of vengeance upon an empire many times their numerical and material strength.

The first advance into Northern Epirus had come in the Macedonian theater of operations. It was actually the defection of a battalion of "Albanians", eager to exchange their hated livery for the tunic of their Greek motherland which heralded the beginning of Italian collapse on that front. As the Greeks advanced on all fronts the number of these "deserters" to their side came to 3,000 well-armed men. They helped their Greek Army buddies solve the important problem of arms shortage, for, as the Greeks pressed forward, they picked up enough Italian artillery to supply a division. These Northern Epirote ex-Albanian soldiers taught the Greek Army behind the lines how to use this captured artillery with striking efficiency against its makers.

After a nine day battle, on November 22, 1940, the first major town of Epirus fell to its liberators. The Greek flag was raised once more over Korytsa to the open joy of the Greek inhabitants and the sullen hatred of the Moslems and the few Christians who had sold their souls to the alien cause. Men who were born and raised under the Albanian yoke were for the first time able to join their rejoicing elders in thanksgiving. The year 1940 joined 1912 and 1914 as a symbol of faith fulfilled. The Northern Epirotes had vindicated the silent devotion they had not dared to show for nearly a quarter of a century.

The Third Liberation

With Korytsa freed the Greek Army stood on the heights of Morava and Ivan. Toward the south Leskoviki and Erseka were soon in Greek hands. The next day after taking Korytsa the Hellenic Army was once again in Moschopolis. The first of December saw the fall of Pogradets and the victorious Greeks moving forward and on. Mussolini's sole answer to these reversals was to replace general after general on the front without holding back the Greeks. His once proud forces were vanquished. Premeti was next to fall.

Meanwhile, the Italian retreat in the west had also turned into a complete rout, with the Greeks advancing faster than the world could learn of each victory. On the 6th of December Porto Edda was once more Santi Quaranta. In two more days the Greek population of Argyrocastron hailed the victorious army of their brothers. Greek morale stood higher than it had been for centuries. In Athens thousands poured into the streets dancing, singing, crying with joy. Theirs were thunderous roars of "To Tirana! To Rome!" A royal proclamation was read to the triumphant troops:

> "Full of rejoicing over the last communiqué regarding the fall of Argyrocastron, proud of the new, bright victories of My troops, I direct toward the Generalissimo, the Unit Commanders, the officers, non-commissioned officers and men, My warm greeting and the expression of My deepest satisfaction. I especially congratulate the unit which brought with such bravery to pass the glorious undertaking of the occupation of Argyrocastron, a center of great moral as well as strategic value.

"I also most warmly express My congratulations to our heroic airforce for its deeds.

"The leaders and men appeared worthy of each other and worthy of the Nation."

"George II"

Argyrocastron was the scene of panegyrics. Metropolitan Panteleimon, with tears of happiness in his eyes, received the Greek troops with his blessing. The hearts of the Moslem Albanians, as they witnessed the Northern Epirote rejoicing, burned with a different desire—revenge. The Moslems had been deceived into believing that nothing short of total annihilation could efface their fellow inhabitants' devotion to Greece. It was not enough to hold Northern Epirus in bondage. Now they lived for the day when they could burn and massacre the Christians until not an infidel soul would draw breath.

Soon the winter storms cut through Greek and Italian alike. Hundreds on both sides were felled by the winter's icy scythe. In the snow and ice the Greeks continued to press forward. Nature held no terrors for the simple Greek soldier. Had not the Italians struck first by violating the shrine of the Virgin Mother of God? To the Christian Greek she was again the "Hypermachos strategos", the defending general to whom belonged the victory.

Klisura fell to the Greeks on January 10, 1941. From Chimarra to Lake Ochrida a portion of Northern Epirus had been freed, but the way from Klisura to Tepeleni proved unexpectedly difficult and, for the first time since their reversal, the Italians were able to counterattack. The Greeks stiffened their lines and defended. Again and again the forces of Mussolini dashed themselves against the Greeks to no avail. The Greeks continued to capture large supplies and hundreds of Italian prisoners, while the Italians could make no headway with their counter-offensive. Italian General Cavallero threw in all the available armored units and mountain infantry in forty-six attacks upon Greek positions at Klisura. The only results were further Italian losses without a single gain.

Early in March, Mussolini came to the front and assumed personal command. After ordering the offensive he departed on its first day, March 9. The only result of this Italian attack was the loss of more than 9,000 Italian soldiers. After eight days the Italians had to admit that it had come to the same end as the previous attempts. The Greeks would not be moved.

The Italians underwent the humiliation of requesting a truce from the Greeks to bury their dead. The Greeks refused. The Italians attacked again from the 17th to the 19th. The Greeks wouldn't budge. Mussolini made another trip to the Klisura front and narrowly escaped being taken prisoner himself!

Winter was becoming Spring, and the Greeks made ready to resume the chase. The Italians had finally become convinced that their own forces could not change their ignominious destiny. Northern Epirus was the grave of the Italian Empire. If his once awesome and resplendent army was not to be thrown into the Adriatic, Mussolini had to down his pride for good and call in the ally who had once regarded him with deep respect, which had now become equally profound contempt—the madman of Berchtesgaden, Adolf Hitler.

The Germans Come

The Italian fiasco in the mountains of Epirus was such that some men in Fascism's inner councils began to question the validity of their political faith. In January, 1941, Mussolini boarded a train with Ciano and went to Salzburg to discuss his terrible dilemma with Hitler and Ribbentrop. Ciano wrote:

> ". . . once again we have had a kick in the pants, leaving many prisoners in the hands of the enemy. The serious thing is that it involves the 'Lupi di Toscana' (wolves of Tuscany), a division which has an excellent reputation and a grand tradition, landed only a short while ago in Albania, and on which we had put many hopes. The Duce talks at length about all this. He repeats his pessimism concerning the Army and the Italian people. He can't explain it all. He keeps repeating, 'If anybody had predicted on October 15 what later actually happened, I would have had him shot.' Then he changes the subject."[86]

At Salzburg the two dictators had a heart to heart talk, and Ciano was able to note in his diary on January 21, "there is absolute solidarity between the countries of the Axis, and we shall march together in the Balkans."[87] What the world was to behold was the Germans marching in with the Italians meekly following them with their tails between their legs. From that moment the European Axis was to be a one man show—Hitler's.

[86] Ciano, *ibid.*, p. 337.
[87] Ciano, *ibid.*, p. 339.

Mussolini was fast to slide down to the level of a Horthy, Antonescu or Laval.

On March 27, 1941, the Yugoslav situation had gotten out of Axis hands. An uprising of the Yugoslav Army and people, burning with resentment against the pact by which pro-Nazi Regent Paul and Premier Cvetkovich had tried to sell the country to Hitler, placed pro-Allied King Peter firmly in the saddle. Germany raged while Mussolini, chastened by his defeats and with visions of the Yugoslavs joining the Greeks in pushing him into the sea, tried to soften the impact.

On Sunday, April 6, the German *blitzkrieg* was striking Yugoslavia. At the same time, the Germans, with Bulgaria as their base, were joined by the Bulgarians in attacking Greece from the east. Rolling along the Vardar, the Germans soon sealed off Greece from Yugoslavia and moved south from Macedonia to conquer all of Greece. In a few days the Adolf Hitler Division was in Florina and then Jannina. The victorious Greek troops in Northern Epirus were sealed off from the rest of Greece.

Despite desperate urging from Athens to fight their way out of the hopeless trap, the Greek choice in Northern Epirus was surrender or suicide. The rank and file and many of the officers were determined to attempt the impossible had not their determination been shattered by one man. Seeing their untenable position, lacking necessary supplies and acting on his own initiative, General George Tsolakoglu surrendered the Hellenic Army in Epirus to the Germans. The Nazi avalanche thundered on.

On Orthodox Good Friday, April 18, 1941, the Germans were rolling on to certain conquest of Greece. Premier Alexander Koryzes, who had become Premier upon the death of Metaxas at the height of Greek victory, could see now only a Golgotha ahead for his nation. He locked himself in his study, an ikon of the Virgin in one hand and a revolver in the other, and calmly shot himself.

On April 27 the German units entered Athens and raised the Swastika over the Acropolis. Germans and their Italian, Bulgar and Albanian camp-followers were soon masters of the birthplace of democracy and European civilization. Tsamouria in southern Epirus and Kossovo in Yugoslavia were annexed to the Greater Albania the Axis had promised to create. Italy and the Albanians returned to Northern Epirus by the grace of their teutonic gods. The Albanians prepared to offer Valhalla the sickly odor of a burnt offering—the Christian villages of Northern Epirus.

Despite the fact that the Nazis were now masters in Athens, the Greeks continued to contest every inch of ground until driven from the Peloponnesus to Crete. Crete fell after a mass assault by Nazi parachute troops, and the remnants of the Greek Army and Government, headed by the King, sought respite and a chance to rebuild the Greek Army in Egypt. Never yielding the battle to an enemy now master of the whole of Europe, the Greeks were to fight at El Alamein, at Rimini, in the mountains of the motherland itself, until the common Allied struggle was won. Theirs was the sacrifice for which small reward was asked and even less would be received, though the world confessed itself forever in their debt.

Chapter XII

EPIRUS IN FLAMES

The Albanians as Fascist Allies

In April 1941, Mussolini and Vërlaci exchanged tokens of love and gratitude over the prostrate body of Axis-occupied Greece. On April 24 the Duce wrote to his stooge:

> "I wish to tell you that Albania too has contributed to the victory of Italian arms. It has contributed by its fighting volunteers, with its works and, above all, by the admirable calm and discipline of its people.
>
> "I wish to render you a token of confirmation of my sympathy for your country and for you.—Mussolini"

Two days later puppet premier Vërlaci sent the following reply to his Duce:

> "Your words addressed to me constitute the best recompense for our faithfulness and the high spirit and fervent will with which the Albanian people have placed themselves at the side of their brother Italians in this war, the victorious end of which will signal the definitive triumph of the Axis Powers in all the Balkans. Your words represent the certainty alive in every Albanian heart that with the peace with justice and in your new order, Duce, through you, Albania will have the certain recognition of her rights and the guarantee of her life within her legitimate frontiers and within the body of the Imperial Community of Rome.
>
> "In the name of the Albanian Government, I express to you, Duce, the highest gratitude and ardent wish of all Albania to work again and always with immutable spirit for the great power and glory of Rome.—Shevket Vërlaci (President of the Council)."[88]

One of the many Axis recognitions of Albanian service to Fascist Italy is from the pen of a Nazi writer who testified:

> "Innumerable are the cases where honorific military distinctions have been conferred on Albanians. The long list of warriors who have received their 'alla memoria' medals fill the official communiques. The citations accompanying these decorations are the constant witness of the irreproach-

[88] Review *Albania,* Rome, Vol. II, No. 5, May, 1941.

able conduct of the Shqiptar soldier. The highest Italian honorific distinction itself, the Gold Cross, has been conferred on Albanians."[89]

Albania breathed in deeply the totalitarian poison of Rome and Berlin. Among the victims of the Albanian Government's attempts to ape the big brothers of Italy and Germany were the Jews of Valona, the only members of that tragic race in Albania, who did not number a hundred families. They were expelled to the accompaniment of an Albanian proclamation of a "Nuremberg Law".

It appears that the overwhelming majority of Albanians had proven themselves collaborationists in whom the Italians could and did rely. When Italy finally surrendered they proved, for a time, just as trustworthy to the Germans. Having joined Italy in the war with Greece, the jackals of Tirana likewise joined Mussolini in declaring war on the United States in December 1941. It was not until the final defeat of the Axis in Europe that the interests of the Albanians differed appreciably from those of their Axis masters.

As has so often been attested by their extraordinary history, the Albanians had a distinct talent for using their masters more than their masters used them. The Axis conquest of Greece gave them the chance, first in black shirts and then in brown, to settle their grim account with the Northern Epirotes.

It did not prove hard for the faithful Albanians to obtain *carte blanche* from the Italians and afterwards the Germans to deal with the Northern Epirote Christians as they wished. The Northern Epirotes, from Korytsa to Chimarra, had shown how dangerous and "unreliable" an element they were for the Axis in the Greco-Italian campaign. What the Albanians had to leave undone under the Fasces and the Swastika they were later permitted to resume by their new Red masters.

Greek Resistance in Northern Epirus

The war in the Axis-occupied countries soon became the drama of undergrounds and guerilla movements. In this bitter though dedicated type of warfare the Northern Epirotes again proved themselves noteworthy components of Greek resistance. Neither Albanian threats and actions nor the Italian concentra-

[89] Kolleger, Willibald, *Albaniens Wiedergeburt,* Vienna, 1942.

tion camps at Durazzo, Porto Romano and elsewhere could lessen their devotion to their age-old ideals.

In May 1942 the first Northern Epirote resistance groups appeared in the Delvino area led by two Northern Epirote officers, Spyridon Litos and John Videles. Lieutenant Videles became the link with General Napoleon Zervas' EDES. Orphaned at the age of four when the Albanians killed his father, he had grown up in Greece, graduating with distinction from the Evelpides, Greece's Sandhurst or West Point. He had fought both the Bulgarians and the Italians in the war. A native of the village Kato Lesnitsa, he returned to the land of his birth to fight against the Axis and its Albanian collaborators. He was later to fall fighting the Germans at the head of his company of Northern Epirote EDES volunteers on January 6, 1944 at Kastrosykia near Preveza.

Later, resistance bands appeared not only in the district of Argyrocastron (Pogonion, Liountzi, Zagoria, Rhiza), but in Chimarra, Valona, Premeti, Leskoviki, Erseka and Korytsa as well. In June 1942 a leadership of these groups in one command was set up as the Northern Epirote National Liberation Organization (E.A.O.B.H.). Its leading spirit was Basil Sachines, a native of Douviani, a village in the Dropolis valley of Argyrocastron. His leadership of the Northern Epirote resistance, which was the local manifestation of the Greek EDES, was to cost him his life. With the aid of George Oikonomides, a schoolmaster from Dervitsiani who fell to EAM assassins in 1945, and others, he sacrified everything in the effort to resist in the name of Greece and her Allies.

As a youth Basil Sachines had studied at the School of Languages and Commerce at Constantinople. Returning to Argyrocastron he prospered as a businessman, but soon became the special target of the Albanian police for his outspoken Greek patriotism. He was frequently an unwilling visitor to Argyrocastron's grim Turkish-built fortress jail where he was locked up and beaten. He was an unregenerate "Grecomane" and the Greek liberation of Argyrocastron found him half-starved and lice-ridden after twenty days in one of the cells. Devoted and undaunted by his trials he was a born leader in the cause to which he dedicated his life. He was assassinated by Hoxha's Partisans when they raided Argyrocastron on November 17, 1943.

Ballists and Partisans

In addition to the Italians and Germans and the official arms of the Tirana régime, the Northern Epirotes had to contend with two other organizations dedicated to their destruction—the terrorist bands of the collaborationist National Front (Balli Kombëtar) and the Partisan bands of a new and alien power—the National Liberation Front (FNC) of the Communist Party.

The Balli Kombëtar, which since the Communist coup represents itself as a legitimate wartime resistance movement, was the Albanian reaction to the Northern Epirotes. Its position in respect to the Northern Epirote resistance organization was similar to that of the government-organized "chetniks" of Nedich in Yugoslavia versus Mihailovich. In other words, this group was organized for counter-resistance by arming irregular bands to supplement the regularly-constituted Fascist Militia. This simplified the problem of the Italians and the German SS and Army in fighting genuine guerilla movements. The reader who is familiar with similar units and groups in other Axis-occupied countries can readily see exactly what the Balli Kombëtar was and what kind of thugs its "chetas" consisted of. As for the top leadership, enough has been said about Messrs. Frashëri and Klisura to make further comment superfluous. Their minions, such as Hysni Lepenica, Safet Butka, Maliq Dushari etc., are now hailed by their exiled comrades-in-arms as "resistance heroes". The reader will shortly judge for himself the extent of both their resistance and their heroism.

Parallel to the emergence of Tito's NOF in Yugoslavia and the EAM in Greece, the Yugoslav-organized FNC and its parent, the Communist Party, were shortly organized in Albania. Before the war Communism in Albania was an abstract idea scattered among tiny groups of disgruntled young would-be bureaucrats who had imbibed it as students in Italian and French universities. It had no Albanian working-class roots, nor could it have since, properly speaking, there was no real Albanian working class. Out of these pseudo-intellectual coteries was born, on November 8, 1941, the Albanian Workers' Party (P.P.Sh.). As in Yugoslavia and Greece it operated behind the facade of the FNC (National Liberation Front) which was organized with the help of Tito's emissaries at Peza on September 16, 1942.

Later, as the Axis power began to fade, the Red star rose.

It gained adherents largely because of its close association with Tito and, to a lesser degree, with EAM. As the Allies won in Europe the Albanians had to jump on a new bandwagon. Allied support of Tito and EAM, the abandoning of Mihailovich and the anti-Communist resistance groups in Greece, was the deciding factor for them. When later the collaborationists were to burn their bridges behind them a considerable number of members of Balli Kombëtar's chetas became Hoxha's partisans. Totalitarians, after all, are all alike underneath.

Against such odds the Northern Epirotes took the field.

Between Two Fires

It is not the purpose of a guerilla movement to capture and hold territory. The prime objective of this type of warfare is to harass the enemy, destroy his supplies, demoralize him when and where he least expects attack and disperse to repeat the action elsewhere. Its nature is sporadic. It if were not, it would cease to be a guerilla movement and become a regular army. Its structure is such that it cannot operate outside territories where its adherents can give it aid and supplies, yet it must constantly shift its base of operations. It is everywhere and nowhere. It is a phantom force so dangerous that whole enemy divisions are sometimes tied up by its operations. The world has seen brilliant applications of it in Arabia in World War I, in the Far East in World War II and by the Communists in many places today. Yet it was in the Balkans where it was born and where it has been developed as the native form of warfare. The Northern Epirotes, no less than their Albanian opponents, are familiar with its techniques.

Wide-spread action was undertaken in December, 1942 in the regions of Pogonion and the Zagoria of Argyrocastron. Attacks on Italian-Albanian frontier posts and gendarmerie stations increased. The villages of Polytsani and Sieperi as well as the surrounding area of Pogonion, Zagoria and Malesiovon were in Epirote hands long enough to establish a headquarters and receive a British mission.

In the mountains at Theologus Monastery the Northern Epirote resistance leaders held a two-day conference beginning on February 12, 1943. It was there determined that "the invaders should be fought with all means, that armed bands should be organized, liaison effected with the resistance organizations in

Greece and funds collected to meet the needs of the struggle."

As a result the Italians and Albanians took concerted action. Operating with units of the Albanian Fascist Militia, the Italians tried to oust the Northern Epirote guerillas from their captured strongholds. Failing, the Italians bombed the villages of Topovon and Polytsani from the air, killing many non-combatant residents. Elsewhere, the Northern Epirote guerillas managed to drive the Italians and Albanians from the Vourko (Delvinon) and Rhizon sectors. In those parts of Northern Epirus where resistance had not yet taken a concrete form the Italians and Albanians applied severe measures. In March 1943, 160 inhabitants of Korytsa were sent to concentration camps for suspected underground activities connected with the Northern Epirote resistance.

Having failed to dislodge effectively the Northern Epirote guerillas, the Italians and the Albanian Militia entrusted their operations to the chetas of Balli Kombëtar which had sprung up for this purpose.

To the Italians the Ballists outlined a plan to swoop down guerilla-fashion on villages suspected of Northern Epirote sympathies and to burn, plunder and murder in such a manner as would demoralize their enemies. With plunder and arson as the bait, they had no trouble recruiting for their counter-resistance bands. The targets chosen by the Ballists offer proof that the masters were again being used for the stooges' purposes. Outside of a limited number of strategically placed Grecophone villages, Moslem fiefs were bypassed and the concentration of these bands was directed against the largely Albanophone Christian villages that were independent of the beys. Before undertaking their operation the Ballists first tried to lure the Northern Epirotes to their own destruction. In terms reminiscent of Ali Pasha's wooing of the Souliotes to their own suicide, the Ballists invited the Northern Epirotes to a conference.

This was held in June 1943 at the Bektashli Teqe (Moslem Monastery) of Argyrocastron. Balli Kombëtar's "offer" consisted of collaboration with the Northern Epirotes against the Axis if the latter foreswore their allegiance to Greece and recognized the new frontiers of "Greater Albania". The Ballists pretended to be willing to bury the hatchet, but, knowing whose skulls would be chosen for the operation, the Northern Epirotes turned a deaf ear.

It was from that conference that the Ballists emerged with

their cards on the table. Their slogan was to be, "Digj shtëpi të bënë Shqipëri"—"Burn a home to build Albania." One does not launch a pogrom without whipping up one's followers with slogans. The Black Hundreds of Tsarist Russia rode to the cry, "Bey zhidov, spasey Rossiyu!" ("Smite the Jews, Save Russia!")

At the same time another opponent with more persuasive means began to feel out the Northern Epirotes—Enver Hoxha's FNC. It assumed the guise of a proposal by the British Liaison that EAM and EDES collaborate. Having thrown their weight with Tito in Yugoslavia, the British and Americans of the Middle East Command felt obliged to support his Greek and Albanian counterparts. The war had reached Italian soil and shortly Mussolini was to fall. In September Italy surrendered unconditionally to the Allies and her place in Albania was taken by Hitler's troops. For reasons that appear clear if one considers the illusion of Soviet-Western relations in World War II as well as the extent of Communist infiltration into OSS and its British counterpart, the task of driving the Axis out of the Balkans was entrusted to totalitarians of another hue—Red.

Meanwhile the Axis and the Albanian Militia were active. Punitive action in the region of Moschopolis-Korytsa in July resulted in the destruction of the historic Monastery of St. John Baptist at Moschopolis as well as ten Moschopolite homes. In August the Italians and the Militia raided the villages of Belovoda and Giantsi. The former, entirely Christian, was totally burned and three refugees from southern Epirus were executed. At Giantsi, the entire Christian quarter was set on fire. Six Moslem homes were destroyed by accident when the blaze spread.

Urged by the British to enter a disastrous collaboration with the Communists, the Northern Epirotes were persuaded to confer with representatives of EAM and FNC on August 1, 1943 at the village of Episcopi, near Argyrocastron. The Argyrocastron Communist Qemal Karagjozi represented the FNC. EAM was represented by Miltiades Kyrgiannes who was to lead Communist forces against EDES in 1944 and who later perished by the hand of a fellow guerilla during the Greek "civil war" in 1948. Because of the vagueness of the Communists and Albanians on a Northern Epirote union with Greece, the conference ended with a decision to re-convene. The very next day, the Ballists struck.

The Ballist campaign of extermination began when the chetas fell upon the villages of Vrachogorantzi and Glyna and the Christian quarter of Libochovo. On the morning of August 2 they had removed every bit of furniture and valuables from the village of Glyna and had set fire to the houses. They then rounded up twenty-five of the villagers and in the afternoon took them out and shot them. Libochovo, eight of the Christian townsmen, including the Orthodox priest, Father Achilles, were executed. The priest was singled out to be burned alive.

Quick to answer the outrage, the Northern Epirote guerillas attacked the Ballists shortly afterward in their Libochovo stronghold. Driven out after a two day battle, the Ballists were still able to take sweet revenge. They singled out two nearby Christian villages—Stegopolis and Upper Lambovon ("of the Cross"). In the former village, after the customary sacking, its sixty-six homes were all destroyed. Those which were of stone and not easily destroyed they dynamited. Nothing was spared. Four inhabitants were executed on the spot. Nineteen were taken captive. At Upper Lambovon, all of the 130 homes met the same fate. Thirteen persons were murdered on the spot and fifteen captives were taken.

As arranged, 150 Northern Epirote representatives of the resistance from all parts of Northern Eprius met on the 8th of August at Memorachi, Delvino, to consider the basis upon which they could meet British demands that they collaborate with FNC. Their decision was embodied in a letter forwarded to FNC headquarters. Its terms were that the Northern Epirotes were to continue complete organic independence from any other movement and would join FNC in attacks against the Axis forces only if the latter and its allies recognized the future disposition of Northern Epirus under the Atlantic Charter's principle of self-determination.

These terms were formalized in the Konispolis Agreement signed by the Northern Epirote resistance organization, by Rexhep Plako for the FNC, by Qemal Karagjozi for the Central Committee of the Albanian Workers' Party (under the pseudonym Çelniku) and Miltiades Kyrgiannes for the EAM-ELAS.

The Northern Epirotes had good reason to mistrust the FNC because it was Albanian. Their suspicion of EAM was not less because it was Greek. Nevertheless, the British military mission, with headquarters then at Polytsani, extended every verbal assurance possible. Ballist attacks on Christian villages were increasing daily in severity. This combination of pressures forced a large number of the Northern Epirotes to deny their own better judgment and follow the line of cooperation with the Communists laid down by the British.

In spite of this uneasy arrangement, Basil Sachines did not cease to warn that, "a time will come when the Albanians, Ballist and Partisan, will unite and strike us together." The British were not then impressed. The FNC secretly marked Sachines for liquidation.

The fall of Italy and the German assumption of command in Albania gave the Balli Kombëtar an even freer hand. A self-appointed "Albanian National Committee", of which a number of members were Ballists, functioned as a provisional government from October 8 until November 6, 1943 under Nazi *gauleiter* Dr. Neubacher. On the latter date a formal puppet government was installed by the Nazis in Tirana, the Premier of which was Ballist Rexhep Mitrovica, a Kossovar. Mitrovica today is one of the most influential of the emigré clique in Istanbul. To his machinations may be credited the hostile attitude against Greek claims on Northern Epirus of a large section of the Turkish press.

The Northern Epirote guerillas were also affected by the Italian surrender. Guerilla battalions under a central command were formed out of the bands that had operated before. This unification of forces was felt throughout the province. Many districts were entirely under Epirote administration and fierce battles took place between Northern Epirotes and a mixed force of Ballist chetas, Albanian Fascist Militia units and Germans. The latter restricted themselves in lieu of a sufficient occupation force, (for the Germans now needed every man they could get for the Russian and western fronts), to providing officers in an advisory capacity to the Albanians. These Nazis were both Wehrmacht and SS.

The large-scale Epirote offensive launched upon the Italian surrender included operations in the region of Korytsa. At Pogradets a particularly fierce battle took place with the outgoing Italians. The town was taken only after the Italians had looted and burnt a part of it in their retreat.

It was not until October that German-Ballist forces undertook to dislodge the Epirotes from the sector. The Epirotes made a stand in the strongholds of the Kiari Mountains, in spite of the fact that many Moslem villages nestled in those hills were also Ballist strongholds. Thus, an unusually large and locally organized Ballist force was ranged against them. The deciding battle in this operation was fought around the village of Borova. As a result of the unequal struggle the Northern Epirotes retreated and the Ballists entered the Christian village. In the presence of German officers, they set fire to it and locked up those inhabitants they found in their own homes to which they set fire. One hundred thirty villagers, irrespective of age or sex, were lined up and shot the same day. The body of the village priest, Father Gregory, remained hanging for a week on the bridge near the village, a mute witness that the Ballists had passed that way.

By December the Ballists had retaken the area almost entirely. Among the villages destroyed was Phlioki. It was not, however, until 1944, when the strength of the Epirote resistance had been spent almost completely, that extensive Ballist punitive expeditions reduced the Christian villages to nearly complete destruction.

Other battles were fought in the west during the same period of intensified activity. Every one of them was met with Ballist reprisals against Christian villages. After one such battle, the Ballists and their Nazi comrades entered the village of Krania and set fire to it after looting, among other things, 400 tons of corn flour. Fighting in the district of Argyrocastron reached its highest intensity in December. One of the villages plundered and completely gutted was Mouzina, where most of the inhabitants of its 200 homes escaped death by fleeing to the hills.

At the same time an attempt was made by the Epirotes to take the airfield at Argrocastron. Failing, they were pursued by Ballist forces under Ismail Golemi, Ruhi Runa, Vehip Runa (son of the Prefect of Argyrocastron) and Seit Shejho.

The retreating Epirotes managed to elude capture, but the Ballists gained revenge by plundering the remaining villages of Liountzi as well as Kato (Lower) Lambovon ("of Zappas") and Lekli. A summarized catalogue of the destructions reached this author from refugees in Athens.

VILLAGE:	NO. HOMES:	NO. BURNED:	PERSONS MURDERED:	CAPTIVES:
Lekli	40	40	8	—
Terbouki	22	22	5	—
Lower Lambovon	75	59	4	12
Khountekouki	18	18	3	—
Kargianni	32	18	2	—
Kakozi	28	13	1	—
Giates	25	17	—	—
Erinti	47	47	7	9
Nokovon	58	52	2	13
Mingouli	33	29	1	8
Kalezi	25	28	3	—
Doxati	42	12	2	—
Kestorati	40	34	3	—
Sarakinista	37	22	3	15
Tranousista	23	23	1	—
Krina	19	19	2	—
Soukha	29	29	4	9
Seltsi	60	8	1	12
Totals 18	653	490	52	78

Thus was a once populous and historic region that had given birth to Greek statesmen and benefactors reduced to ashes. Not one village in the area was left intact. Stegopolis and Upper Lambovon, not included above, had been first in the general destruction, as previously related.

In the village of Doxati, Father John Telis, the village priest, was among the dead. In several well-substantiated instances which recall the Middle Ages several persons, among them an old man of eighty, were impaled alive and roasted in their death agonies.

For all their activities, the Epirotes were caught between two fires and doomed by the inability of the British and Americans to cope with the Communist forces the west had chosen to back. In the larger game played on a world scale they appeared too small a pawn to survive a situation over which they had no control. They were then, as now, in the power of friends who did not recognize their value in the game of expediency that surrendered half the earth to Soviet tyranny.

Hoxha's Yugoslav Communist advisers knew their holy writ well. Lenin had schooled his followers to, "Surprise your antagonists while their forces are scattered, prepare new successes, however small, but daily; keep up the moral ascendency which the first successful rising has given to you; rally those vacillating elements to your side which always follow the strongest impulse, and which always look out for the safer side; force your enemies to a retreat before they can collect their strength against you; . . ."[90]

These have always been the standing battle orders of the world revolution, and Hoxha followed them scrupulously and to their final conclusion.

The bad faith in which the Communists had entered the alliance with the Northern Epirotes—a bad faith since recognized universally as a Red trademark—became increasingly dangerous throughout August-November, 1943. Added to the savage Ballist reprisals was the Red stab in the back.

Hoxha succeeded both in swaying the British into accepting his thesis that organic unity of the Northern Epirotes and FNC was necessary for concerted anti-Axis action and in destroying the effectiveness of the Northern Epirotes.

On more than one occasion the Northern Epirotes and the FNC attacked jointly only for the FNC to withdraw, leaving the Germans free to surround and annihilate the Epirotes. The climax of Communist perfidy was reached when, in mid-November, the FNC shot Basil Sachines and almost provoked open warfare with the Northern Epirotes.

If this had happened, the Epirotes would have faced openly two foes devoted to their destruction. This was prevented by the British mission which, following higher instructions to play along with the FNC, called for a compromise or, in blunter language, told the Northern Epirotes to give in for the sake of a "united front" or suffer the consequences. One of the consequences was a threat to stop all Allied supplies to the Northern Epirotes.

Again following tactics which since have become more familiar in other areas of East-West conflict, the Communists smoothed over their most blatant double-crosses with declarations of their friendly desires to compose all differences in a conference—on their own terms, of course.

Another conference with the FNC, this time at Polytsani, followed. The Greek Communist EAM was also represented by an observer. The following paper compromise was worked out: Subject to approval by an FNC congress, the right of the Northern Epirotes to full separation from the Albanian state

[90] Lenin, V. I., *Can the Bolsheviks Retain State Power?* tr., *Selected Works*, Vol. V., N.Y., 1942, pp. 291-292.

after the war, i.e. to union with Greece, was recognized. Meanwhile, the fighting forces of the Northern Epirotes were to remain autonomous under leaders who would become a special FNC Northern Epirote bureau until they decided to detach themselves from the Albanian state.

This seemed to satisfy the British and offered a way out for those Northern Epirotes who felt the situation was otherwise hopeless. Naturally, the Communists played false as they have always done and destroyed those whom they embraced.

As a result, half of the Northern Epirote resistance was swallowed up by the FNC, scattered, rendered impotent and then physically liquidated. Half of it formally joined the uncompromisingly anti-Axis and anti-Communist EDES of General Napoleon Zervas.

Those who chose the latter path eventually lived to find themselves destitute post-war exiles in southern Epirus, an iron curtain between themselves and the homes they had struggled to free. The others were destroyed in a manner made clear by the following illustration:

One of the immediate results of the great upsurge of Northern Epirote activity had been the liberation of Chimarra. A provisional three man committee set up a local Greek administration in anticipation of an Allied invasion of the Balkans. The FNC, in treating with this situation, issued the following secret directive to its forces:

"From the Central Committee
"Secret Orders
'To the Regional Committees of Valona and Argyrocastron:
"February, 1944.

"The region of Eastern and Western Chimarra must be taken immediately. You must defend yourselves against a possible German attempt to seize this region. In case it is impossible to achieve this, the Germans must be provoked to set fire to the villages of these regions. All Greek nationalists must be seized and sent to I.K.*

(s) "Nako Stavro
"Secretary of the Central Committee of the National Liberation Front"

Thus, when the Northern Epirotes were cleared out of the region of Chimarra, Valona and Santi Quaranta, the Partisans were able to take their places. The story of how the British failed to profit by the bad advice given the Northern Epirotes followed

(*A designated place of execution.)

later the same year when British troops finally landed in the Balkans.

> "During this period 40 R. M. Commando, now under the command of Lieutenant-Colonel R. W. Stankey, was engaged in operations . . . of the Royal Marines. Landing in Albania in October, 1944, together with 2 Army Commando, they took part in the capture of Sarandë, the only port available for the evacuation of the German garrison in Corfu."[91]

The epilogue to this British action was that there was now no Northern Epirote resistance movement to greet the British, thanks to the mistakes of the British themselves. Only isolated Epirote bands, hunted by Ballist and Partisan alike, still existed. Thus, instead of a welcome, the British commandos found that no "anti-fascist" partisans would lift a finger to help them against the Germans. But that was not the worst of it.

A Northern Epirote band which had miraculously survived intact then bolted the FNC into which it had been incorporated and attacked the Germans. Ten Germans, among them the German colonel in command, fell into the hands of the Northern Epirotes whose chief, Demetrius Maxacoulis, promptly delivered them to Colonel Stankey. As a result, the FNC Partisans, Britain's erstwhile allies, turned their guns on the British and Epirotes, taking a British Commando officer, two soldiers and Maxacoulis prisoners. The British prisoners were freed from a Communist jail at the end of World War II. Maxacoulis later escaped to Greece.

A Commando unit which had been detached upon landing and sent to the villages to distribute food to the hungry population was surrounded by Partisans outside of the village of Phoenice (Delvinon), disarmed and given a severe thrashing. As a result, the British withdrew their forces from Santi Quaranta and went to Greek Corfu where they received the surrender of the German garrison. They had begun to pay the price of their betrayal of the Northern Epirotes to Hoxha.

The bombing of British cruisers later, the expulsion of British missions, the indignities suffered by the British since, are all installment payments of that price, which may yet be paid in full.

With Mihailovich, whose fate was their own, the Northern Epirotes of the resistance can say in retrospect, "Fate was merci-

[91] Lockhart, Sir Robert Bruce, K.C.G.M., *The Marines Were There*, pp. 150-151.

less to me when it threw me into this maelstrom. I wanted much, I started much, but the gale of the world carried away me and my work."

The Last Flame of Vengeance

As the European phase of the Second World War neared its finish, the Ballists saw their hopes fading with the retreating Swastika. The Partisans, thanks to Allied blunders which had made them possible, began to fill the vacuum in Albania as their comrades-in-arms, the Yugoslav NOF and the EAM-ELAS were doing. They had no need to consider anything except the promise of utter and ruthless power. Moscow's red star was casting its baleful light on the Balkans.

The Ballists, in a final spurt of savage frenzy, put the remaining Christian villages to the torch. Out of the catalogues of horror, the real authors of which unfortunately continue to enjoy British and American patronage, a sampling is given here, culled from refugees from Northern Epirus shortly after World War II. It is a partial list of the atrocities in the villages of the Korytsa, Premeti and Moschopolis regions:

1. The village of *Liavdari,* Christian: was burned entirely in January, 1944, by the Ballist band of Dylber Xerhia. Three villagers, one named Lazaros Samaras, were executed.

2. *Karbanios,* Christian: was burned entirely in January, 1944 by the Ballists under Maliq and Cane Dushari. Nine villagers, among them Constantine Alexiou, Basil Alexiou and Athansius Letsos, were executed.

3. *Osoyia,* mixed: The Christian quarter was burned in January, 1944. The Moslem quarter (Goraçani) was untouched. The Ballists who did the burning were led by Maliq Dushari and Riza Bej Moglica. Nine villagers were executed, four of whom were Panos Delis, John Delis, Anestos Poulakis and Menelaos Papagregoriou.

4. *Ginikasi,* Christian: Burned entirely in January, 1944, by the Ballists under Mustafa Qeroshi, Mete Strelca and Mako Treshova, after it was completely looted. Two villagers were executed.

5. *Pounmira,* Christian: Burned entirely in May, 1944, by the Ballist bands led by Haqi Losmi and Nihas Çesma. Six villagers, among them Alekos Theodosiou and Athanasius Ziou, were executed.

6. *Opari,* Christian: Burned entirely by the band of Haqi Losmi.

7. *Misrasi,* Christian: Six homes were burned.

8. *Moschopolis,* Christian: Burned once by the Italians, twice by the Ballists. The second and third burnings occurred in January, 1944. The Ballists were led by Dervish Bejo from Georgevitsa. Its 24 churches were completely razed. Sixteen Moschopolites, three of whom were Andreas and Anastasius Samis and Michael Panis, were executed.

9. *Sipiska,* Christian: Thirty two homes burned after the whole village was sacked by the band of Haqi Losmi.

10. *Polena,* Christian: Burned entirely and 60 persons executed by the Ballists of Zade and Husejn Dershniku, October, 1944. Among the executed were Raphael Mingas, Raphael Polenas and Elias Apostolou.

11. *Orman Tsiflik,* Christian: Burned entirely by the Ballists. Sixty-four inhabitants were tortured to death by order of the Prefect of Korytsa, Xhevat Bej Starova, October, 1944. Among the victims were Pantelis Kitas, Markos Kitas, Michael Kitas, Lazaros Gatsis and his wife.

12. *Ravonik,* mixed: The Christian quarter alone was burned by the Ballist band of Mece Turani in October, 1944. Forty-four persons were executed among them Evangelus Stratis.

13. *Bobostitsa,* Christian: Of its 300 homes only 26 were saved. It was first sacked and then burned by the bands of Pasko Kolaneci and Bajram Bej Goca in February, 1944. Sixteen persons, among them women and children, were tortured to death.

14. *Rembetsi,* Christian: Half of the village was burned after most of the inhabitants were physically maltreated and the whole village sacked by the Ballists under Rahman Zvarishti and Gani Zablaku. Sixteen inhabitants, among them Epaminontas Charalampou and Spyridon Sioros were executed.

15. *Pogianni,* mixed: In February, 1944, the Christian quarter was burned entirely by the Ballists. Eight persons, among them Anestis Vrettos and his brother-in-law were executed. Only one Moslem home, previously burned by the Italians, was touched.

16. *Kamenitsa,* mixed: Burned in April, 1944, by the Ballist band of Zade Dershniku.

17. *Dyshnica,* mixed (Moslem majority): The Christian quarter was burned entirely in the presence of German officers by the Ballists one month before the German withdrawal.

Sixteen persons, among them a pregnant woman, were beheaded. The killers were Ballists led by Gani Zablaku, Mece Turani and Qamil Kosnica. This happened in September, 1944. Not a single Moselm home was touched.

18. *Nitsa,* Christian: Entirely burned by the band of Kajo Treshova, July, 1944. Among the thirteen persons executed was the priest Father Papageorgiou.

19. *Lekna,* Christian: The village was burned and 44 inhabitants executed by the Ballist band of Njazi Çesma in June, 1944.

20. *Grabotska,* Christian: The village was burned and 16 persons were executed in June, 1944, by the band of Njazi Çesma.

21. *Podgoziani,* Christian: Was burned and 14 inhabitants executed by Njazi Çesma's band.

22. *Bourgaletsi,* mixed: In reprisal for the death of notorious Ballist terrorist Sabri Panariti at Korytsa, half the Christian quarter was burned by the Ballists. Four persons, among them Argyrios Ginis, were executed.

23. *Pogradets,* mixed: In April, 1944, the entire Christian quarter as well as all the market shops owned by Christians were burned after looting and 44 inhabitants were executed.

24. *Aliaroupi,* mixed: The entire Christian neighborhood was burned by volunteer Kossovar irregulars. Four inhabitants were executed.

25. *Svirina,* mixed: The Ballist band of Edhem Bej Frashëri burned 11 Christian homes and executed three persons.

26. *Soviani,* mixed: Edhem Bej Frashëri's band burned eight Christian homes and executed two inhabitants.

27. *Darda,* Christian: Thirty homes were burned by the Ballist band of Demir Shehu and 11 persons were executed.

28. *Sinitsa,* Christian: The Ballist bands of Demir Shehu and Qamil Kosnica looted and burned the village.

29. *Kiouteza,* Christian: Six homes were burned by the bands of Demir Shehu and Qamil Kosnica.

30. *Bratvitsa,* Christian: The village priest was included among 16 persons executed. Eighteen homes were burned.

31. *Zitsista,* Christian: Twenty-two homes were burned and nine inhabitants, including the wife of Dimetrius Petropoulos, were executed by the Ballists.

32. *Chotsista,* Christian: The Ballist band of Gani Zablaku burned the larger part of the village, including all the churches, and executed 32 inhabitants.

33. *Progri,* mixed: Gani Zablaku's band here burned nine Christian homes and executed four inhabitants.

34 *Treni,* mixed: Six Christian homes were burned by Gani Zablaku's band.

35. *Pliousi,* mixed: The Ballist bands of Safet Butka and Mehmet Elmisi burned 16 Christian homes and executed four inhabitants.

36. *Lioubonia,* mixed: Ten Christian homes were burned and five persons executed by the bands of Safet Butka and Mehmet Elmisi.

37. *Kiafzezi,* mixed: Eight Christian homes were burned and seven persons executed by the Ballist band led by Pasko Kolaneci.

38. *Roziani,* mixed: Four homes were burned.

39. *Stika,* Christian: Twenty-two homes were burned and a number of villagers executed by the band of Safet Butka.

40. *Skorovoti,* mixed: Seven Christian homes were burned. Not a single Moslem home nor person suffered the slightest injury.

41. *Gostivisti,* mixed: Thirty Christian homes were burned. Then, the Ballist bands of Rahman Zvarishti, Asllan Dolaneci and Safet Butka took 11 of the Christian villagers and led them to the village church where they were slain before the altar.

42. *Sialesi,* Christian: A number of villagers were executed after the place was burned entirely by the Ballists in the presence of German officers.

43. *Germeni,* Christian: The village was burned in the same manner as *Sialesi* and a number of inhabitants were executed.

44. *Ponta,* mixed: A mixed neighborhood of Christians and Moslems was destroyed by the Italians. On a later occasion, the Ballists burned the remainder of the Christian quarter.

45. *Voditsa,* mixed: Eight Christian villagers were executed and the entire Christian quarter burned by the Ballists.

46. *Erseka,* mixed: Most of the Christian homes as well as the marketplace were burned by the Ballists. Among numerous persons executed were Nicholas Mingas and Soterios Priphtis.

47. *Leskoviki,* mixed: The Ballists and Germans burned most of it and many of the Christian inhabitants, among them Antonios Kitas, were executed.

48. *Tserka,* Christian: The village was entirely burned and 35 persons were executed by the Ballists.

49. *Viglista,* mixed: The entire Christian quarter was burned. The marketplace was then looted by the Ballists in the presence of German officers. Responsible for this, as well as for the atrocities at Leskoviki and Tserka, was the Ballist band of Safet Butka.[92]

50. *Katoundi,* Christian: The village was burned and a number of persons were executed by the Ballists led by Demir Starovecka and Pile Backa.

51. *Treska Stratoberda*: The village was entirely burned and a number of persons were executed by the above bands.

52. *Trebitska Kabliari*: ditto.

53. *Mitsani*: ditto.

The list can be extended to cover many more pages. The entire carnage, arson and imprisonment suffered by the Northern Epirotes at the hands of Balli Kombëtar and its Italian and German masters came to over 2,000 murdered, 5,000 imprisoned, 2,000 taken hostages to concentration camps, over 15,000 homes, churches and schools burned, over 50,000 head of livestock stolen, and the equivalent of more than 200,000 gold sovereigns looted.

This terrible period, however, was but another chapter in the continuing horrors visited upon these Greek captives of Albania. It was followed immediately by the advent to power of Albanian communism and the expropriation of the tattered remains of once-flourishing towns and villages. Without a break in the pathetic series of circumstances, yesterday became today and the martyrdom of Northern Epirus entered its present phase. The end does not appear in sight.

[92] In connection with Safet Butka and Hysni Lepenica, it is interesting to note the fondness with which they are remembered by their now-exiled comrades in crime. On Page 1 of the Ballist organ *Flamuri,* No 56-57 of 11-10-1954, we read: "The strength of Balli Kombetar consists in the sacrifice of its martyrs: HYSNI LEPENICA, Commander-in-Chief of Balli Kombetar . . . His death left an emptiness in the ranks of the national resistance . . . The first shot of the civil war against us was fired by the Reds in the region of Korça where valiant Professor SAFET BUTKA was at the head of the Balli Kombetar forces."

Chapter XIII

THE RED TERROR

The "People's Republic"

Jungle anarchy was the immediate prelude to the consolidation of Communist rule in Albania following the German withdrawal from the Balkans late in 1944. Some of the Albanian quislings fled abroad, while others, such as the Fascist militia commander Riza Kodheli, the late Dr. Omer Nishani and others, were expediently accepted and used by the Albanian Communist leadership until they died or were purged.

The all-too-familiar pattern of government by purge, arbitrary confiscation and forced labor—hallmarks of the Stalin era—became the style of the years that followed. At first, before the borders could be effectively sealed, Northern Epirotes fled as best they could, arriving in free Greece with no more than the clothes on their backs. Tent cities housed whole families as international relief organizations and the Greek government attempted to cope as best they could, despite the fact that Greece was herself engaged in a bitter Moscow-created turmoil.

A 21-gun salute greeted Enver Hoxha and Mehmet Shehu in December, 1944, when they entered Tirana. The same scene was being repeated throughout Eastern Europe where, with or without benefit of the Soviet Army, total terror installed itself in the seats of power. On November 10, 1945, Albania's Red regime received provisional recognition from Britain, the United States and France. The Americans and British, however, withdrew that recognition shortly thereafter when Hoxha tore up his country's adherence to international law and expelled representatives of the West from Albania. A slender link remained in the French Legation that stayed on, joined later by an Italian trade mission. This non-recognition, however, did not prevent a horsetrade in the U.N. some years later whereby Albania, though still unrecognized by the United States and Britain, was admitted into the international organization.

The legal farce of rigged elections with near-100 percent results was over in December, 1945. While the hand of the Soviets was heavy throughout the land, new victims were added daily to the martyrdom of Greek freedom in Northern Epirus. Hundreds were executed as "Anglo-American spies and *agents provocateurs,* Greek monarcho-fascists, Kulaks" and the like. What little had been saved from destruction under the Axis and its Albanian collaborationists was expropriated in the name of the "People's Republic" by the Albanian Workers' Party.

There was to be no mercy for anyone. Even women, many advanced in years, were torn from homes no longer theirs to toil and die constructing railways and canals as "volunteers." The chastity of Northern Epirote womanhood was violated by Red bravos who were done with "bourgeois morality". Children were egged on by Communist instructors to betray their elders and a handful of wheat became the reward for denunciation.

At first, Albania's dynasts looked to Belgrade for tutelage. Yugoslav "advisers" were everywhere in the country and huge signs in Tirana bore the legend "Tito-Enver".

Tito may now have just cause to regret that, while the Soviet-Yugoslav honeymoon was on, he did not annex Albania as Stalin suggested, for soon, from a mere stooge, Hoxha was to become a thorn in his side.

Almost on the eve of the Stalin-Tito break, Stalin astounded the Yugoslavs with just this proposal. Milovan Djilas relates:

> ". . . to my surprise, Stalin said: 'We have no special interest in Albania. We agree to Yugoslavia swallowing Albania! . . .' At this he gathered together the fingers of his right hand and, bringing them to his mouth, he made a motion as if to swallow them.
>
> "I was astonished, almost struck dumb by Stalin's manner of expressing himself and by the gesture of swallowing, but I do not know whether this was visible on my face, for I tried to make a joke of it and to regard this as Stalin's customary drastic and picturesque manner of expression. Again I explained: 'It is not a matter of swallowing, but unification!' At this Molotov interjected: 'But that is swallowing!' And Stalin added, again with that gesture of his: 'Yes, yes. Swallowing! But we agree with you: you ought to swallow Albania—the sooner the better.' " [93]

To understand the context of Yugoslav desires for "unification" of Albania is to realize that there are, in fact, two Albanias—half of geographic and ethnic Albania (Gegnija) having been occupied by Serbia since 1912 and being now the

[93] Djilas, Milovan, *Conversations With Stalin,* N. Y., 1962, p. 143.

Kossovo-Metohija ("Kosmet") region of Yugoslavia. For the Albanians, joining northern Albania to Yugoslavia as a Federated Republic would double the population of Albania and would erase a boundary that cuts across the land of the Gheg "malesori" or mountain tribes. For Yugoslavia, it would eliminate an internal minority problem that has been allayed but not solved by the creation of "Kosmet".

For both the United States and the Soviet Union, it would today—20 years later—remove from the troubled Balkans Peking's only European ally.

When the Tito-Stalin break did come, Hoxha opted for Moscow. In the Khrushchev era, with the easing of tensions in Soviet-Yugoslav relations, he swung over to Peking in an effort to keep the grip of Stalinist terror firm in Albania. In each instance, the heads of his opposition rolled.

And Yet They Hope

Submerged in this tide of internal terror, the silent hope of Northern Epirus would be easy to forget, were it not for reminders that it persists, needing only circumstances to reassert itself. However much this small but important fact is overlooked in Moscow and Washington, it is an ever-present reality in Tirana and Athens.

The Greco-Albanian border is a visible symbol of this today. Twelve years ago, a veteran British observer of the Balkans noted:

> "Russia's other Balkan satellite, Albania, has not with the years become more reasonable, more willing to acknowledge that the Greek claim to Northern Epirus is founded on justice and on the aspirations of the people who live there. Albania's attitude has not changed since I was in that hapless region some dozen years ago. Around the frontier the Greek Army, the *gendarmerie* and the villagers are inextricably woven together. Peasants are armed and trained under the command of the military unit of their area. Men from three villages are formed into a company; nine villages for a 'battalion.' In Florina, a town of only 1,200 people, where only one man—the doctor—owns a private car, there are 70 gendarmes stationed." [94]

Another observer, this time nearly a decade later and from the other side of the border, writes:

[94] Baerlein, Henry, in *Fortnightly*, London, Jan. 1954, p. 25.

"More instructive still than all the stories about 'spies' and 'subversive elements' was my trip along the Greek frontier from Argyrocastro to Leskovik. Needless to say, no Albanian may travel this route without special permission. The barbed-wire entanglements in the river along the border, the dead man's strip, the numerous watchtowers, and the innumerable checks by Albanian military control points were all symptoms of political hysteria. We had the greatest difficulty in getting past the controls, in spite of the bundle of special passes my escort had been given by the authorities in Tirana and Argyrocastro. At the most important control point, a few hundred yards from the Greek border, the sentry vanished into the checkpoint building with all our papers and did not reappear for a long time, the time it took to clear everything to his satisfaction." [95]

This same observer makes quite clear the reason for this extraordinary vigilance. He notes:

"While I do not claim that any concrete conclusions about the state of political affairs in South Albania can be drawn from these few indications, there is probably some basis for the particularly stringent security precautions being applied there. The leaders in Tirana may well have to face action from the Greeks as well as from the Yugoslavs. Minorities are always a delicate subject, particularly those living in strongly nationalist states under totalitarian rule. Moreover, Athens has said for years that when the Cyprus question was out of the way, the Greek Government would energetically tackle the matter of North Epirus, *and there is little doubt that the Greek population of southern Albania has been following the Greek Government's intentions with both interest and sympathy.* [italics mine]."

How justified this apprehension may be may be judged from events that have transpired in Albania since the fall from grace of Nikita Khrushchev. Current headlines elucidate further. The following is a news item that appeared on October 30, 1964, on the front page of the New York Greek-American daily *Atlantis*:

"IOANNINA, Oct. 29—Reliable sources indicate that last week, after a betrayal, the Albanian secret police uncovered the spark of a conspiracy by a group of Albanian officers who were intending to overthrow Enver Hoxha. The sources say that at the head of this group was found a general of Northern Epirote origin and that the officers moving to overthrow Enver Hoxha, upon being informed that they had been discovered, made an unsuccessful attempt to flee to Italy, Yugoslavia and Greece. These were arrested and all shot without trial.

"Following this, the Albanian authorities began a drive against the Northern Epirote Greek element and arrested many persons. As a result of this drive, the following fled and turned themselves over to

[95] Hamm, Harry, *Albania-China's Beachhead in Europe*, N.Y., 1963, p. 71.

the Greek border posts, many of these Northern Epirote Greeks stating that they have relatives or friends in the United States: Stavros Bratsikas, 16, from the village of Dritzani, a student at the academy in Argyrocastron; E. Pappas and E. Tsingas, both from the village of Alkion of Delvino; Michael Tsikas from Baltsika, Santi Quaranta; Basil Bitzis from Delvino, aged 15; Basil Kokovetsis, 16, from Kakavia; Christos Bitas and George Giorgiadis, from Dropolis, Argyrocastron; George Evangelou from Leskoviki.

"Among them are included also two students of the University from the village of Darda, Korytsa, the names of whom were not made public.

"The above Northern Epirote escapees into Greece describe in darkest terms the life of the Greeks in Northern Epirus as well as that of the Albanian people in general."

Chapter XIV

GREECE, THE UNITED STATES AND NORTHERN EPIRUS

Greece, Ever Hopeful

Despite the blood that ran in Greek streets as a result of the Communist conspiracy, the Greek people emerging from World War II cherished the somewhat romantic notion that their sacrifices entitled them to justice before the seats of the mighty. The forthcoming Peace Conference, they believed, could not fail to recognize their sacrifice—the "No" they had thrown in the Axis' teeth and the five years of passion and crucifixion that followed.

A gigantic rally of 150,000 Athenians on Nov. 18, 1945, cheered exiled Bishop Panteleimon of Argyrocastron as he demanded justice for Northern Epirus. This was the greatest mass demonstration held in modern Greek history. Premier Panagiotes Canellopoulos pointed out to foreign newsmen from his hotel balcony, "You are beholding the population of Athens in mass meeting to express with dignity and modesty the national pain at the sufferings of their brethren in Northern Epirus."

The Greek people believed that the United States and Great Britain were with them. Many recalled that at the time of the Peace Conference in 1920, the United States Government had not been unsympathetic, though it had been outfoxed by Italy. On May 17, 1920, the United States Senate had unanimously adopted Resolution 324 during the Second Session of the 66th Congress. Introduced by Senator Henry Cabot Lodge, it had unequivocally stated:

> "Resolved: That it is the sense of the Senate that Northern Epirus (including Corytza) . . . where a strong Greek population predominates, should be awarded by the Peace Conference to Greece and become incorporated in the Kingdom of Greece."

Explaining his vote, a future president of the United States,

Sen. Warren Gamaliel Harding stated on Oct. 24, 1920 to the president of the Massachusetts Greek Republican Club:

> "I voted for the Lodge resolution declaring the sense of the Senate that Northern Epirus . . . should go to Greece.
> ". . . I stand for a settlement which will do full justice to the Greek people. America will always do its full and humane part in the world while insisting that it be directed by its own conscience and its own conception of right and justice."

American friends of Greece gave hope to the Greek people that the issue would be decided with America on their side. As early as 1945, these American friends organized a "Justice for Greece" Committee. The list of sponsors of this American organization was headed by such philhellenes as Mrs. Calvin Coolidge, Honorary Chairman, Mr. Chauncey Hamlin, Chairman, and former Undersecretary Sumner Welles, Chairman of the Advisory Board.

Largely due to this reawakening of American concern in the just solution of this complex problem, the Senate of the United States, on July 29, 1946, unanimously reaffirmed the 1920 resolution by adopting Resolution S.82, again resolving:

> ". . . it is the sense of the Senate that Northern Epirus (including Corytza) . . . where a strong Greek population predominates, should be awarded by the Peace Conference to Greece and become incorporated in the territory of Greece."

Greek hopes that a favorable response could be expected from Great Britain were based, in part, on the statement of British Foreign Minister Anthony Eden in Commons on Dec. 17, 1942, in a declaration of British foreign policy:

> "His Majesty's Government regard of the question of the frontiers of the Albanian State after the war is a question which will have to be considered at the peace settlement."

That the above was intended by Sir Anthony to refer to Greece's claim is confirmed by a statement made by Canellopoulos as spokesman of the National Unity Party parliamentary faction on July 26, 1946. We quote from the minutes of that session Mr. Canellopoulos' statement:

> "I do not wish to go back to the past except to open one page that I think I ought to make known to the parliament. On Dec. 16, 1942, the British Foreign Secretary Mr. Eden was to make a certain declaration concerning Albania. Being in Cairo at the time, I fortunately learnt of the text of the declaration that was to be read in the House of Commons,

though only 24 hours previously, and considered it my duty to protest as to its tenor. The declaration recognized the moral obligation of the regeneration of Albania, without any allusion being made to any of our claims in Northern Epirus, and without any allusion even to the necessity for the rectification of our frontiers.

"As a consequence of my protest, the communication of the Foreign Secretary was postponed for 24 hours and the phrase, that the problem of the frontiers would remain in abeyance, was added to the declaration, as I concluded from the Note given me by the Minister for the Near East, Lord Moyne.

"The question, to wit, was created internationally at that moment, though only by an inadequate phrase, and Great Britain found herself bound in regard to the matter."

Although hopes among the people ran high, Greek political leaders were extremely cautious in their optimism. During the same session of the Hellenic Parliament, Mr. George Melas gave his views:

". . . that when the Four assembled last September to prepare the treaties with Italy and the other satellite states, I at once foresaw that the question of Northern Epirus would be put off 'ad calendas Graecas'. I have therefore considered since, that the only way of ever obtaining justice would be for Greece to demand, as she has the right to do, that the question be examined by the Conference, as an inseparable part of the Italian Treaty. I know that the Allies by their declaration of 1942 of the same import had assured the independence of Albania, but that did not prevent the matter being connected with Italy as an inseparable part of the Adriatic question. On Jan. 13, 1920, a decision was taken by the Allied Supreme Council, adjudging Northern Epirus to Greece, but it was to have been taken over by her after the Adriatic question was settled. Relying on this authentic precedent, Greece could and ought to have demanded the introduction of the matter before the Four. . ."

The Paris Peace Conference

At the plenary session of the Paris Peace Conference at the Palais du Luxembourg, Greek Premier Constantine Tsaldaris, heading the Greek delegation, presented the case for Northern Epirus on Aug. 3, 1946:

"Less than a week ago the Senate of the U.S.A., by an unanimous vote, recognized the Greek character of Northern Epirus and recommended its incorporation in Greece.

"Yet, a policy of denationalization has been systematically carried out in that region. It remains no less true that, immediately after the Balkan Wars, and again when the Peace Treaties of 1919 were being discussed, a series of international acts recognized that Northern Epirus should belong to Greece. Europe at the time yielded, not without regret, first to Austrian and later to Italian pressure, thus committing an injustice against an allied country. Greece paid dearly for this injustice. Only yesterday she saw fourteen Albanian battalions ranged against her at the side of the Italian divisions. She saw a contingent of the Albanian army march past in Athens in the aggressors' victory parade. She was forced to pay reparations to Albania. I refuse to believe that today, after all that has passed on the very borders of Greece and Albania, after so much Greek blood has been shed on this soil, which has for centuries been a cradle of Hellenism, our allies would wish to confirm this injustice by according legal recognition to the deeds of oppression and systematic denationalisation pursued by Albania's leaders.

"Greece insists that her claims on this subject be heard. At the appropriate moment, the Greek Delegation will present before competent committees the arguments advocating an equitable settlement of a question that cannot continue to remain in abeyance. We are all determined to reestablish peace in a region so sadly afflicted. The state of war existing between Albania and ourselves must come to a natural and just end through the cession of Northern Epirus to Greece.

"The war, as I mentioned previously, has not given us a legal title to oppress other peoples. But it has certainly given us all a right to be accorded the justice that is due, in the widest and deepest sense of that word. And, if this word has a meaning that makes it of capital importance in the lives of peoples, this meaning consists above all in the recognition of a place of honor for those who, in defending the cause of Right, have not failed in their duty.

"But what a sad travesty of the ideals of justice it would be to grant to nations guilty of aggression the advantages of certain rules of diplomatic procedure and of their tardily rallying to the cause of Justice, and so to end by ignoring the legitimate aspirations of their victims!

"On the borders of Northern Epirus a wonderful page in the history of the war has been written. The Greek people have sealed the destiny of this region with their blood. By their victories—the first in this long war—they cast the first rays of hope upon a humanity in distress. Is it possible to recognize today, on some flimsy pretext, the legality of Austrian and Italian infiltration towards the Straits of Otranto?"

This official post-war bid for Northern Epirus had, in fact, been submitted before the Council of Foreign Ministers in a series of memoranda in April, 1946. A "Report of the Greek Government Concerning the Greek-Bulgarian and Greek-Albanian Frontiers" (*Greek Documents,* Series B, No. 1) was submitted to the Secretariat of the Big Four Foreign Ministers' Council in Paris, July, 1946. The relevant portion is reproduced below:

". . . the present boundary facing Albania forms a flank in relation to the main body of Greece, and covers the extremely important plain of Thessaly, which is the very heart of Greece. This means that she is exposed to a two-front war with a threat to the rear of the troops fighting on one of the other frontiers.

"IX. The present boundary facing Albania has the following defects:

"a. It has the great length of 300 kms;

"b. It leaves within Albanian territory and close to the vitally important Greek provinces of Epirus and West Macedonia bases permitting rapid offensive operations against these provinces;

"c. The defence of these provinces is extremely difficult owing to the absence of strategic communication between them. This is due to the Pindus mountain range which lies between them.

"X. Added reasons in favor of the rectification of the border area:

"a. Since ancient times Northern Epirus has always been Hellenic. When Albania was made into an independent State, Northern Epirus was inhabited by a majority of Greeks;

"b. Albania came into being as an independent State in 1913 thanks to Italian and Austro-Hungarian diplomacy. Greek Northern Epirus was then incorporated into Albania for the purpose of keeping Greece away from the Valona (Avlon) region, which controls the Straits of Otranto, and of depriving the Straits of the Island of Corcyra (Corfu) of their strategic importance. The little island of Sasseno (Sason), Greek until 1913, was incorporated into Albania then, and later occupied and fortified by Italy;

"c. Since her creation as a State, Albania has constantly persecuted the Greek element of Northern Epirus;

"d. Albania has always served as a center for extra-Balkan intrigues and interventions, and was wilfully turned over to Italy (Italo-Albanian Agreements of 1926 and 1927). The fact that Albania, alone with Austria, refused to participate in the sanctions imposed on Italy by the League of Nations in 1935 is added proof of Albania's close collaboration with Italy;

"e. Various international acts since 1914 have officially recognized the Greek character of Northern Epirus;

"f. Southern and Northern Epirus have always formed one indivisible geographic, economic and commercial unit. Under Turkish rule the Korytsa region belonged administratively to Macedonia, while commercially it was connected exclusively with the Thessalonica market;

"g. The road from the Port of Santi Quaranta and from Ioannina to Leskoviki-Korytsa (Korcë)-Florina is the only communication line serving the trade of the whole of Epirus and the only natural traffic route between it and Macedonia (Thessalonica). This road is broken up by the present boundary."

Greece's concept of the strategic value of Northern Epirus was more than justified by succeeding events. Valona and Saseno were turned into Soviet submarine bases. British warships were fired upon and damaged by mines in the Straits of Otranto and Soviet warships, paying "friendly calls" in Albanian ports, used the Albanian pretext to sail in and out of the Dardanelles. As for the danger to Greece herself resulting from Albanian occupation of Northern Epirus, the events of the so-called Greek "civil war" bore ample witness. In its 1949 report, the United

Nations Special Committee on the Balkans awoke to the fact that:

> "An important road in Albania . . . runs from Korcë to Leskovik . . . All the evidence obtained by the Special Committee indicates that the whole strategy of the guerrillas in the Albanian-Greek border area has been based on the unrestricted use of this main lateral road through Albania; and that, with the use of Albanian trucks and drivers, the guerrillas have been able to bring up supplies from Albania and to by-pass Greek Army units."

Despite arguments that had been proved valid by the past and would be proven even more valid in the difficult years to come, Greece found that her friends at the Paris Peace Conference had no intention of bucking the Red conspiracy to aid her. The request for a rectification of the Bulgarian frontier was thrown out. In view of this, it was a certainty that the matter of Northern Epirus would meet the same fate if Greece insisted that it be decided then and there. Greece had no choice but to withdraw her claim from the Peace Conference for resubmission to the Council of Foreign Ministers. A portion of a letter signed for the Secretary of State by Gordon P. Merriam, Chief of the Division of Near Eastern Affairs, and addressed to the chairman of the public relations committee of the "Justice for Greece Committee" on Jan. 17, 1947, sheds some light.

> "As you know, representatives of the Greek Government withdrew from the Paris Peace Conference their claims against Albania for Northern Epirus. Officials of the Greek Government have asked that the Council of Foreign Ministers consider their claim for a territorial adjustment by which this territory would be ceded to Greece.
>
> "Under the agreement creating the Council of Foreign Ministers, the Council was directed to consider first the treaties of peace with enemy states. There is no treaty of peace with Albania, and therefore until the treaties have been disposed of a request of Greece for a transfer of territory from Albania to Greece cannot be considered. The United States will support the desire of Greece to have that question considered by the Council when, in accordance with the agreement creating the Council the peace treaties have been disposed of."

The United States Department of State and the British Foreign Office assured the Greeks that the Greek case for Northern Epirus would be heard before the Council of Foreign Ministers, a promise that it has proved impossible to fulfill in view of Soviet intransigence. In 1948, replying to Soviet charges of aggression, the Greek permanent undersecretary for foreign affairs, Mr. P. Pipinelis stated this Greek position in the United

Nations General Assembly. He said, on Oct. 30, 1948, that since the Peace Conference: "Greece, taking her stand on the new and recent aspects of this problem, has avoided anything which could embitter the conflict with Albania. In doing so, she has shown good faith and a spirit of appeasement and understanding. All she has done is to ask that this problem should be discussed by a competent international body, that is, the Council of Foreign Ministers. If the question has not been discussed in that Council it is due, if I am not mistaken, to a persistent refusal on the part of the Soviet Government.

"This is the sum of Greece's alleged aggressive intentions against Albania. I think I have said enough to show that there is nothing unprecedented or shocking in a country which has taken part in war in circumstances which are well known to you putting forward its legitimate claims at the end of the war. The Greek Government, in doing so, and in adopting an attitude which has been calm, correct and honorable, has not been guilty of any unprecedented action in its relations with its neighbors."

Since then, Greece has watched the martyrdom of the Northern Epirotes with heavy heart, but with her hands tied. It is a claim which has not been abandoned, nor will it ever be until justice is done.

Is There a Solution?

Yet, in what might be called their eleventh hour, the Greek captives of Albania—with official Greece and the entire Greek nation standing by—still cannot abandon hope that the United States and Britain will awaken to their common interests in support of their aspirations.

Far from the borders of divided Epirus, the emigrated and exiled keep anxious watch. Over 15,000 American citizens, found in almost every Greek-American community from the Atlantic to the Pacific, are the husbands, sons or brothers of these victims of Red Albanian terror and some have lived under it themselves. They are not indifferent to the fate of the captive land they left behind.

As early as 14 years ago, the former editor of the British periodical *The 20th Century* suggested, "The West could have established itself without difficulty in Albania—and can, in fact, still do so. The Soviet Union could not have, and cannot do anything to prevent it. Once established in Albania, the West could be able to gain a real foothold in Yugoslavia . . . and in time perhaps bring about the restoration of much or all of Southeast Europe to the European Community."[96]

Much that has happened since then has not made this observation less astute. With or without a Soviet-U.S. detente, this can still be done. The solution to the problem presented by Albania is not simple, but it is not impossible.

The United States has seen the futility of placing any hope in Albania's "liberation" by the flotsam of Albanian politicos who "have no real leadership and spend their energy intriguing against one another or, in some cases, in trying to explain away their taint of collaboration with Mussolini and the Nazis."[97]

Albania's masters, be they Zogist, Fascist or Communist, have continued the initial prostitution of their country's independence to Ottoman Turkey by serving—and betraying—every subsequent master of the southern Balkans. Any solution of the perennial Albanian question that relies upon them is doomed to founder on the shoals of Albanian treachery and cupidity.

[96] Vogt, F. A., in *New Leader,* N. Y., Dec. 4, 1950.

[97] *Collier's* Sept. 15, 1951.

NORTHERN EPIRUS. A rough map showing the area inhabited by Albania's captives. (From "Memorandum on Northern Epirus" presented to the Paris Peace Conference of 1919 by the former Provisional Government of Northern Epirus).

BIBLIOGRAPHY

A. In English

Albania, Basic Handbook (marked *Secret.* Copy in author's possession is numbered *877*), London, 1943-44.
(Prepared by a British government agency as one of a series on Axis-occupied countries. Supplements 1 and 2 contain biographical data on Albanian quislings and others.)

Amery, Julian, *Sons of the Eagle, a Study in Guerilla Warfare,* London, 1948.
(Personal account of World War II operations in Northern Albania by a British officer and afterwards cabinet minister. Scrupulously honest but not particularly well-informed on operations in the south in which he was not personally involved.)

Athene, Winter 1963, Vol. XXIII, No. 4. Chicago, Ill.
(Quarterly publication, the above issue of which contains numerous enlightening facts about ancient, mediaeval and modern Epirus.)

Atwood, William, and Freidin, Seymour, "Russia's Most Mysterious Colony," in *Collier's Magazine,* Sept. 15, 1951.

Baerlein, Henry, *Under the Acroceraunian Mountains,* London, 1922.
(Account of a post-World War I visit to Northern Epirus.)

Capps, Edward, *Greece, Albania and Northern Epirus,* Chicago, 1963.

Cassavetes, Nicholas J. ed., *Greek Northern Epirus, a Peace Conference Issue,* N. Y., 1943.

Cassavetes, Nicholas J., (Brown, Carroll Neide, Ph.D., ed.) *The Question of Northern Epirus at the Peace Conference,* N. Y., 1919.

Cassavetti, Demetrius J., *Hellas and the Balkan Wars, London,* 1914.

Central Committee of Northern Epirotes (KEBA), *Memorandum to the United Nations Special Committee on the Balkans, Sub-Committee III on Refugees and Minorities, Prot. No. 5139, Jan. 26, 1948.*
(Mimeographed memorandum re conditions in Northern Epirus and Northern Epirote refugees in Greece.)

Comstock, John L., MD., *History of the Greek Revolution.* N. Y., 1828.
(Despite some inaccuracies, forgivable under the circumstances, this volume struck off by an American in the heat of the Greek War of Independence itself contains much of value obtainable elsewhere only with difficulty.)

Department of State, United States, *The United Nations and the Problem of Greece,* Washington, D. C., 1947.

Diehl, Charles (Ives, G. B., tr.) *History of the Byzantine Empire,* Princeton, 1925.

Djilas, Milovan, *Conversations With Stalin,* N. Y., 1962.

Elliot, Sir Charles, *Turkey in Europe,* London, 1908.
(Written originally under the pseudonym "Odysseus" by a former British Ambassador to the Porte and an authority on his subject.)

Gibbon, Edward, *The Decline and Fall of the Roman Empire* (Modern Library edition, 2 vols., N. Y.)

Gibbons, Herbert Adams, *New Map of Europe,* London, 1915.

Gibbons, Hugh, (ed.), *The Ciano Diaries, 1939-1943, Garden City,* N. Y., 1946.

Greek Documents, Series B., No. 1, (Military Questions), *Report of the Greek Government Concerning the Greek-Bulgarian and Greek-Albanian Frontiers, Submitted to the Secretariat of the Foreign Ministers' Council of the Four Great Powers,* Paris, 1946.

Greek Ministry of Foreign Affairs, *The Greek White Book, Diplomatic Documents Relating to Italy's Aggression Against Greece,* (American Council of Public Affairs, pub.), Washington, D. C., 1943.

Greek Under-Secretariat for Press and Information, *The Conspiracy Against Greece,* Athens, June 1957.

Griffith, William E., *Albania and the Sino-Soviet Rift,* Cambridge, Mass., 1963.

Hamm, Harry, *Albania, China's Beachhead in Europe,* N.Y., 1963.

Helmreich, Ernst Christian, *The Diplomacy of the Balkan Wars, 1912-1913, Harvard Historical Studies, Vol. XLII,* London, 1938.

Hobhouse, John Cam, (1st Baron Broughton), *Journey through Albania,* London, 1813.

(Lord Byron's travelling companion constantly confuses language with nationality, but otherwise gives a not inaccurate picture of Epirus in the the time of Ali Pasha.)

House, Edward M., and Seymour, Charles, *What Really Happened at Paris in 1918-19,* n.p., n.d.

International Justice, Permanent Court of, (Hague Tribunal), *Fascicule No. 64, Series A./B., XXXIV Session, Minority Schools in Albania, Advisory Opinion of April 6, 1935.* (Text also in French).

Justice for Greece Committee, *The Hellenic Character of Northern Epirus, A Handbook of Diplomatic and Other Sources,* Washington D. C., (n.d.).

Konitza, Faik (Bey), *The Background of the Italo-Greek Conflict,* Washington, D. C., 1940.
(A pro-Axis, anti-Greek assault by the last Albanian minister to the United States.)

Manning, Clarence A., *The Axis Satellites and Greece, Our Ally,* N. Y., 1946.

Marriott, Sir John A. R., *The Eastern Question,* Oxford, 1925.

McLain, Glenn A., *Albanian Expose, Communism versus Liberation for Albania* (Albanian-American Literary Society, sponsors), Quincy, Mass. 1952.
(A publication by Bishop Lipa's church faction backing the then NCFA and attacking the pro-Communist Fan Noli-Vatra orientation.)

Miller, William, *The Ottoman Empire and its Successors* (rev. ed.), Cambridge. 1934.
(This and Marriott's work, *Vid. Supra,* are the standard works on the Eastern Question in English).

Moore, Clement C. Ll.D., *George Castriot, Surnamed Scanderbeg, King of Albania,* N. Y., 1850.

Nicol, D.M., *The Despotate of Epiros,* Oxford, 1957.

Nicolson, Harold, *Peacemaking, 1919,* London, 1933.

Noli, Fan S., *George Castrioti Scanderbeg (1405-1468),* N.Y., 1947.

Oost, Stewart I., *Roman Policy in Epirus and Acarnania in the Age of the Roman Conquest of Greece,* Dallas, 1954.

Puaux, René, *The Sorrows of Epirus,* London, 1918 (reprint Chicago, 1963).
(Translation of *La Malheureuse Epire,* written by a distinguished French journalist and eye-witness of the war in Epirus, 1912-14.)

Peace Through Justice League, Eds., *The Resistance Movement of Northern Epirotes,* 1941-1945. Athens, 1947.

Photos, Dr. Basil J., *A Brief History of Albania,* Chicago, 1965.

Photos, Dr. Basil J., *The History of Northern Epirus Through Postage Stamps,* Chicago, 1963.

Pipinelis, M. P., *Europe and the Albanian Question,* Chicago, 1963.
(A sound diplomatic survey by a veteran Greek diplomat who has served as a caretaker prime minister of Greece.)

Plutarch, *Parallel Lives* (Pyrrhus) ed. B. Perrin, Loeb Classical Library.

Polybius, *The Histories* ed. W. R. Paton, 6 vols. Loeb Classical Library, 1922.

Polybius (Pseud.), *Greece Before the Conference,* London, 1919.

Pouqueville, Charles Francois, *Travels in Greece and Turkey,* London, 1820.
(Translation of an important and knowledgeable account by Napoleon's ambassador to the court of Ali Pasha. See also present bibliography in French.)

Raditsa, Bogdan, "How the Soviets Gained Control of Albania," in *New Leader,* N. Y., Aug. 30, 1947.

Ruches, Pyrrhus J., "Terror in Lilliput," in *New Leader* (pub.), N. Y., March 12, 1949. (Reprint in *Catholic Digest,* June 1949.)

Ruches, Pyrrhus J., "Can Albania Survive?" in *New Leader* (pub.), N. Y., Feb. 8, 1954.

Ruches, Pyrrhus J., "The Puppet's Puppet," in *Plain Talk* (pub.), N. Y., April 1948.

Sadik, Hito, "An Albanian Letter" *(Italian Library of Information, Outline Study No.* 38), 1940.
(Sponsored by Mussolini's government, the above gives the classic Albanian nationalist exposition of the point of view respecting Greece and Northern Epirus.)

Sigalos, Louis, *The Greek Claims on Northern Epirus,* Chicago, 1963.

Skendi, Stavro, *Albania,* N.Y., 1956.

Skendi, Stavro, "Albania Within the Slav Orbit: Advent to Power of the Communist Party, in *Political Science Quarterly* Vol. LXIII, No. 2, June 1948.
(Frashërist viewpoint by an active professional Albanian nationalist intellectual.)

Skendi, Stavro, "The Northern Epirus Question Reconsidered," in *Journal of Central European Affairs,* Vol. *XIV,* July 1954, pp. 143-153.

Toynbee, Arnold, *Greek Policy Since 1882,* London, 1914.
(An early and penetrating work by the great philosopher of history.)

Trapmann, A. H., Capt., *The Greeks Triumphant,* London, 1916.

Vasiliev, A. A., *History of the Byzantine Empire, 324-1453,* Madison, Wis., 1952.
(An authoritative history with a stupendous bibliography.)

Venizelos, Eleutherius K., *Greece Before the Peace Conference,* Paris, 1919.

Woodhouse, C. M., *The Greek War of Independence, Its Historical Setting,* London, 1952.

In French:

Andreades, A., *La Grèce devant le Congrès de la Paix,* Paris, 1919.

Baudy-Bovy, D., *L'Epire, Berceau des Grecs,* Geneva, 1919.

Carapanos, Alexis C., *Memoire sur L'Epire du Nord,* Paris, 1919.

Carapanos, Alexis C., *Appel Adresse á la Conference de la Paix au nom des Populations de l'Epire du Nord.*

Driault, Edouard, et Lheritier, Michel, *Histoire diplomatique de la Grèce,* Paris, 1925.

Duruy, Victor, *Historie de la Grèce depuis les temps les plus reculé, jusqu'a la reduction de la Grèce en province romain,* Paris 1887-89, (3 vols.).

Léréque, Pierre, *Pyrrhos,* Paris, 1957.

Maccas, Leon, *La Question Greco-Albanaise,* Paris, 1921.

Moschopoulos, Nicephore, *La Question de l'Epire du Nord,* Athens, 1946.

Noti Botzaris, D., *Carte des èglises et des ècoles helleniques de l'Epire du Nord en 1913,* Athens, 1920.

Noti Botzaris, D., *Carte Ethnographique de l'Epire du Nord en* 1913, Athens, 1919.

Papadakis, B. P., *Documents officiels concernant l'Epire du Nord, 1912-1935,* Athens, 1935.

Papadakis, B. P., *Histoire Diplomatique de la Question Nord-Epirote, 1912-1957,* Athens, 1958.

Peace Through Justice League, ed., *La Participation de l'Albanie a la Guerre Mondiale, 1939-1945,* Athens, 1946.
(Documented)

Pouqueville, Charles François, *Histoire de la Régénération de la Grèce,* Paris, 1824.

In Italian

Amadori-Virgilj, Giovanni, *La Questione Rumeliota e la Politica Italiana, Biblioteca Italiana di Politica Estera, No. 1,* Bitonto, 1908.
(The most thoroughly exhaustive study of the nationalities of European Turkey ever made, pinpointing the churches and schools of each native nationality in the tiniest hamlets of the Balkan vilayets.)

In German:

Kolleger, Willibald, *Albaniens Wiedergeburt,* Vienna, 1942.
(A German account of Albanian contributions to the Axis in WW II).

Musulin, Frieherr von, *Das haus am Ballplatz,* Vienna, 1923.
(A post-World War I unravelling of the tangled skein of Austro-Hungarian foreign policy, especially illuminating with respect to the creation of Albania. Written by an architect of that policy.)

In Russian:

Petriaew, A., *Albaniya i Albantsii,* in *Russkaya Mysl',* Petrograd, Vol. V., 1915.
(The author was the Russian imperial representative on the International Control Commission that was set up to act as midwife for the birth of the Albanian state.)

In Albanian:

Central Commission for the Exposure of the Crimes of the War Criminals and Enemies of the People, *The Truth about the Traitors to the Fatherland,* Tirana, October 1949.
(A valuable and documented expose of Ballist activities in World War II when separated from Communist hyperbole by the knowing eye. Some of the supporting evidence is in photostats of undoubted authenticity.)

In Greek:

Agathos, Eustathios A., *The Italians in Corfu,* Athens (n. d.).
(Background and account of the Corfu incident of 1923)

Antonopoulos, Stamatios, *The Treaties of London, Bucharest and Athens,* Athens, 1917.

Aravantinos, Peter, *Chronicle of Epirus,* Athens, 1856.

Aravantinos, Spiros P., *History of Ali Pasha Teplenti,* Athens, 1895.

Argyrocastrites, Nicholas, *The Sons of the Mercenaries,* vol. I, Athens, 1956.

Argyropoulos, Pericles J., *Greece's Claims,* Athens, 1945.

Asteriou, Asterios, *The Greco-Slavic Boundaries: Macedonia-Thrace-Albania, with an appendix concerning autonomous Albania,* 1916.

Bekker, Immanuel, (ed.) *The History of Epirus by Michael Nepotas Ducas,* Bonn, 1869.

Charisiadis, Stylianos, *Northern Epirus Enslaved,* Athens, 1951.

Christopoulos, Constantine P., *The Greek Problem,* Thessalonica, 1945.

Christopoulos, George Ch., *Diplomatic History of the New Europe, 1919-1939,* Athens, 1939.

Dimiteas, Mergaritis, *Critical Researchs on the Origins and the Nationality of George Castriotis Scanderbeg,* Athens, 1877.

Evangelides, Demetrius E., "The Antiquities and Byzantine Monuments of Epirus," in *Neos Hellenommemon.* (Spyridon Lambros, ed.) Vol. X., Athens, 1913.

Evangelides, Demetrius E., *The Ancient Inhabitants of Epirus,* Athens, 1947.

Evangelides, Demetrius E., *Northern Epirus,* Athens, 1919.

Hestia, Epirotike, (pub.), Ioannina, 1952 et seq.

Keramopoulos, Antonios D., *The Greeks and their Northern Neighbors,* Athens, 1945.

Kyritsis, Photius P., *The Question of Northern Epirus,* N.Y., 1946.

Kyrou, Alexis A., *Greek Foreign Policy,* Athens, 1955.

Lilles, John, *Liountzi (History, Folklore, Manners and Customs),* Athens, 1947. (Traditional life in seven Albanophone villages of Northern Epirus. The Northern Epirote social pattern and the deep involvement of these villages in the life of Greece as a whole, through notable sons, is told simply and without hyperbole.)

Mammopoulos, Alexander Ch., *Epirus, Folklore, Customs, Ethnography,* Athens, 1961. (Vol. I); 1964. (Vol. 2).
(This is nothing less than the oral history of Northern Epirus. The author has transcribed, with meticulous zeal, the unwritten anecdotes and traditions preserved in the memories of Northern Epirotes and passed down through the generations. Unique.)

Metallinou, Angelica B., *Our National Claims, Northern Epirus,* Thessalonica, 1950.

Michalopoulos, Phanes, *Gregory the Argyrocastran and the Revolt of Euboia,* Athens, 1955.

Michalopoulos, Phanes, *Moschopolis, the Athens of Turkish Times, 1500-1769,* Athens, 1941.

Neos Kouvaras (Pub.), 1961- (Annual of Epirote Chronography), Athens.

Papadopoulos, Nicholas K. (ed.) *Northern Epirus, Essays by Fifth Form Students at the Tositsaion-Arsakion School,* Athens, 1959.

Papamanolis, *Flameswept Epirus,* Athens, 1945.
(Albanian operations in the region of Thesprotia occupied by Axis Albania in World War II.)

Paparrhegopoulos, Constantine, *History of the Greek Nation,* Athens, 1930. (3 vols.)
(The standard modern Greek history of Greece.)

Papastavrou, Christos B., *Greece and Northern Epirus,* Athens, 1945.

Patselis, Nicholas B., *Delvinakion In Epirus,* Athens, 1948.

Patselis, Nicholas B., *Northern Epirus and Her Natural Boundaries,* Athens, 1945.

Perrhaebus, Christopher, *Greek Revolution, Collected Works.* Athens, 1956.

Pop, Alexander G., *This is Albania,* Athens, 1946.

Rentis, Constantine Th., *The Northern Epirote Question,* Athens, 1922.

Sathas, Constantine N., *Turkish Occupied Greece, 1453-1821,* Athens, 1869.

Skenderes, Constantine, *History of Autonomous Northern Epirus, 1913-1916*, Athens, 1930.
(One of the few detailed, documented histories of the Autonomy and a prime source in the absence of the autonomist archives scattered here and there. The author was MP from Korysta in the Greek Parliament.)

Spyromilios, Miltos M., *Grece and Albania*, N.Y. (n. d.)

Stoupes, Spyros, *The "Foreigners" in Corfu*, Corfu, 1960.
(The story of the Epirote community in Corfu founded and maintained by refuges from the mainland and their descendants.)

Stoupes, Spyros, *Pogonisiaca and Vessaniotica*, Patras, 1962.
(A study of several villages along the present Greco-Albanian frontier.)

Tzovas, Costas I., *To Northern Epirus, Laurels and Chains*, Athens, 1964.

Zotos, Demetrios A., *The National Conscience of Epirus through the Centuries*, Athens, 1940.

INDEX

L